Autism in a Decente

Autistic people are empirically and scientifically generalized as living in a fragmented, alternate reality, without a coherent continuous self. In Part I, this book presents recent neuropsychological research and its implications for existing theories of autism, selfhood, and identity, challenging common assumptions about the formation and structure of the autistic self and autism's relationship to neurotypicality. Through several case studies in Part II, the book explores the ways in which artists diagnosed with autism have constructed their identities through participation within art communities and cultures, and how the concept of self as 'story' can be utilized to better understand the neurological differences between autism and typical cognition. This book will be of particular interest to researchers and scholars within the fields of Disability Studies, Art Education, and Art Therapy.

Alice Wexler is Professor Emeritus of Art Education at SUNY New Paltz, USA.

Routledge Advances in Disability Studies

New Titles

Towards a Contextual Psychology of Disablism
Brian Watermeyer

Disability, Hate Crime and Violence
Edited by Alan Roulstone and Hannah Mason-Bish

Branding and Designing Disability
Reconceptualising Disability Studies
Elizabeth DePoy and Stephen Gilson

Crises, Conflict and Disability
Ensuring Equality
Edited by David Mitchell and Valerie Karr

Disability, Spaces and Places of Policy Exclusion
Edited by Karen Soldatic, Hannah Morgan and Alan Roulstone

Changing Social Attitudes Toward Disability
Perspectives from historical, cultural, and educational studies
Edited by David Bolt

Disability, Avoidance and the Academy
Challenging Resistance
Edited by David Bolt and Claire Penketh

Autism in a Decentered World
Alice Wexler

Forthcoming Titles

Intellectual Disability and Being Human
A Care Ethics Model
Philosophical Debates on Being Human
Chrissie Rogers

Disabled Childhoods
Monitoring Differences and Emerging Identities
Janice McLaughlin, Emma Clavering and Edmund Coleman-Fountain

Inner Limits: New Encounters Science Fiction Plan Alternative Guide to the Universe of the Peace on Earth by William Scott

Autism in a Decentered World

Alice Wexler

LONDON AND NEW YORK

First published 2016 by Routledge

2 Park Square, Milton Park, Abingdon, Oxfordshire OX14 4RN
711 Third Avenue, New York, NY 10017

Routledge is an imprint of the Taylor & Francis Group, an informa business

First issued in paperback 2018

Library of Congress Cataloging-in-Publication Data
Names: Wexler, Alice, 1942- author.
Title: Autism in a decentered world / by Alice Wexler.
Description: New York : Routledge, 2016. | Series: Routledge advances in disability studies ; 8
Identifiers: LCCN 2015034061 | ISBN 9781138818576 (hbk) | ISBN 9781315745152 (ebk)
Subjects: LCSH: Autism.
Classification: LCC RC553.A88 W456 2016 | DDC 616.85/882—dc23
LC record available at http://lccn.loc.gov/2015034061

ISBN: 978-1-138-81857-6 (hbk)
ISBN: 978-0-815-38188-4 (pbk)

Typeset in Sabon
by Apex CoVantage, LLC

To the Creative Growth Art Center and all the artists

Contents

Illustrations

Foreword

The last fifteen years have witnessed a flowering of autistic writing and art. From published books and blog posts to gallery exhibitions and virtual displays, this flowering has put pressure on conventional understandings of the disorder. No longer is it appropriate to suggest, as Oliver Sacks once did in a profile of Stephen Wiltshire, that autistic drawing is unworthy of the appellation "art" because the consciousness that produced it is "defective." While the normal/abnormal binary continues to hold sway, particularly in medical and scientific arenas, the strict distinction between cultural "insiders" and "outsiders" has started to crumble. Part of a wider neurodiversity movement, this renaissance has elicited attention from both autistic and nonautistic critics, but we don't yet fully know what the concept of neurodiversity might mean or, as important, what it might still achieve.

Along comes Alice Wexler, the author of a number of important books about disability. She brings to the task of investigating neurodiversity both knowledge of autistic autobiography and art and a commitment to ethnographical research. In her book we learn about, among other autistics, Dan Miller, whose work is part of the permanent collection at the Museum of Modern Art in New York. As a result of perseverative behavior and a difficulty communicating, he carries the label of "low-functioning autism," even though in the context of art he "functions" perfectly well, if not in a manner superior to the nondisabled artists who support him at Oakland's Creative Growth Art Center, to say nothing of the doctors who label him and who probably couldn't make compelling art if their lives depended on it.

"In his drawings," writes one critic,

> [Miller] superimposes words, letters or numbers with other words and numbers. Sometimes he accumulates the strata of graphic elements until the center of the surface becomes completely black. . . . The words he writes are the names of the people he knows, the places he has visited, the activities he has been engaged in or everyday objects. (http://www.abcd-artbrut.net/spip.php?article1340)

Another critic describes the impact of his work like this:

> Layered elements appear to be in a constant flux emerging into view while being scratched out of existence. Simultaneously poetic and artistic, expressive and conceptual, his work renders distinctions between such categories meaningless.

Wexler herself suggests that Miller's art is "the outcome of an intense investigation into the graphic form and the visual representation of language."

If neuroscience has taught us anything over the last decade, it is that autism is primarily, although by no means exclusively, a visual intelligence. Temple Grandin has famously called this proclivity "thinking in pictures," and research has shown that autistics do indeed rely to a much greater degree on posterior sensory regions of the brain, especially the visual cortex, to think. A study from 2005 found that autistics possess a "nonverbal, visually oriented processing style" and, even after becoming literate, remember printed letters as if they were shapes and not just the instrumental signifiers that neurotypicals take them to be. Put simply, autistics engage with printed language—and, it turns out, with spoken language, too—as if it were akin to art: something to behold as much as to unpack or decode. Here, an appreciation for the materiality of language may have a conspicuously neurological origin. If so, autism would offer Miller a significant aesthetic advantage. The distinction between the verbal and the visual breaks down, and the context of art, which for autistics is often much more hospitable than the context of everyday life, allows language to be any number of things at once.

It may be that Miller's art also reflects the difficulty that some otherwise literate autistics report when looking at printed text: they simply *see* too much; the medium refuses to disappear and, as a result, it often moves and swirls and jumps and, in general, drives them crazy. For this reason they prefer to listen to text being read aloud. How tempting, from a neurotypical point of view, to reduce Miller's art to a struggle with literacy rather than a complex unfolding of "a gift with a shadow side," as the writer Suzanne Antonetta calls her bipolar disorder. None of this is to suggest that Miller simply projects a different neurology onto the canvas; nor is it to assert that his art lacks intention or refinement. Rather, he works with a different set of neurological predispositions, just as neurotypical artists do.

While proposing a number of theories about autistic cognition, Wexler never forgets that she is hypothesizing. As she listens to autistic people, as she takes their writing and art seriously, she tries to account for neurological difference without presuming pathology and without allowing it to devolve into something static or immune to influence. The autistic renaissance we are currently witnessing is the product of neurocultural intermingling. There are no fixed forms of cognition: autistics aren't simply one thing and neurotypicals another. We are all hybrid creatures whose very plasticity can stretch the limits of our own biological organization. By stretching these limits we can stretch our capacity for empathetic understanding.

There is much to be found in this book. May it be one of many that seek to realize a neurodiverse future.

Ralph James Savarese
Professor of English
Grinnell College

Acknowledgments

Many people have generously offered their time and expertise during the writing of this book. I especially want to express my gratitude to the staff, artists, and the families of the artists at Creative Growth Art Center. Studio Manager Matt Dostal read the short biographies of the four artists in Part II, and gave me invaluable advice that helped me align my own goals with the wishes of the staff who so carefully make sure that the artists are represented respectfully and truthfully. He also read each chapter to the artists, or in some instances to a family member, for their input. As a result, I was able to challenge my own assumptions about what was most important to communicate. Gallery Manager Catherine Nguyen also offered wise suggestions based on her knowledge of the artists' lives and her sensitivity to their privacy. Projects Manager Jennifer State O'Neal afforded her anecdotal and insightful knowledge of the artistic development of the artists. Kathleen Henderson, Anna Marta Dostourian, and Veronica Rojas, staff artists who worked closely with the studio artists, generously and patiently answered my many questions. Maria Hartikainen, who at the time was Dan Miller's ceramics mentor, allowed me to film their interactions during a studio project, which illuminated the Center's difficult to describe non-teaching ethos, which as Director Tom di Maria believes, can only be understood through prolonged observation. di Maria's presence and intelligence were felt in the intention and thoughtfulness of the daily activities of the studio.

I would like to recognize three scholars who afforded me their expertise in email correspondences and personal interviews. Matthew Higgs, Director and Chief Curator of the White Columns gallery in New York City, is an eloquent art historian who has exhibited the works of the artists I write about in Part II. His knowledge of the art world as a gallerist and curator, his personal relationship with the Creative Growth Art Center, and his appreciation for its historic place in the art world were essential in bridging these worlds. Roger Ricco, co-founder and owner of the Ricco/Maresca gallery, one of the earliest galleries to feature Outsider Art, has supported me in researching and negotiating the often contested labels of this art form. Douglas Biklen, the former Dean of the School of Education at Syracuse

University, and author of many articles and books about his advances in and advocacy for facilitated communication, guided me through this difficult and complex terrain.

Finally, thank you to James Brent, Director of The Museum of Everything, Joe Coleman, Leon Borensztein, and the White Columns Gallery, for their permission to use their works of art.

Introduction

The politicized disability identity—the self-conscious use of the category—has become one of the most potent since the forcible implementation of the Americans with Disabilities Act (ADA) in 1990 by the disabled population. The formation of new disabled identities is the result of taking back the category that has been the domain of clinical discourse in medicine, biology, and education. These transformed identities signal the end of an era of objectification in which the disabled person can be spoken for.[1] Individuals with disabilities who read what medical practitioners write, and write their own versions of their lives through memoir, poetry, performance, and the visual arts, self-designate the disability category with their lived experience.[2]

The implosion that caused the reckoning with the federal government prior to the passage of the ADA was led mainly by individuals with visible physical disabilities. They fought for the civil right of equal and competitive employment in a social democracy. The members of ADAPT (American Disabled for Accessible Public Transit) gathered a "hidden army of civil rights,"[3] a resistance against the perpetuated myth that disabled people are helpless and dependent on charity and welfare. They wanted access to buses, buildings, offices, and public places. In March 1990, ADAPT staged a protest they called the Capitol Crawl; hundreds of people abandoned their wheelchairs at the bottom of the capital steps and crawled to the top. The metaphor was clear: the locus of power was inaccessible to them (Dolmage, 2008).

As recently as 1988, Lisa Carl rolled up in her wheelchair to a movie theater in Tacoma, Washington and was turned away. This story was told in front of the ADA panel, which would extend the same protection that had been given minorities in the 1964 Civil Rights Act (Shapiro, 1994). Carl's incident was not the only act of discrimination. According to Joseph Shapiro, 66% of people with disabilities were unemployed, of which two-thirds were capable of working. "No other group of citizens was so insulated or so removed from the American mainstream. . . . For the first time, people with disabilities were asking Americans to recognize that the biggest problem facing them was discrimination" (p. 106). After a long battle, the ADA bill was signed into law by George H. Bush on July 26, 1990.

Even after the passage of ADA, the collective psyche remained the same, despite more sensitized terminology, such as the language of people first before disability (e.g., individuals *labeled* autistic or individuals *with* or *who have* a disability). In addition, the narrow interpretations of the ADA have limited its efficacy and set a precedent in the ways it has framed a minority group model. McRuer and Mollow (2012) interpret the backlash against ADA not as a theoretical rejection of a minority group model, but as a result of its punitive application of a narrowed-down minority group. Nevertheless, after its passage, disability activism was free to move from political praxis to academia, problematizing the disabled as invisible in cultural studies dominated by race and gender. The postmodern and cultural constructivist movements that challenged the unexamined assumptions about race and gender now opened the way for disability as a discursive category. A new paradigm expanded the repertoire of models of physical difference as a cultural process rather than a biological condition, a nuanced subject of identity and representation in all cultural forms, both aesthetic and popular.

Disability studies discourse, however, has leaned heavily toward the disabled body. Disability scholars such as Mark Osteen (2008), in his groundbreaking anthology *Autism and Representation*, takes note of the "blindsightedness" of disability studies discourse in its virtual elimination of developmental disabilities. He suggests that we have left out of our discourse individuals who cannot compete intellectually in our particularly American brand of individualism and productivity. "Are academics—even disabled academics—unaware of our cognitive privilege? Is disability studies guilty of cognitive ableism—a prejudice against those who cannot compose articles and books, compete for advocacy space, and contribute to disability scholarship?" (p. 5).

Disability studies' focus on visible physical disability could be explained by its historical relationship and indebtedness to activists such as ADAPT. But Osteen brings up an equally important position that has not yet been examined fully, that the inclusion of intellectual disabilities in the conversation exacerbates the tension between impairments and disability: the former as a bodily reality, the latter as a sociopolitical-cultural construction. One of the reasons for the resistance to theorizing the place that impairment has in disability discourse is that medical definitions of disability as impairment have positioned disability as a problem, while disability studies sought to invert this perception by re-directing causation toward social, political, and cultural access, bias, and concepts of normal. Simi Linton (1998) writes:

> When disability is redefined as a social/political category, people with a variety of conditions are identified as *people with disabilities* or *disabled people*, a group bound by common social and political experience. These designations, as reclaimed by the community, are used to identify us as a constituency, to serve our needs for unity and identity, and to function as a basis for political activism. (p. 12)

Linton recognizes that disability studies has not yet theorized impairment with the complexity and nuance that it does disability as a social, political, and cultural construction, fearing that to do so would essentialize and isolate disability as an individual's problem with negative value. Since publishing the autobiography, *Life as We Know It: A Father, a Family, and an Exceptional Child*, the deeply pragmatic Michael Bérubé (1998) has been writing about Jamie, his son with Down syndrome. Bérubé's preoccupation is with a just society: how prudently it treats individuals with impairments. If a society is to foster independence, it must take into account his son's impairment and dependency, "or it will be of no account of all" (p. 248).

Bérubé conjectures the exclusion of nonstandard communication as a side effect of the Aristotelian concept of life as a hierarchical system whereby lowly creatures are connected to superior creatures through a sort of trickle-down benevolence from God, to humans, to animals, to plants, and so on. Revised throughout western civilization, the eighteenth century's Great Chain of Being utilized this concept, which continues to persist in ableist misconceptions about disabled people, to justify the moral rightness of a superior class of the rich alongside a common class. Bérubé suggests redefining the Chain of Being such that disabled people are invited inside the privileged circle of typical communicators without euphemisms or denial, without theorizing disabled people as having supernatural powers, or mythologizing them with fearsome figure stereotypes. To be part of the Chain of Being is to have the privilege of representing oneself, particularly in a more favorable way than the public images and stereotypes that obfuscate the disabled identity. Without self-representation, communication exists *about* and *without* you.

Artists and writers with disabilities are composing narratives that intentionally respond to the intrusion of representations of people with disabilities by the non-disabled. Through literary, visual, and performative narratives, they disrupt "the way disabled subjects are often used, then erased," from the public sphere (Brueggemann, 2002, p. 318). The paradox that confronts this large minority is the instability of the category itself, which in its ambiguity attempts to normalize and justify its boundaries. These narratives produce critical and experiential insight and, thus, they destabilize the binary relationship between the signifier and signified as theory gives way to raw lived experience and continues to rattle the developing field of disabilities in the arts and humanities. Rather than simply an academic pursuit, the theories of disability studies now exist side by side with profound questions of social and cultural justice, corporeality, social construction, and aesthetic and political representation (Brueggemann, 2002).

The embodied view of the world, from and of the body, is changing how we think and talk about disability. Postmodern Feminist standpoint theory has increased the status of the experiencing subject and encouraged authors such as Anne Finger (1990), Nancy Mairs (1996, 2002), and Susan Nussbaum (1997) to share the double bind of femaleness and disability.

> I speak as a crippled woman. At the same time, in the utterance I redeem both "cripple" and "woman" from the shameful silences by which I have often felt surrounded, contained, set apart; I give myself permission to live openly among others, to reach out for them, stroke them with fingers and sighs. No body, no voice; no voice, no body. That's what I know in my bones. (Mairs, 1996, p. 60)

With a view of the body as a site of contested cultural discourses (Swan, 2002), an inherent contradiction ensues, as it often does in analytical discourse across disciplines, a problem recognized in cultural studies. The subject is thus rendered static while, in fact, it is dynamic and negotiable, in constant flux, and with changing meanings.

> Consequently, the notion of a subject of discourse can have two contradictory meanings. It is either one who is *subject to* the hegemony of cultural ideology that is internalized and therefore inaccessible and nonnegotiable; or it is one who acts as agent and *subject of* cultural meanings that are understood to be contingent, negotiable, and revisable. (Swan, 2002, p. 285)

The subject of cultural meanings, specifically individuals with disabilities who write, perform, and paint their experience, is contested by some theorists as placating to the non-disabled, appealing for their approval. However, without embodied stories, conceptualization of disability easily remains static (Swan, 2002). For example, the nature of space and time is called into question from the lived experience of the blind (Fittapaldi, 2004; Hull, 1992), or the definition of language itself from the perspective of the deaf (Bauman & Murray, 2013; Davis, 1997, 2002). Disability affects one's daily sense of body in space, whether impairment is neurological, physical, or cognitive. Impairment de-centers social environments constructed for a public unaware of its entitlement. For example, Mairs (1996) describes in humorous detail her "descent," both real and metaphorical, into a wheelchair, reducing her "to the height of a seven-year-old" (p. 56).

Not only does a wheelchair limit mobility and access, but it also affects how Mairs processes information and, in turn, how she is seen and not seen. This is the voice of cognitive difference, one version of the world that poses the speaker as an agent of negotiable meanings as well as the subject of ideology.

While the narratives of Mairs, Finger, and Nussbaum are written by "high functioning"[4] women with physical disabilities, few people with developmental disabilities have left discursive accounts of their experience. What we have instead is often mysteriously compelling, poetic, non-linear prose. Larry Bissonnette and Tito Mukhopadhyay (2003, 2005, 2011), an artist and author respectively, are two examples. Both men are autistic without spoken language, although they have learned to write with assistance: Bissonnette with facilitated communication (FC),[5] and Mukhopadhyay with a similar technique his ingenious mother, Soma, invented called the rapid prompting method. Bissonnette narrated a documentary about his life entitled *My Classic Life as an Artist* (Biklen & Rossetti, 2005), performed as the subject of the Gerardine Wurzburg (2012) documentary, *Wretches and Jabberers*, and presented papers, such as "Letters Ordered through Typing Produce the Story of an Artist Stranded on the Island of Autism," at the Narrating dis/Ability conference at Syracuse University (2002). Mukhopadhyay has authored several monographs, poems, and essays in which he describes his frustration and exhilaration with autism.

In this book, I turn to the less visible disability of the autism spectrum, the "unusual" minds, as Osteen describes them. Since about 1985, we have seen a proliferation of autobiographies by people who do not typically produce textual first-person narratives. And since the emptying of institutions across the nation in the 1970s, we have seen all forms of visual narratives. In Chapter Five, I present the embodied narratives of autists who have become writers through technologies such as facilitated communication, and in Part II, artists who have found art centers that welcome and inspire their visual narratives.

I will not debate if the terminology that is currently used is the best we can do, or what counts as a disability. It has become all too clear that our designations are incomplete and imperfect. My focus instead is the epistemology of autism, the limitations within the neurotypical observer who makes claims about the nature and reach of the autistic mind. I question what neurotypicals perceive as unusual, particularly what we call "low functioning," and what that perception reveals about the neurotypical brain and a "normalized identity."[6] In the following paragraphs, I discuss historical and current neurological and philosophical theories that call into question the neurotypical perspective.

NORMALIZATION AND NARRATOLOGY

Alluded to earlier, the eighteenth century Cartesian mind/body dualism set the stage for the construction of hierarchal values, such as independence, mastery, and competence, that persist today in an essentialist selfhood. A few value-laden descriptors that arise from this concept of selfhood are autonomy, stability, continuity, and unity. In "What is the Western Concept of the Self? On Forgetting David Hume," D.W. Murray (1993) argues that the discrete yet continuous notion of self is ubiquitous, and can be traced back to Plato, Descartes, Kant, and Christianity. But philosophers such as Hume, Sarte, and Merleau-Ponty present conflicting notions of the self as contingent, embodied, fragmented, relational, pluralistic, and inconsistent. Western culture, however, inherited the predominant Greek and Christian selfhood, and we measure and are measured by these standards. These measurements led to our subjective definition of normalcy, and its inevitable opposite, abnormality.[7]

According to David Hume (1978), we empirically sense that our lives are continuous, a sum total of our experience and memory. The multifarious appearances of objects are confabulated in our brain so that their identities remain secure and solid. Our sensations, although volatile, maintain a coherency as they are connected to causal relations with the environment and attached to the constant of the self. As a result of the brain's confabulations, we are conscious of a consistent and enduring self from our earliest memories. Hume, however, found no evidence of a continuous self whose reality existed in our own perceptions and sensations. The instability of perceptions and sensations, and the lack of scientific proof that they provide, might just as easily be isolated phenomena with no connection to the self.

> 'Tis certain there is no question in philosophy more abstruse than that concerning identity, and the nature of the uniting principle, which constitutes a person. So far from being able by our senses merely to determine this question, we must have recourse to the most profound metaphysics to give a satisfactory answer to it; and in common life 'tis evident these ideas of self and person are never very fix'd nor determinate. 'Tis absurd, therefore, to imagine the senses can ever distinguish betwixt ourselves and external objects. (p. 189)

Hume's argument that the continuity and wholeness of the self is fiction and, therefore, so are our perception of the universe, is the thesis of this book. The theory that I examine began with Hume's rumination about the efficacy and plausibility of autobiography as self-representation, as it is the nature of humans to re-narrate themselves at every moment to cohere a fragile selfhood. In order to avoid contradictions of self, Hume considered all forms of his writing autobiographical and narratological practices. Hume wrote his autobiographical story just before his first philosophical text in 1734 in the form of a letter, or epistle, and his final autobiography, *My Own Life*, along with his will and testament in 1776 (Valenza, 2002). So inseparable is Hume's philosophy from the story of his life that Robin Valenza suggests in her essay, "Editing the Self: David Hume's Narrative Theory," "instead of considering autobiography as a context for Hume's philosophy, how do we read Hume's philosophical texts as a theoretical context for his autobiographical writings?" (p. 139).

Unlike the more enduring concept of "unity of action" as it has applied to literary narrative since Aristotle's coining of the phrase, Hume saw only inconsistencies that disrupted the continuity of identity. In other words, a notion of identity depends on a narrative succession. The unconscious habit of narrating a sequence of perceptions into a single identity is exposed only in cases when the narrative process breaks down, such as in memory loss, brain trauma, or in the autist identity. What written narrative can and does do, then, is enable the writer to put lost connections back in place, or simply to recognize their absence.

Before making the comparison between Hume's notion of self and the autist identity in Chapter Two, I introduce a subgroup of thinkers in Chapter One who have maintained Hume's position. Many of these thinkers are anthropologists, philosophers, neuroscientists, and neuropsychologists. The theory of a fictitious self has gained currency since the latter part of the twentieth century. Our fairly recent ability to see the brain puts us in the self-conscious position of searching for the narrating "I" and coming up with little evidence to support it. Evidence supporting a discontinuous, fragmented, pluralist, relational, inconsistent self, however, has been found not only in diagnostic images of the brain in which no self-aware center can be found, but also through the personal experience of not only their injured subjects, but also the scientists themselves. Other evidence comes from Michael Gazzaniga's split-brain surgery,[8] in which the corpos-allosum is severed, producing two separate hemispheres. Because post-operation patients seem not to be affected, Gazzaniga's view is that "this does not so much show that the patients have preserved their pre-surgical unity as that the unity of normal life is an illusion" (as cited in Dennett, 1986, p. 6). As a result, several of these scientists have abandoned traditional clinical reports in favor of stories, fiction, narratives, and autobiography.

Anthropologist Katherine Ewing (1990) suggests that a pluralistic identity and inconsistencies in self and self-representation are experienced not only in non-western cultures in which self is contextual and relational, but also in the western identity, even though it is typically described as autonomous and independent, which

> illustrates a universal semiotic process by which people manage inconsistency. . . . People construct a series of self-representations that are based on selected cultural concepts of persona and selected "chains" of personal memories. Each self-concept is experienced as whole and continuous, with its own history and memories that emerge in a specific context, to be replaced by another self-representation when the context changes. (p. 253)

Ewing asks how self-continuity can be explained in light of the evidence against it, and how we function within an equally inconsistent and contradictory environment. "Why are we not all psychotic?" (p. 263). In order to maintain the efficacy of the self, she reduces the illusion to "a semiotic process that highlights and organizes certain fragments of experiences" (p. 263). Daniel Dennett (1986) solves the problem of defining the self by comparing it to the center of gravity of sentient and insentient phenomena, which have no physical properties or mass of their own. Self is not, then, real in the "real" sense, "but it is a fiction that has a nicely defined, well delineated and well behaved role within physics" (p. 1). You can see where Dennett is leading with this metaphor. The center of gravity, he says, is as robust and familiar as anything we can know in the universe. Strictly, according to physics, "[T]he self is also an abstract object, a theorist's object" (p. 2), and as such it exhibits the same features as other fictional objects. "They have only the properties that the theory that constitutes them endowed them with" (p. 3). But from an anthropological or phenomenological perspective, the interpretation of "realness" is much more complex.

Returning to Hume's analogy of our lives as fiction, we engage with fictitious characters in novels in ways similar to how we interpret people in the world. Dennett writes that we demand consistency; as we read we cannot tolerate inconsistencies and discontinuities of characters as they develop in the story, and compensate by bifurcating them. According to this theory, we are adding a layer of our own fiction to prop up the author's fiction. Our need for coherent narration is embedded in our perception and organization of the world. But if we had a pluralistic sense of the self as inhabiting possibly two selves, one for each side of the brain, which seems to be acceptable to some neurologists, then we might make coherence around two imaginary points.

> We are all, at times, confabulators, telling and retelling ourselves the story of our own lives, with scant attention to the question of truth. . . . Why are we all such inveterate and inventive autobiographical novelists? As Umberto Maturnana has (uncontroversially) observed: "Everything said is said by a speaker to another speaker that may be himself." But why should one talk to oneself? (Dennett, 1986, p. 5)

Mind/Body Duality

At the same time as Descartes famously located evidence for his existence in his thoughts, he rejected his body as not the "I" that he knew. "I am not this assemblage of limbs" (as cited in Broks, 2003, p. 106). The effects of Descartes continue to hold sway in the collective unconscious even though the inseparability between mind and body is well established in bio-neurology. The Cartesian "I," which most of us still hold consciously or unconsciously to be true, is irreducible to both body and experience, and ubiquitous because of its similarity to the belief in the soul. In other words, I own my mind, body, and experience, but they are not me (Glover, 1989). The Cartesian ego is a disembodied mental state that is conscious of, and gives unity to, all experience.

It was clear to scientists such as Paul Broks (2003) that the brain could not be understood without the body, since the tightly connected functions between them are embedded in it, as well as embodied in the physical and cultural landscape. As sensory and perceptual observers, however, we instinctively conceive the essence of identity as located somewhere in the brain. We have a long history of identifying our face—as somewhat separate from our body—to be the self's representative. And as observers we intuit the minds behind other faces. "Irresistibly, we still see the vision of minds in the light of other people's eyes . . . if this illusion begins to fade then so does the observer" (p. 21). The face is the entry point into the selfhood of the other and, therefore, by extension, our mutual knowing. I could argue that this assumption is emblematic of the theory of mind, our ability to perceive the thoughts of others at some point behind the eyes and "to place oneself within the context of a developing social story" (Belmonte, 2008, p. 171). This illusion is an essential piece in our story of the self and, therefore, our belief that we understand other selves, conceiving them not only through the spoken word but also through the signals of facial expressions. Broks's objection that nothing is "there" in the mind/brain but organic matter is the post-postmodernist dilemma of reconciling the numinous qualities of subjective experience with the physical matter of the brain.

The Autistic Self

Because we believe our mind and the minds of others house the continuous, unbroken self, we depend on the homogeneous reactions of others to support this intuitive belief about personhood. Each of us, says Broks (2003), takes an inferential step in this mental process of locating our selves among other selves. The autistic self, therefore, presents a seepage in our tenuous hold on our illusion, which works only if everyone is part of the illusion. Because of the breakdown between the neurotypical observer and the autistic participant, the neurotypical can only speculate about atypical brains (Biklen, 2005). In Chapter Two, I call into question the shaky ground upon which theory of mind is conceived, given the neurotypical's tenuous grasp of his or her identity.

Autists are known for their lack of eye contact and pronoun confusion. They will often tell their stories in the third person. They are also assumed not to have a theory of mind, the awareness that the thoughts and feelings of others are different from one's own. As a neurotypical, I infer the identity of others as others infer mine. Yet, I am not given my identity, but cohere the fractious memories and experiences of my life into a coherent whole—the story that I tell myself. My brain is telling the story to the listening "I;" experiences that do not fit get edited out. However, the autist's story is never edited and never completed. Temple Grandin explains to Oliver Sacks (1995) in *An Anthropologist on Mars* that she doesn't have an editor, a subconscious that represses memories. "There isn't enough painful emotion that would cause the amygdala to lock the files of the hippocampus. . . . There are no secrets, no locked doors—nothing is hidden" (p. 287).

Narratives such as Grandin's make clear that the story the neurotypical tells is an ironic one: the brain understanding the brain by the brain. The brain understanding itself is a situation in which the observer is limited by the story he or she tells. It is a story told by the ego, its roots, believes Glover (1989), are in language, "in the way we think of our own body and of our mental states, in our experience of perceiving things and of acting, and in the unity of our experience" (p. 90). It is the persistence of this mental state in language that perpetuates the notion of the cognitive "I" and gives coherence to experience. Along similar lines, Broks (2003) theorizes that language fulfills the primary purpose in the brain's evolution, which was to promote a system for adaptive negotiation between the organism and the world. In the western tradition we live simultaneously in nature and culture, subject to the laws of physics in the first and customs and beliefs in the second. Neuropsychology, says Broks, has been engaged in the brain's process of developing systems that are dedicated to the social functions of thought, communication, and action. The brain thus constructed an interior representation of the organism in relationship to organisms similar to the self, the self that negotiates social interaction. "Tightly bound to language, these brain mechanisms are the channels through which biology finds expression as culture, as means of distributing mind beyond biological boundaries" (p. 51). In Chapter Three, I explore how the genesis of "I" is embedded in the world through language.

Neurotypicals build stories from language, memory, and experience qualitatively different than autistic language, memory, and experience. Stories are usually dependent on language developing in the early years because we construct ourselves in relationship to the world through language acquisition, which forms a particular kind of memory and experience. Since autists acquire language later in life, if at all, their memories are usually formed by de-contextualized sensory images. New communication strategies and technologies have made autistic narratives available to neurotypicals and, therefore, have provided a window into autistic experience. These narratives are reframing prevailing ideas and theories about autism (Biklen, 2005). Chapter Four presents augmentative alternative communication (AAC), which might range from the highly contested facilitated communication (FC) to simply pointing to letters and numbers. In many cases, children and young adults who do not use spoken language reveal a competent, sometimes highly competent, use of written language. Many of these young people were classified as mentally retarded, such as Sue Rubin, who was tested at a 29 IQ. After learning to type at 13, she was reassessed with a 133 IQ, enabling her to graduate from high school with a 3.98 GPA and complete college with the help of a keyboard and facilitator (Wurzburg, 2005).[9] In each of the cases in which AAC has been used, a prompt or gentle cueing was needed from the facilitator to organize the client's mental impulse into action. The intention of the mental message and its target in the autist's body—volition and action—are not usually in harmony.

Neurotypicals do not require a conscious understanding of the causal relationship between mind and body in order to accomplish a task. Autists, however, must put forth conscious and deliberate effort to follow through on an internal or external command. On the other hand, autists describe compulsive or automatic movements that impose themselves on their bodies (Biklen, 2005). Autism calls into question our ambiguous understanding of how mental events cause physical events, from the initiation in the brain to action in the body. We still cannot explain this process without lapsing into the Cartesian model of body/brain connection or without using a metaphysical explanation in which mental states transcend physics.

Narrative versus Theory

Herein lays the conundrum. "Experience is a first-person business. Science operates in the third person" (Broks, 2003, p. 139). As mentioned earlier, because of the interaction with like-organisms, our brains assembled an interior picture of the body, or body schema. In their narratives, autists describe an altered internal perception of the body, such as seeing their limbs in multiples. Atypical boundaries and relationships among language, memory, cognition, and the sensory system in autism will be explored in Chapter Five and throughout the book. For example, Lucy Blackman (2005), who began using FC when she was 14, describes the facilitator's role in mediating the gap between mind and body.

> If a tree falls in a forest and no one hears it, can one say it made a sound? That is, I point at a donut and no one sees! That is not communication. This is where the facilitator also has a role in my speech. This often happens. I believe that I have spoken but only in my brain, not in my throat. In fact often I make a sound I believe to be a word, but it has no form. (p. 148)

Tito Mukhopadhyay (Mukhopadhyay & Biklen, 2005) describes his mind and body confusion:

> Am I made of thought or am I made up of my body? I usually experience either, one at a time. For a long time I had no idea of waking or dreaming concept because everything looked as an extension of thoughts. Thoughts would get alive like anything that is alive. (p. 121)

Narratives by non-verbal individuals on the autism spectrum are particularly valuable because they invite the neurotypical into their subjective experience and, therefore, shift the authority from the medical and rehabilitative professions toward a contextualized and socially constructed concept of disability (Biklen, 2005). The autistic writers in Chapter Five, such as Donna Williams, Lucy Blackman, and Tito Mukhopadhyay, describe their inability to translate events into a mental structure, sequence, or representation. Written narratives are attempts to cohere the world through their tenuous but developing grasp on language.

Autistic texts and memoirs take on intensity and deliberation as a defense against the discontinuous "I" and a conscious effort to constrain experience (Belmonte, 2008). Their voices inevitably produce a compelling version of reality. They are fragmented accounts of heightened awareness of the arbitrariness of social norms and superficial communication and relationships. Autists also fill their narratives with honest and introspective descriptions of their pre-verbal lives and realizations of their limitations. In *Autism and the Myth of the Person Alone*, Blackman (2005) writes about her sudden urge to use speech socially. "This wasn't a learned skill but something like an urge that had developed two decades too late" (p. 160). Watching her one-year-old nephew, she acutely understood that her overloaded sensory system misfired this urge in infancy. She ruminates on how these early stages determine the course of one's life:

> Because he learned to smile and babble, he and his family tossed this back and forward in even the most unconscious encounter so that I could see the building blocks of language in place before he had the words with which to cement them. (p. 160)

Matthew Belmonte (2008) argues that the network of integrated perceptions located throughout the brain is easily organized into narrative by the neurotypical, but not for the autist. The social urge to narrate and communicate experience, which comes late in life for autists such as Blackman, intensifies and magnifies awareness of the mind's and body's underdeveloped roles in making the narrative process possible. This existential awareness of one's marginalized place in the world, as a consequence, powers their narratives with exigency. The authors' absence of a coherent "I" does not make autists "lesser than" other humans, says Belmonte (2008), but more than.

The Artist Self

In Chapter Six of Part II, I turn toward the art work, or visual narratives, of autists who emerged from the deinstitutionalization movement in the United States during the latter half of the twentieth century. The chapter investigates identities constructed according to medical misconceptions, institutionalization, and misrepresentation in the mid-twentieth century, and their reconstruction through deinstitutionalization and participation within art communities.

A number of important events unfolded that precipitated government intervention and closings. The infamous Willowbrook asylum in Staten Island, New York—misleadingly called a State School—was scandalized by the revelation of the young reporter Geraldo Rivera. In 1972, Rivera entered the institution with a stolen key and filmed the mistreatment of fifty developmentally disabled children under the supervision of a single attendant.[10] A few years before, Burton Blatt's and Fred Kaplan's hidden camera revealed similar treatment of inmates at five state institutions. Many institutions across the country soon closed, while various outpatient centers opened to help the inmates transition into the community. As the oldest art center in the world for physically, developmentally, and intellectually disabled artists, the Creative Growth Art Center in Oakland, California established a model for professional art making. The artists were understood as valuable makers of culture rather than passive recipients of therapy. Dwight Macintosh, who spent 55 years in an institution, and Judith Scott, 36 years, became the most praised and documented among the artists at Creative Growth.

Because of Creative Growth's long existence, it has established a broad range of media, such as sculpture, printmaking, wood, ceramics, fiber arts, and rug making, with the recent addition of digital film and animation. Painting and drawing are the mainstays and have served as the entry point for new artists. Creative Growth opened in 1974 as a part-time program with six students under founders Elias Katz, a psychologist with training in developmental disabilities, and his partner, Florence Ludins-Katz, an artist and art teacher. They recognized the aesthetic value of the body of work made known by German psychiatrist Hans Prinzhorn. Prinzhorn's collection was the precursor of Art Brut, the term that artist Jean Dubuffet used for his collection of artwork in Lausanne, Switzerland. Prinzhorn began his collection as both an art historian and psychiatrist at the psychiatric clinic at the University of Heidelberg. Although Prinzhorn's project began for diagnostic purposes, as an art historian, his interest in the art of his patients was more subjective than clinical. After Roger Cardinal (1972) wrote *Outsider Art* as a study of Art Brut, "Outsider Art" became the favored terminology, although art historians and critics debate which artists fit into this label.

Case Studies of Visual Artists

The Director of Creative Growth, Tom di Maria (2013), is not deliberate about labeling the artists "outsiders," but they are not immune to such labels, or to the aesthetic and political conflicts that they invite. However, di Maria does not categorically reject the outsider label because to do so would mean to exclude a segment of the art world that identifies the Creative Growth artists among this family of artists and the exhibition opportunities that come with the label. The artists in Part II of this book have exhibited loosely under the outsider label, as well as with no signifiers other than as contemporary artists. Maintaining their mercurial position in the art world is one of the advantages of being in a community. Other benefits have been learning self-advocacy and responsibility for the protection, promotion, and integrity of their work.

Three of the four artists in the final chapters, Gerone Spruill, William Scott, and R.B., are aware of their success and how it has affected their lives. Both R.B. and Dan Miller are non-speakers, but Miller's awareness of his success is uncertain, while R.B. is an aggressive self-promoter. Nevertheless,

Miller enjoys the admiration and attention of the many visitors who seek him out in the studio. The irony of his indeterminate awareness of the excellence of his work was evident in a routine report from the Regional Center that provides daily living services for several of the artists. Among a case manager's memorandums, such as his ability to count to 100, follow directions, and other behavioral information, was a notation that he brought in a 142 page glossy colored catalogue of his one person show at the prestigious La Galerie Christian Berst in Paris, which sells his work for many thousands of dollars.

The four artists are at different levels of cognition, speech, and communication. R. B. and Miller use few words but understand speech. Along with the autism label, Miller has also been classified intellectually disabled, and R. B. has been labeled with paranoid schizophrenia. In my encounters with R. B., I sensed a sharp awareness of self and how she wants to be seen in the world. Her work is fetishistically representational, with highly stylized characters dressed in costume and disguise. Miller's numerical and textual layers of ink and paint invite us into his world of utilitarian objects such as light bulbs, electric sockets, and toilets. Scott's work also has utility, although his subjects are his family and his city. He uses paint to undo the errors of his past and to design a more socially just San Francisco for the future. Both Scott and Spruill search for the ideal woman. Scott, a devout Baptist, paints wholesome and healthy church women; Spruill, who is also a DJ with a penchant for "pretty feet," paints 70s hipster women in black tights, black socks, and penny loafers.

The final chapters devoted to these artists reveal affecting narratives, sometimes humorous or tragic, of longing, overcoming abuse, sexual searching, and speculating about the limitations and possibilities of the future. The artists use idiosyncratic metaphors, symbols, and "the debris of the social order" (jagodzinski, 2012) to stake their places in the Great Chain of Being. Sometimes consciously, for others unconsciously, they take back the right of self-narratization with the meaning and representation of their beingness. Their iconoclastic texts and schema disrupt the normalized boundaries of "insider" and "outsider" art, rendering cultural constructs contingent, negotiable, and dynamic, like the artists who make them.

NOTES

1. Some disability scholars, says Osteen (2008), "view disabilities as artifacts of the disciplines that measure them, and as possessing no physical reality apart from the discursive practices that assess them" (p.1). Osteen suggests that disability studies has set up a binary position in which impairment and the somatic conditions of disability are ignored, a separation that produces "a neo-Cartesian mind/body dualism . . . and that dissolves the body into an aftereffect, or symptom, of discourse" (p. 3).
2. Ian Hacking (1999) describes people with disabilities who influence and change their own category with their collective response to the classification as "interactive kind."

3. "A Hidden Army of Civil Rights" is the title of the fourth chapter in *No Pity* authored by Joseph P. Shapiro (1994).
4. The terms "low" and "high functioning" are used by neurotypicals to refer to the cognitive functions of developmentally disabled people. I use it here to emphasize the impressive intellectual ability of these women writers compared to the intellectual capacity of autists as they are *perceived.*
5. In facilitated communication, the facilitator touches the arm, shoulder, or wrist of the typist; autists explain that initiating an action is one of their most frustrating problems. The desire to take action is in the mind, but the mind cannot command the body to follow through. This is one of the reasons that autists do not do well when tested by external assessors without their assistants. There are also problems about the tests themselves, such as unfamiliarity with testing and lack of preparation, lack of confidence, and test anxiety (Biklen & Cardinal, 1997).
6. I use "normalized identity" to mean the confabulated self, the self that is constructed by our brains to give the illusion of cohesion and continuity.
7. For a comprehensive historical account of the genesis of normal, normalcy, the norm, see Davis, L. J. (1997). Constructing normalcy. In L. J. Davis (Ed.), *The disability studies reader* (pp. 9–28).
8. "According to Gazzaniga, the normal mind is *not* beautifully unified, but rather a problematically yoked-together bundle of partly autonomous systems. All parts of the mind are not equally accessible to each other at all times These modules or systems sometimes have internal communication problems which they solve by various ingenious and devious routes" (Dennett, 1986, p. 6).
9. Sue Rubin is the subject and narrator of *Autism is a World*, directed by Gerardine Wurzburg.
10. Rivera's film, *The Unforgotten*, was followed by Jack Fisher's *Twenty Five Years After Willowbrook* in 2008.

REFERENCES

Bauman, H. D., & Murray, J. (2013). Deaf studies in the 21st century: "Deaf-gain" and the future of human diversity. In L. J. Davis (Ed.), *The disability studies reader* (pp. 246–260). New York, NY and London, England: Routledge.

Belmonte, M. K. (2008). Human but more so: What the autistic brain tells us about the process of narrative. In M. Osteen (Ed.), *Autism and representation* (pp. 166–179). New York, NY and London, England: Routledge.

Bérubé, M. (1998). *Life as we know it: A father, a family, and an exceptional child.* New York, NY: Vintage Books.

Biklen, D. (Ed.). (2005). *Autism and the myth of the person alone: Qualitative studies in psychology.* New York, NY: New York University Press.

Biklen, D., & Cardinal, D. (Eds.). (1997). *Contested words, contested science.* New York, NY: Teachers College Press.

Biklen, D., & Rossetti, Z. (Producers and Directors). (2005). *My classic life as an artist: A portrait of Larry Bissonnette* [Motion picture]. U.S.: The Center on Disability Studies, Law, and Human Policy, Syracuse University.

Blackman, L. (2005). Reflections on language. In D. Biklen (Ed.), *Autism and the myth of the person alone: Qualitative studies in psychology* (pp. 146–167). New York, NY: New York University Press.

Broks, P. (2003). *Into the silent land.* London: Atlantic Books.

Brueggemann, B. (2002). An enabling pedagogy. In S. L. Snyder, B. Brueggemann & R. Garland-Thomson (Eds.), *Disability studies: Enabling the humanities* (pp. 317–336). New York, NY: The Modern Language Association of America.

Cardinal, R. (1972). *Outsider art*. New York, NY: Praeger.

Davis, L. J. (1997). Constructing normalcy. In L. J. Davis (Ed.), *The disability studies reader* (pp. 9–28). New York, NY and London, England: Routledge.

Davis, L. J. (2002). Bodies of difference: Politics, disability, and representation. In S. L. Snyder, B. Brueggemann & R. Garland-Thomson (Eds.), *Disability studies: Enabling the humanities* (pp. 100–108). New York, NY: The Modern Language Association of America.

Dennett, D. (1986). The self as a center of narrative gravity. In F. Kessel, P. Cole & D. Johnson (Eds.), *Self and consciousness: Multiple perspectives*. Hillsdale, NJ: Lawrence Erlbaum. Retrieved from http://ase.tufts.edu/cogstud/papers/selfctr.htm

DiMaria, T. (2013). *Cultures of the maker*. San Francisco/Oakland CA: San Francisco Art Institute/Creative Growth.

Dolmage, J. (2008). Mapping composition: Inviting disability in the front door. In C. Lewiecki-Wilson & B. J. Bruegemann (Eds.), *Disability and the teaching of writing: A critical sourcebook* (pp. 14–27). Boston, MA: Beford/St. Martins.

Ewing, K. (1990). The illusion of wholeness: Culture, self, and the experience of inconsistency. *Ethos, 18*(3), 251–278.

Finger, A. (1990). *Past due: A story of disability, pregnancy and birth*. Seattle Washington: Seal Press.

Glover, J. (1989). *I: The philosophy and psychology of personal identity*. London, England: Penguin.

Hacking, I. (1999). *The social construction of what?* Cambridge, MA: Harvard University Press.

Hull, J. (1992). *Touching the rock: An experience of blindness*. New York, NY: Vintage Books.

Hume, D. (1978) *A treatise on human nature* (2nd ed.). Oxford, England: Oxford University Press.

jagodzinski, j. (2012). Outside the outside: In the realms of the real. In A. Wexler (Ed.), *Art education beyond the classroom: Pondering the outsider and other sites of learning* (pp. 159–185). New York, NY: Palgrave Macmillan.

Linton, S. (1998). *Claiming disability: Knowledge and identity*. New York, NY: New York University Press.

Mairs, N. (1996). *Waist-high in the world: Life among the nondisabled*. Boston: Beacon Press.

Mairs, N. (2002). *Sex and death and the crippled body: A meditation*. In S. L. Snyder, B. Brueggemann, & R. Garland-Thomson (Eds.), *Disability studies: Enabling the humanities* (pp. 100–108). New York, NY: The Modern Language Association of America.

Mukhopadhyay, T. R. (2003). *The mind tree: A miraculous child breaks the silence of autism:* New York, NY: Arcade.

Mukhopadhyay, T. R. (2011). *How can I talk if my lips don't move?: Inside my autistic mind*. New York, NY: Arcade

Mukhopadhyay, T. R., & Biklen, D. (2005). Questions and answers. In D. Biklen (Ed.), *Autism and the myth of the person alone: Qualitative studies in psychology* (pp. 117–143). New York, NY: New York University Press.

Murray, D. W. (1993). What is the western concept of the self? On forgetting David Hume. *Ethos, 21*(1), 3–23.

Nussbaum, S. (1997). Mishuganismo. In K. Fries (Ed.), *Staring back: The disability Experience from the inside out* (pp. 367–401). New York, NY: Plume.

Osteen, M. (Ed.). (2008). *Autism and representation*. New York, NY and London, England: Routledge.

Shapiro, J. P. (1994). *No pity: People with disabilities forging a new civil rights movement*. New York, NY: Three Rivers.

Swan, J. (2002). Disabilities, bodies, voices. In S. L. Snyder, B. Brueggemann & R. Garland-Thomson (Eds.), *Disability studies: Enabling the humanities* (pp. 283–295). New York, NY: The Modern Language Association of America.

Valenza, R. (2002). Editing the self: David Hume's narrative theory. *The Eighteenth Century, 43*(2), 137–160.

Wurzburg, G. (Director). (2005). *Autism is a world* [Motion picture]. U.S.: CNN and CNN Presents.

Wurzburg, G. (Director). (2012). *Wretches & jabberers* [Motion picture]. U.S.: Institute of Community and Inclusion, Syracuse University.

Part I

Theories of Selfhood

1 Beyond the Cognitive (Cartesian) "I"

If you want to know more about me I'll tell you a story.

(Paul Broks, 2010b)

In this chapter, I reexamine how several philosophers, neurologists, and neuropsychologists determine the meaning of "self," a term that I will use interchangeably with "I," "subject," "object," "personhood," "ego," and "identity." These scholars proceed from the primary platform in each of their respective fields, in which the self—the awareness of an "I," or a subjective perspective that produces self-consciousness—is inexhaustible.

Most of these scholars make use of the atypical subject/self, because in examples of neurological anomalies, they might take new positions and frameworks as observers in a hall of mirrors, in the "strange loop" (Hofstadter, 2007) of minds observing minds. For example, V.S. Ramachandran (2011) observes that people with disturbances in self-representation can lead to the discovery of how the sense of self arises in the typical brain: "Each disorder becomes a window on a specific aspect of the self" (p. 250).

I suspect that the reason that scholars such as Paul Broks (2003), Daniel Dennett (1991), Jonathan Glover (1989), Douglas Hofstadter (2007), and Derek Parfit (1984) resort to fiction, poetry, and outlandish metaphors and analogies is because they are humbled by the infinitely fractured, destabilized nature of the "subject." Scientific, cool objectivity belies our uncertainty as we approach the "strange loop" of our minds. Given the fallibility of understanding consciousness, I turn toward the experts of autism with skepticism later in the chapter. Particularly the concept of theory of mind,[1] when applied to both primates and humans, highlights the overwrought confidence of experts when they purport that it is within the power of "normal" human beings to know not only the nature of one's own mind, but also the minds of others.

MANY MINDS/ONE BODY

In *A Treatise of Human Nature*, in "Of Personal Identity," Part IV, section VI, which David Hume wrote in the years 1739–1740, he alludes to a "bundle theory" in which he defines the mind as a collection of perceptions.

Hume (1978) begins: "There are some philosophers who imagine we are every moment intimately conscious of what we call our Self; that we feel its existence; and are certain beyond the evidence of a demonstration, both of its perfect identity and simplicity" (p. 251). If we doubt the certainty of self, says Hume, of what can we be certain? Certainty of self is without doubt a pre-condition of a stable life, the homeostasis and balance to which we Homo sapiens strive (Damasio, 1999; Dennett, 1991; Glynn, 1999). Homeostasis is the standard of "normal," which biologists often define as the achievement of bodily and mental health.

The question from where the impression of self is derived is in itself a contradiction, says Hume, since there is not one impression of self, but a bundle, or collection of impressions that must then remain constant and unchanged throughout the arch of our lives. At which moment and in which of our many conditions can we capture the self? "It cannot therefore, be from any of these impressions, or from any other, that the idea of self is deriv'd; and consequently there is no such idea" (p. 252). When entering into what Hume calls "self,"[2] he finds perceptions and sensations, but never does he observe a single identity. The question Hume asks is how do we presume that these sensations and perceptions belong to something we imagine as a self? And beyond these sensations and thoughts in rapid succession, Hume could find not "a single power of the soul, which remains unalterably the same" (p. 253). In a direct objection to Descartes, Hume suggests that these perceptions appear *as if* in a theater, but resists the notion that they exist in a physical space.

Then how are we to explain our experiential sense of self that is beyond a doubt our identity, and the inference of other selves with their own identities? What makes our identities secure over time, from the first moment of self-awareness to the present? This object (self), "invariable and uninterrupted thro' a suppos'd variation of time; and this idea we call that of *identity* or *sameness*" (p. 253). To be sure there are moments in life when we feel a sense of interruption and disruption, but these feelings can be rationalized by our imaginations. And this is where the story of self begins.

> Thus we feign the continu'd existence of the perception of our senses, to remove the interruption; and run into the notion of a *soul*, and *self*, and *substance*, to disguise the variation. But we may farther observe, that where we do not give rise to such a fiction, our propension to confound identity with relation is so great, that we are apt to imagine something unknown and mysterious, connecting the parts, beside their relation. (p. 254)

In the wake of Descartes's (1637) unwavering certainty of his mind, and therefore other minds, Hume comes forth with a self that exists only in the ideal world produced by our imaginations. The "something unknown" is a rebuttal to Descartes's flimsy solution to the materiality of the brain versus the immateriality of the soul. The unanswered question in physics, and elsewhere, is how they interact with each other. As briefly mentioned in the Introduction, Descartes set up the mind/body, subjective/objective, observer/observed dualities that still exist in scientific systematic observation and experimentation in the search for objective knowledge. This split most affects the investigation of consciousness, which "in essence, is subjective and private" (Broks, 2003, p. 139), because dualism also produces the notion that the mind is distinct from the brain, "composed not of ordinary matter but of some other, special kind of stuff" (Dennett, 1991, p. 33). There can only be one sort of stuff—matter—which is material and physical—of physics, chemistry, and physiology, all governed by physical laws, which includes the brain. Descartes introduced a mysterious presence in consciousness ungovernable by physics, which Gilbert Ryle (1949) later called "the ghost in the machine,"[3] as the solution to the intensely real metaphysical feeling of a self located in and connected to, but not entirely governed by, the body's brain.[4] A ghost is useful only if it can move physical matter, says Dennett, but if it can move physical matter, then the ghost itself must be physical matter.

The Absoluteness of Self

The contradiction between the contingency and contiguity of the parts of self and one's insistence on its absoluteness gives the notion of self its evanescence. But what happens when, as Hume (1978) asks, a few inches are taken away from the body, enough to change its appearance or identity? "And therefore, since this interruption makes an object cease to appear the same, it must be the uninterrupted progress of the thought which constitutes the imperfect identity" (p. 256). Similarly, in the aging process, which can seem imperceptible from day to day, the mind will not be aware of successive changes and, therefore, no interruption. "But whatever precaution we may use in introducing the changes gradually, and making them proportionable to the whole, 'tis certain, that where the changes are at last observ'd to become considerable, we make a scruple of ascribing identity to such different objects" (p. 257). The passage of time that changes us so drastically is a topic of philosophical mystery that we handily explain by the connecting forces of memory and imagination.

But what of considerable mental and bodily changes? We all become disabled unless we die first, says Mark O'Brien (1996) in *Breathing Lessons* (Yu, 1996). In Hume's terms, we technically become a different object. Imagination smoothes the way for interruptions . . . until it can't. The story we've told about our identity will carry us so far until a change is so powerful—such as a traumatic brain injury that takes away short-term or long-term memory—that we must re-make ourselves from moment to moment. Medicine's fairly recent ability to keep TBI survivors alive inspired a renewed interest in what consciousness is and certainly what we call identity.

Finally, Hume asks:

> But, as, notwithstanding this distinction and separability, we suppose the whole train of perceptions to be united by identity, a question naturally arises concerning this relation of identity; whether it be something that really binds our several perceptions together, or only associates their ideas in imagination. (p. 259)

Although volatile and inconsistent, memory is often posed by neurologists, such as Antonio Damasio (1999), Oliver Sacks (1995), and V.S. Ramachandran (2011), as the unifier of our experiences, the faculty that continues the story of the "I." But again, Hume suggests that memory is the image or representation of perceptions, not the perceptions themselves, as are the relationship and resemblance among the perceptions. But if memory itself is produced from the imagination, what can we hold to be concrete and real, other than what we perceive in the moment? In other words, do perceptions have existence beyond the moment? If not, what does that mean to our continuous selves? But even while our memory is intact, what happens to identity during the innumerable moments and days that we can't remember? "In this particular, then, the memory not only discovers the identity, but also contributes to its production by producing the relation of resemblance among the perceptions" (Hume, 1978, p. 261). Experience instructs us about the past, as habit determines what we expect in the future, says Hume, and both operate on the imagination to form images from memory to be conceived as true pictures of the past. Hume concludes that memory, senses, and understanding must come from an ideational imagination.

> No wonder a principle so inconstant and fallacious shou'd lead us into errors, when implicitly follow'd (as it must be) in all its variations. 'Tis this principle which makes us reason from causes and effects; and 'tis the same principle, which convinces us of the continu'd existence of external objects, when absent from the senses. (pp. 265–266)

THE BIOLOGY OF CONSTRUCTING STORIES

Language and Memory

The intuitive feeling and certainty of "I" can be traced to the evolution of language (Damasio, 1999; Dennett, 1986, 1991; Glover, 1989; Jaynes, 2000; Ramachandran, 2011). The feeling of certainty of self is embedded in self-awareness, the subjective knowing of one's own existence. The evolution of language is inevitably linked to self-knowledge, since our verbal commentary is often used as evidence of a conscious self. For example, "talking to oneself" is a term for which Julian Jaynes is well-known, and the foundation of a theory that he and Dennett propose as the construction of self-consciousness.

Neuroscientist V.S. Ramachandran (2011) introduced the science of specialized locations of language in the brain as a polarizing topic in academia, particularly for linguists. He notes that the evolution of consciousness and language, which science is so far—or possibly forever—unable to verify with evidence, attracts geniuses and crackpots. Without "evolutionary intermediates or fossil languages" (p. 163), theories cannot be proved or disproved. He offers balanced and rational theories of language evolution based on his studies with patients with Broca and Wernicke's areas aphasia, the former being dedicated to grammar and syntactical rules of language, and the latter to semantics and understanding, or representation of meaning. These neural circuits that have evolved to specialize in language in humans are part of a larger network, an interconnected system. Ramachandran asks questions that Dennett (1991) and Jaynes (2000) also query and attempt to answer with more unconventional theories. First, Ramachandran (2011) queries, how autonomous are the Broca and Wernicke's areas?

> How does language interact with thought? Does language enable us to think, or does thinking enable us to talk? Can we think in a sophisticated manner without silent internal speech? And lastly, how did this extraordinarily complex, multicomponent system originally come into existence in our hominin ancestors? (p. 161)

Ramachandran's predilection for mirror neurons colors his observations and informs his theories about autism. Ramachandran looks for the transitional phase that led to complex thought and language, possibly 75,000 to 150,000 years ago. Jaynes (2000) offers a more florid theory of the transitional period in which language prepared the way for self-awareness, or consciousness.

From Ramachandran's perspective, the evolutionary theory proposed by Stephen Jay Gould is the most sound. Gould suggests that "language is rooted in a system that gave our ancestors a more sophisticated way to mentally represent the world . . . a way to represent themselves within that representation" (as cited in Ramachandran, 2011, p. 166). Gould hypothesizes that this system was repurposed as language, the way many systems are exapted (opportunistically evolved) from one function into another in natural selection.[5]

The thinking-first-before-language theory is in direct opposition to Jaynes's, in which he claims that speaking out loud, or talking to oneself, eventually became private and silent. Ramachandran proposes a slightly different framework than Gould's, which is more closely aligned with Jaynes's theories related to metaphorical thinking and abstraction. Ramachandran builds upon a possibly hardwired, cross-modal sensory communication system, particularly the visual and auditory maps in which "the link is nonarbitrary and grounded in a true resemblance of the two in a more abstract mental space" (p. 172). He also suggests that these metaphorical abstractions influence our motor maps, which mime corresponding shapes in the contours of our mouth that produce sounds.[6] The emphasis on abstraction and metaphor in language development will be revisited in this and later chapters when we turn to atypical language development in autism.

Included in this cross-modal network are hand gestures, a theory championed by genomist Matt Ridley (2003). The protolanguage of gestural communication might have easily been translated into words, particularly because, Ramachandran notes, the cortical areas of both mouth and hand sit next to each other. The angular gyrus, located between touch, vision, and hearing in the brain, plays an important role in metaphor and abstraction. Two angular gyri exist, one in each hemisphere, the right for visual-spatial and body-based metaphors, the left for language-based metaphors. Ramachandran (2011) suggests that the escalation of higher forms of abstraction—the ability to form common sensory attributes among dissimilar entities and objects—was the result of a need by primates to

> achieve an exquisitely refined, fine-grained interaction between vision and muscle and joint position sense while negotiating branches on tree tops. This resulted in the capacity of cross-modal abstraction, for example, when a branch is signaled as being horizontal both by the image falling on the retina and the dynamic stimulation of touch, joint and muscle receptors in the hands. (pp. 179–180)

It is not far-fetched to extrapolate this ability and to imagine the final result as poetry and other sophisticated products of culture.

A significant question for which there are also no hard scientific answers, however, is whether language is necessary for logical thinking. "Does language precede propositional logic, or vice versa? Or perhaps neither is necessary for the other, even though they mutually enrich each other" (p. 185). Let us return to Dennett (1991) and Jaynes (2000), who imagine a time in Homo sapien history when language was just beginning to develop in significant ways, beyond the "special-purpose vocalization" of primates (Dennett, 1991, p. 194). Speech, which surpassed these spontaneous utterances, was not only intentional but also dependent upon the audience's understanding of the speaker's intention, and therefore made way for a new phase of cultural evolution in human development. Usually sharing of information came about by asking for help. Then one day, imagines Dennett, a request was made for help but no one was around to hear it.

> When it heard its own request, the stimulation provoked just the sort of other-helping utterance production that the request from another would have caused. And to the creature's delight it found that it had just provoked itself into answering its own question. (p. 195)

This hypothetical vocal auto-stimulation would facilitate new connections within the brain and later lead to talking silently to oneself, the awareness of an "I," the owner of the brain. Jaynes (2000) had a similar and highly contested, somewhat cultish theory, with an elaborate hypothesis that suggested human consciousness was preceded by talks with internal voices of gods hallucinated in the right hemisphere as language was in its nascent stage. He called this pre-consciousness the bicameral mind. During the breakdown of pre-consciousness by the first millennium B.C., the mind was transformed into a metaphorical mental space. Jaynes also suggests that the duality of the "soul" and the body began with this metaphysical subjective mind-space in opposition to the material body, and then was cemented by Plato, religion, and finally Descartes.

> So dualism, that central difficulty in this problem of consciousness, begins its huge haunted career through history, to be firmly set in the firmament of thought by Plato, moving through Gnosticism into the great religions, up through the arrogant assurances of Descartes to become one of the great spurious quandaries of modern psychology. (Jaynes, 2000, p. 291)

Thus, the gods' voices departed and were replaced by an interior voice that maintained some of its original mysticism. The lost religiosity that was our pre-conscious has never quite left us, says Jaynes, and we can recognize it in our search for absolute authorization—our contemporary substitution of mysticism, "the same nostalgia for the Final Answer, The One Truth, The Single Cause" (p. 443). The theme of lost innocence and certainty is evident not only in all human religions (e.g., the myth of Eden and the fundamental fall), but also in philosophy and psychology (e.g., Platonic dialogues, Kant's transcendental ego, Marx's lost childhood, and Freud's causes of neurosis). These are the driving narratives of a vague memory of pre-conscious innocence, according to Jaynes.

Metaphor

Jaynes hypothesizes that the metaphorical use of language, such as "seeing" in western culture, generated and gave access to consciousness, and anchored mental events in visual physical space.[7] The "I," or a transcendent ego, is necessary to do the seeing or introspecting in a visual physical space.

> Consciousness is constantly fitting things into a story, putting a before and an after around any event. This feature is an analog of our physical selves moving about through a physical world with its spatial successiveness which becomes the successiveness of time in mind-space. (Jaynes, 2000, p. 450)

Metaphor is not "a trick of language" but rather grounded in the human body (p. 50). The roots of language influenced by bodily feelings in space are often obscured by phonemic change. The most simple and seemingly abstract word in the English language, the verb "to be," is traced to the Sanscrit *bhu*, which means "to grow." Similarly, "am" or "is" evolved from the Sanscrit *asmi*, which means "to breathe." Jaynes points out that the bodily words "grow" and "breathe" preceded the abstract word "existence," for which there was no independent word. Jaynes is himself a skilled metaphor-user, characterizing abstract words as "ancient coins whose concrete images in the busy give-and-take of talk have worn away with use" (p. 51). In this early age, metaphor functioned as the bridge between the concrete meaning of words and their abstractions. The pervasive feeling of touch became particularly significant via the skin, for example the way we use phrases such as "stay in touch," "thin skinned," "rub the wrong way," and "a touching experience" (p. 50). Metaphor transformed consciousness with our ability to reach beyond the concrete moment into new forms of perception and understanding of the world. The most transformative of changes, mentioned earlier, was the metaphor of "I" that exists in the metaphorical space of the mind.

But if we are to follow the implications of Jaynes's theory, we will find no metaphor for consciousness, "For it should be immediately apparent that there is not and cannot be anything in our immediate experience that is like experience itself" (p. 53). According to Jaynes, all explanations of consciousness have been failed attempts at using metaphors. Even the suggestion that consciousness *does* something in a metaphorical space is a metaphor. "For to *do* things is some kind of behavior in a physical world by a living body" (pp. 53–54). If consciousness is a thing it must have a location in physical space, which it does not.

Jaynes defines consciousness as an analog of the "real world" built from metaphors and behaviors in physical space to describe mental behavior, such as "quick," "slow," "nimble-witted," "strong-" or "weak-minded," "narrow-minded," "deep," and "open" (p. 55). Jaynes then takes us deeper into the affect of metaphor. The bodily feelings on which metaphor is based make it impossible to separate the body's affect from metaphor. These are the complex metaphors that carry the deep-seated associations that come with bodily experience in the world. Jaynes uses an example of Seamus Heaney's poem from "Mossbawn (for Mary Heaney)," "my love is like a tinsmith's scoop, sunk past its glean in the meal-bin" (as cited in Jaynes, 2000, p. 57). The affective associations with one's body is apparent in "the enduring careful shape and hidden shiningness and holdingness of a lasting love deep in the heavy manipulable softness of mounding time . . . of such poetry is consciousness made" (p. 58).

The process of generating and organizing consciousness by metaphor is bound in the structure and organization of the world of past experiences and anticipation of future experiences. The similarity of structure allows us to understand the world on which consciousness is based. These organized "spaces" are not only what it means to be conscious, but also to assume consciousness in others. We even spatialize phenomena that do not have a spatial quality. Time, for example, cannot be understood without our conscious spatialization (e.g., from left to right), or seen in what Jaynes calls "side-by-sideness" (p. 60). Excerpts of time can also be described in terms of a succession of events. Excerpts or abstractions from life are not the things themselves but rather they are the raw material of stories and treated as if they are the "true nature" of things. They are the stories of ourselves and the stories we tell about others. Jaynes makes a distinction between excerpt and memory, the former being the representation of something or someone on which memories depend and are retrieved. Before going into greater detail about the narrative "I," I will turn toward the eternal Cartesian problem that eludes reconciliation between the brain and the mental events it produces.

The Problem of "I"

> *What is needed is something we do not have: a theory of conscious organisms as physical systems composed of chemical elements and occupying space, which also have an individual perspective on the world, and in some cases a capacity for self-awareness as well.*
>
> (Nagel, 1986, p. 51)

How are free-floating subjective thoughts generated from what appears to be the brain's physical matter? "The concept of the self," says Thomas Nagel (1986), "seems suspiciously pure—too pure—when we look at it from inside" (p. 32). As an "ultimate private object," it shares no allegiance to physical matter, and yet it arises from it (p. 32). How do I know that I am the same person in the past and will be the same person in the future if I am independent of bodily and mental continuity? Or can the sum total of memories be adequate in defining the self? (Nagel thinks they're not). These are the central problems of Nagel's book, with the suggestive title, *The View from Nowhere*.

The betwixt and betweeness of the "I," which is both observer and actor, perceiver and conceptualizer, must own features that are as yet to be known. Nagel ceaselessly asks what these qualities might be, not as an empty existential exercise, but rather from philosophical angst. He searches for a unifying principle that he admits is not within the mental power of either philosophy or science. Nagel asks where the person Nagel fits into a centerless world—with a view from nowhere—if he is to be contained in the world. How is the particularized subjective Nagel part of the objective world? The contradiction is in fitting both subjective and objective views into one world. No matter how complete the concept of a centerless world, Nagel will always be omitted from it.

> The conception of the world that seems to leave no room for me is a familiar one that people carry around with them most of the time. . . . But

> if it's supposed to be this world, there seems to be something about it that cannot be included in such a perspectiveless conception—the fact that one of those persons, TN [Thomas Nagel], is the locus of my consciousness, the point of view from which I observe and act on the world. (p. 56)

When we conceive of a centerless world, says Nagel, we conceive of it without our own perspective or, in other words, without us in it. Conceptualization, Nagel says, is the cause of our detachment from the world, the illusion that we might know the world from an objective view from nowhere. Only a certain kind of truth can come from the first-person perspective in the present tense, he says, for example "I am Thomas Nagel." Something essential in being an "I" has been left out of this universal view, the objective third-person quality of science and the first-person subjective experience being irreconcilable and untranslatable.

"There's something quirky at the philosophical centre of neurorpsychology," says Broks, a lack of certainty and completeness beyond what he calls "Articles of Faith" (2003, p. 128). They are the fundamentals of neuroscience; the circular certainty that the brain is the organ of a modular mind, and the brain's function is evidence of its modularity. But this certainty does not resolve the sort of de-centering philosophical questions about self, such as Nagel's. Neuroscience's "Articles of Faith" overlooks the qualities of mental life that Nagel wrestles with: self-awareness, or consciousness itself. "One has to be bilingual, switching from the language of neuroscience to the language of experience; from talk of 'brain systems' and 'pathology' to talk of 'hope,' 'dread,' 'pain,' 'joy,' 'love,' 'loss' " (Broks, 2003, p. 130).

Nevertheless, neuroscience is replacing the language of psychoanalysis with both hypothetical and concrete answers about who we are (Broks, 2007). But because of his poetic imagination, Broks is painfully aware of neuroscience's shortcomings and the consequences of making presumptions based on the "Articles of Faith." As a young trainee, he met a 17-year-old patient who fell three flights from an empty elevator shaft. After surgery his face was frozen in anguish, which set off in Broks (2003) a reverie about the accessibility of the face in communicating subtle emotions—humanity itself.

> The chaos of his face drained my sympathy. It broke the rules. A face should allow public access to the private self. It's an ancient convention of the human race. There is a universal system of signals. But this young man's facial displays worked like a subterfuge, denying knowledge of what lay behind. Perhaps nothing lay behind. (p. 19)

Broks's wondering whether the boy existed behind the face was both shocking and revelatory. He witnessed later the boy's interaction with his mother, which brought her son back to life. His shock was the horror of writing off a human being and his realization about the transformative effect of relationship; that we are, in fact, greater than the sum of our parts. For the moments that his mother was with him the rage disappeared from his face. What crystallized from that experience is the necessity of a multi-dimensional model of neurology, and the abjectness of the "crude biomedical model" that reduces people to a "subpersonal biological mechanistic" level (2007, p. 5).

The Narrating "I"

> *As to causation; we may observe, that the true idea of the human mind, is to consider it as a system of different perceptions or different existences, which are linked together by the relation of cause and effect. . . . I cannot compare the soul more properly to anything than to a republic or commonwealth, in which the several members are united by the reciprocal ties of government and subordination.*
>
> (Hume, 1978, p. 261)

Broks (2003), Dennett (1986), and Jaynes (2000) suggest that the first-person subjective "I" is an illusion, which in turn affects the third-person objective view of the world. These scientists and philosophers employ terminology that denotes "I" as a collection of selves working in unity, such as in a confederacy, nation, or republic. "The self has no location, however natural it seems for us to believe otherwise" (Broks, 2003, p. 125). The preponderance of the mystery of putative non-physical mental events that arise from the physicality of the brain has led to many viewpoints. The most ubiquitous comes from the compelling instinct to imagine a self that orchestrates mental events.

Like the all or nothing viewpoints—materialism and idealism[8]—the Cartesian duality solution is mistaken, says Broks. The self requires us to find an alternative form of analysis, yet neuroscience is restrained by a wall that resists a broader concept of self. A concept that does not put mind and body on the same plane would hold back the inevitable lapse into duality. Science has made strides in how we theoretically understand memory and language. Yet, how memory, language, and experience produce the conscious self is unknown. Because memory, language, and experience bind the self (selves) together, Broks implies that to imagine a broader concept of self it would need to be plural—the self in relationship—more than a single brain can reveal. "So it's how brains are an interaction that produces meanings and emotions and selves. To understand emotions you have to understand more than one person, you have to understand brains in interaction rather than in isolation" (Broks, 2010a). But these social and cultural first-person experiences are yet to be translated into neurons.

Broks often frames dialectic within stories, mythology being the most appropriate vehicle to disturb the holders of certainty in his profession. In the chapter called "Right This Way, Smiles a Mermaid" in *Into the Silent Land: Travels in Neuropsychology*, Broks (2003) scripts a scenario during an imagined black-out from a biblical-like storm in Manhattan. The President of the Academy, Collicula Brodmann, escorts Broks to the Investigatory Panel of the Disciplinary Council on the grounds that he is "drifting toward mysterianism"[9] in an otherwise "Broad Church" of neuroscience (p. 133). Three figures whom he identifies by number interrogate Broks. His interrogators want hard certainty while Broks hedges. One figure asks if he believes that neuroscience can find the solution to the eternal mind-body problem.

> 'I'm not sure neuroscience has even found the problem.'
>
> 'What do you believe?' she asked.
>
> 'Nothing,' I replied. 'Sometimes I wonder "How does meat become mind?" and it seems absurd.' . . . 'Then, other times, I see it as a pseudo-problem, a screen of confusion . . . behind which there is empty space' (p. 135).

Broks's internal dialogue in narrative form presents characters with contradictory perspectives—each negating the other—with which he must do battle. Ultimately, he says, science has set up a problem crystallized by Descartes that essentially splits "the fabric of reality" (p. 139). Science is expected to conduct systematic, objective experimentation, "the world *as it is*, independently of personal feelings and opinions" (p. 139). In contradistinction, consciousness is subjective and idiosyncratic. We have essentially set up an inner and outer world, the inner world grounded in the physical matter of the outer world, yet ultimately beyond the reach of scientific scrutiny. Consciousness can either be experienced by its "owner" from the inside, or observed in a lesser form (conjectured) from the outside via neural activity, bodily states, and verbal behavior. Yet, "The quality—the feel—of our experience remains forever private and therefore out of bounds to scientific analysis. . . . Privateness is a fundamental constituent of consciousness" (p. 140). Thought might be dependent on neural activity, and sight on photons, but it is the point of view of the poet we humans are interested in, not his or her visual cortex or neural patterns. As a scientist Broks knows the brain as a physical device, "three pounds of fats, proteins, sugars and salts" (2007), but knowing the brain at this level alone insufficiently describes the complex and intangible experiences on the private level.

Broks's narratives are replete with ambiguity, whether he is pondering a collection of brain specimens suspended in jars or visiting a patient who wakes up to a world she mistakes to be 25 years earlier. In each story he recoils from the role of confident scientist. He confesses to his interrogating peers that although neuropsychology is his area of expertise, it fills him with a sense of profound ignorance, particularly of the relationship between the brain and consciousness.

> An ocean of incomprehension heaves beneath the textbook-confident surface of plain facts and technicalities that I present to my colleagues

> and patients. I have a clear picture of the material components of the brain and am prepared to ad lib at length about features of its functional architecture—the interlocking systems and subsystems of perception, memory, and action. But quite how our brains create that private sense of self-awareness we all float around in is a mystery. (pp. 91–92)

Broks confesses that even the assumption that the brain generates consciousness is suspect. The more he looks for consciousness in the brain, the more elusive "it" becomes.[10] From this vantage point, Broks says, "It is no more to be found in the hills and dales of the frontal lobes or on the slopes of the Rolandic fissure than in the chair you are sitting on" (p. 95). Broks does not, as his interrogators rush to question, resort to a soul-related solution. He would rather have no solution at all. Nor will Broks rush to the we-are-the-sum-of-our-parts solution, having seen his patients maintain a conscious self with less than a whole brain. Because of the intense vagueness of scientific solutions, however, he concedes to the natural inclination and biologically embedded tendency to bifurcate the world into mind and brain, immaterial soul and physical body.

In order to "untie this knot of knots perhaps the first move is to acknowledge that we are not only physically *embodied*, but also *embedded* in the world about us" (p. 101). Our evolutionary social embeddedness, says Broks, determined this bifurcation. Our own mental states and those of others may have led to the belief in the soul. We view ourselves as integrated mental entities with an agenda of intentions and actions, authors of our own destiny. Broks suggests that our sense of self begins in the early biological moment of interaction with the world. The "I" that reflects on experience is the by-product of what Broks calls the affect programs—the limbic system that prepares us for action through the input of affective sensory information. Affect, whose evolutionary purpose is survival in the external world, has also provided us with an internal sense of self and the coherency of experience. In cognitive science this embeddedness in the social world is called *the extended mind*. Its precursor was described by Alexander Luria (1966) 50 years ago, who conceived of the relationship between mind and body as an open biological and social system. This concept also extends science into the subjective and complex sphere of human relationships. A new neuroscience would embody the socially constructed self and the biological brain in one paradigm.

The internal sense of self as embodied, and externally embedded in the world, centers us within the inner limits of our physical shape and the outer limits of our skin. "I have a strong sense that I'm located *in* my body. . . . My body also contributes to my sense of continuity—the feeling that I am the same person from one day to the next" (p. 107). How we maintain continuity despite the aging and changing process of the body is a phenomenon that Dennett (1986), Hume (1978), and Glover (1989) also contemplate. The mirror image of our body contributes to our continuity on a daily basis, yet it is perplexing that we can identify with a photographic image of a visually different object that was our self as an infant or other stage of life. Other problems are the permeability of the body: where we begin and end. Do we accept as part of ourselves the various bacteria and viruses in our digestive system? The length of our occupancy in our bodies over the life span is also not within our control. Neurotypicals can usually sweep these issues under the rug. But for autists an awareness of foreignness and lack of control within one's own body in a capricious and random world is part of the daily experience of being alive. In subsequent paragraphs, I will revisit this phenomenon and question the reliability of neurotypical clinical observation of autistic experience.

Autism and Consciousness: The Intersection of Enigmas

> *If "I" is inescapable, it is also true that the place I am at is always here, and the time is always now. Tomorrow never comes.*
>
> (Glover, 1989, p. 66)

If the affect programs formed the notion of a neurotypical self, how might atypical social relationships form the autistic self? If emotions give cohesion to neurotypical experience, how might atypical emotions affect the experience of being autistic? Autistic perceptions, thoughts, emotions, and actions are not organized in a way that would accord the sense of coherency and continuity as they would in the neurotypical self. There is no central location from which autists feel perceptions, thoughts, desires, and actions. There is also no central core from which past and present cohere.[11]

Oliver Sacks (1996) ruminates on this phenomenon while observing the well-known British artist Stephen Wiltshire. Sacks met Wiltshire as a young adolescent, so much of Sacks's descriptions of him are outdated since the young man is now in his thirties. While on a train to Leningrad with Wiltshire, Sacks watched the continuous flow of images from his window and wondered whether Wiltshire experienced the world in similar un-integrated, un-synthesized images; whether his mind acted as a storage container for images to be filed and retrieved in the future but without connection or meaning to his life. Sacks makes the imperceptible leap from quasi-objective observation to a subjective neurotypical assumption that a differently-experienced consciousness has no meaning. If the universe has a special place in us (Broks, 2007), how do autists internally represent the world? If there is no stronger intuition than our ownership of our bodies, in what way do autists "feel" that they occupy their bodies? Do autists' bodies contribute to, or are they indifferent to, a sense of continuity? Do they, as neurotypicals do, expect to look and feel the same from one day to the next? These are questions I will revisit and develop throughout the text.

In an interview with the Australian Broadcast Corporation (ABC) in 2007, Broks describes in a few words the ambiguity, confusion, and angst that the "deep problems" of our existence have on us in childhood. To speak very generally, we sense these ontological problems and ask the big questions: "who am I?" "How did I get here?" "Where am I going?" Most importantly, who is the "I" that wonders? Perhaps children in their yet-to-be-indoctrinated minds experience the visceral ambiguity of being a self in the world. And then we go to school and take comfort in the education of a simplified version of life. But the big questions remain, says Broks. A simplistic view of the quality of our conscious selves and the satisfaction of unproblematic answers might stand as metaphors for our naive assumptions about, and categorizations and diagnoses of, autism. But in the shift in understanding the self as a bundle rather than an ego, the neurotypical's relationship to autism changes dramatically. From what certainty do we claim to analyze what we describe as a fragmented, permeable, contingent, pluralist, relational, and inconsistent autistic self?

In this book I argue that autists experience, probably in excess, the "bundle-like" quality of self. While neurotypicals inherit the evolutionary skill of cohering the brain's sequence of experiences into the illusion of a unified self, autists do not lay claim to this ability. It is not within the scope of this text to presume a "coherent" reason why this might be so, which would also derail the point of the book.[12] Rather, I question the stability of the neurotypical self in a postmodern era that has been given substance by neuroscience: the illusion of the hard and fast boundary between neurotypicality and otherness.

Like postcolonial and racial discourses, disability studies underlines the political implications of binary opposites and their inherently asymmetrical power relationship in defining selfhood. Margrit Shildrick (2012) analyzes the social and psychological compulsion of setting apart the other as a way of holding back the "contamination" of disability, disavowing and denying the vulnerability of mind and body, and securing the illusion of stability, self-control, and predictability. Shildrick's scholarship is primarily in physical embodiment and the anomalous body's reminder of our mortality. In the same way, autism reminds us of the fragility of identity, the lack of absoluteness of "I," and the porous borders of the self.

My point is not to diminish the neurotypical or put her on the defensive, but rather to equalize the playing field of human conditions and disrupt the asymmetrical polarized discourse. As Shildrick (2012) writes, the point is to hold the neurotypical responsible within the human continuum rather than isolate him as a normalized subject against which all other humans conditions are measured. From his autistic perspective, Eugene Marcus (1998) addresses his search for personhood in a neurotypical world in his keynote presentation, *On Almost Becoming a Person*, at the Facilitated Communication conference at Syracuse University in New York.

> All people are real, in the deepest sense of that word. That means that there is no such thing as a non-human human. But if you look around

> this room, you will see people who look at least non-standard. And that is where the problem begins. We live in a country where image is kind of a reality more real than reality. (p. 2)

Broks (2003) suggests that our mental narrative and body produces our sense of personhood, and our imagination completes the rest. Autists' stories are not typically sequential, their sensory and perceptual systems do not work in an order that is logical to the neurotypical. The mental functions that bring the neurotypical's world into view, such as the construction of concrete time and space, are also not available to the autist. Thus, body in time and space is differently organized. I suggest that autists have organization, but must function in a world constructed by the logic of neurotypicals' perceptual and sensory systems and the survival imperative of social existence.

Social and cultural existence requires communicative language and a complex memory system, since language and memory contribute to the consistency of stories. As mentioned above, autists, whose early development excludes language, construct an essentially different form of self, and thus a very different story. Autists' stories do not cohere in a neurotypical construction of time and space, but rather, I hypothesize, are re-written each moment, which would explain the neurotypical's difficulty in following their storylines. I quote Marcus again as he introduces himself to the conference audience.

> What I want to talk about today is about life and fairy tales, and how you know which one you are in at the moment. Seems easy, doesn't it? But sometimes life becomes magical, confusing, and familiar all at once, just like a fairy tale. And so there are times I feel more like Pinocchio than I do like Eugene Marcus. . . . And eagerness by parents to cure autism or retardation or compulsiveness will not drive great distances toward the final solution to the actual problem. Because the person who believes, "I will be real when I am normal," will always be almost a person, but will never make it all the way. (p. 1)

If neurotypical consciousness is made from the poetry of metaphor, described by Jaynes as the predecessor of language, then we speak of a quality of consciousness that cannot measure an alternate consciousness by the standards of language. Given the theory of language as inextricable with self, neurologists make an error when applying the same meaning-making to an essentially non-language-based "ego." The question then is whether autists embody an ego in the sense that ego is produced by social language. We might consider the cultural challenges of a non-native speaker negotiating the dominant world view of the host country. Language contains nuanced, contextualized, often untranslatable meanings. Imagine the autist navigating a language-filled world without a disposition toward any kind of language at all, to language itself.

Then how do autists internally represent the self and the self in the world, which automatically give rise to narrative structures in neurotypicals? Matthew Belmonte (2008) theorizes that the autist's process of narratization is disrupted from weakened connections made among perception, attention, and memory throughout the brain. "Since there is no neuroanatomical Cartesian theater," writes Belmonte, a location where the elements of personhood come together, the neurotypical narrator is dependent on a functional connectivity among all the regions of the brain to cohere experience (p. 169). Thus, Belmonte's theory of the neurotypical "narrative defense against sensory chaos" is compromised in autists, and results in their highly calculated, ritualized, and conscious narratives (p. 170).

Local coherence is well described by Kamran Nazeer (2006) in *Send in the Idiots: Stories From the Other Side of Autism*. Autists tend to establish a local coherence in the environment as an organizational strategy that substitutes for the neurotypical's abstract or global coherence. Belmonte describes local coherence as beginning with the detail and working up to the concept, while neurotypicals begin with the concept and work downwards to the detail. Nazeer describes his need to establish local coherence when confronted with unpredictable situations. He keeps a set of keys in his pocket that he twirls incessantly to offset social unpredictability and make it workable.

Bundles and Boundaries

Broks (2010a), like other Bundle theorists, does not believe in an inner essence of the self. He has witnessed the stripping away of the "bundle" in neurological disorders, and "the bundle rolls on until it stops. But there's nothing in the middle of it," or as he paraphrases Derek Parfit (1984), the self is not caused by neural behavior, it *is* neural behavior.

In the sometimes half-fictionalized stories of Broks's patients with such self-shifting diseases as Cotard and Capras syndromes, dramatic changes of personality and narratives might also serve as metaphors for kinship with the estranged other, a closing in on the overwhelming separation between neurotypicals and autists. Cotard and Capras syndromes highlight two states of existence, the core and extended self. Neurologist Antonio Damasio calls the core self, the self in the moment, "a transient entity, re-created for each and every object with which the brain interacts" (as cited in Broks, 2012). The extended self is the autobiographical self, the beginning, middle, and end of a story projected through time. Patients with Capras syndrome recognize their friends and loved ones but have lost a shared extended story with them—their extended selves—and so believe they are impostors. People with Cotard can tell their stories but have lost their core selves and therefore believe that they have ceased to exist in the present, resulting from "a neurological decoupling of feelings and thoughts. Thinking that one exists was not enough: the notion had also to be felt—'I feel I think, therefore I am'" (Broks, 2006, p. 3). One of Broks's (2006) Cotard patients thought that all that was left was her interior voice. This voice that never ceases is part of the autobiographical scheme that insures that we maintain the experience of self. Without it we would live in an extended and unmediated present. Broks embellishes the evanescence of self, even in ordinary life, with a description of how the author not only interpellates the reader, but also becomes the reader's voice.

> But these words you are now reading, whose are they? Yours or mine? The point of writing is to take charge of the voice in someone else's head. This is what I am doing. My words have taken possession of the language circuits of your brain. I have become, if only transiently, your inner voice. Doesn't that mean, in a certain sense, that I have become you (or you me)? It's a serious question. Written text is a primitive but powerful form of virtual reality. In the beginning was the word. And in the end? A liberating truth. There are no souls, only stories. (p. 4)

Broks (2010b) shared a story on National Public Radio about a patient with a severe head injury he called Jeff. At one point Jeff became volatile and angry, throwing the test materials on the floor. Later Broks asked Jeff's wife how she handled her husband's outbursts. "That's not really him, it's not really Jeff," she said. Then who is Jeff, Broks thought? The essence or soul that remains of Jeff is precisely what Bundle theorists argue against. Where would the soul go? Would it be mutilated with the brain? Dennett (1986) suggests that when the behavioral control system breaks down, the best story we might tell about the individual is that there is more than one protagonist that inhabits the body. In effect, there are "two centers of gravity, two selves. One isn't creating or discovering a little bit of ghost stuff in doing that. One is simply creating another abstraction" (p. 8).

Shildrick (2012) writes that it is not that we have fears and anxieties about the old, sick, and disabled because they are foreign, but rather because they are too familiar. Neurotypicals are simply a slip away, as Broks (2010b) says, from an extra-ordinary existence. I hypothesize that neurotypicals and autists are on similar ground based on what we know of neurotypical automatic construction of autobiography and the random self-stories of autists. Stripped of the story-telling device, where "I" end and "you" begin would be as unclear to the neurotypical as it is to the autist. Without this device, neurotypicals would need to recreate themselves in the continuous present. With this device, neurotypicals do not think according to the laws of logic, but think somewhat magically, holding two opposites to be true. The neurotypical individual identity, itself, says Broks (2012), is an act of imagination. Autists have been known to think illogically as well:

> [W]e human beings are creatures of the natural world subject to the Laws of Logic, physics, biology. But the self . . . the compelling illusion

> that we're more than that, that we somehow transcend biology and physics. . . . But illusion is not quite the right word. It implies that there might be a way of stepping outside the frame of the false perception to see ourselves as we really are. But no, we inhabit the illusion, we're built into it, the illusion is who we really are. (Broks, 2012, http://vimeo.com/45242445)

In Chapter Five, we will revisit autists who have crafted their own life narratives by learning to write through alternate communication strategies. As mentioned above, their narrative organization has been disrupted and the conscious effort to construct it is arduous. And, as Belmonte points out, this hyper-conscious effort usually produces intensely perceptive insights.

NOTES

1. For a good explanation of theory of mind, see V.S. Ramachandran (2011, p. 138).
2. Nelson Pike (1967), in his article "Hume's Bundle Theory of the Self: A Limited Defense," infers that Hume's use of the term "self" refers to "mind" and not to the whole person.
3. In Ryle's classic attack on Descartes's theory, he calls it the dogma of the ghost in the machine. Since then dualists have been on the defensive (Dennett, 1991). Broks (2006) writes in the *New Scientist*, "If we found a ghost in the machine we'd have to start looking for the machine in the ghost," suggesting the hall of mirrors conundrum (para., 5). "There was no homuncular assembly point where a little soul-pilot sat watching the dials of experience and pulling the levers of action. We were, neuropsychologically speaking, all over the place" (para., 5).
4. Descartes was aware of the problem of dualism and so he formulated that the pineal gland was the site of interaction between the body and brain through which messages are transmitted. "These, *ex hypothesi*, are not physical; they are not light waves or sound waves or cosmic rays or streams of subatomic particles. No physical energy or mass is associated with them. How, then, do they get to make a difference to what happens in the brain cells they must affect, if the mind is to have any influence over the body?" (Dennett, 1991, pp. 34–35). Dennett emphasizes that it is not that Descartes made the mistake of thinking the Pineal gland was the locus of interaction, but that there is any location in the brain at all that would be a locus of mind-brain interaction.
5. Ramachandran (2011) offers the following example of exaptation: "For instance, feathers originally evolved from reptilian scales as an adaptation to provide insulation (just like hair in mammals), but then were exapted from flight" (p. 66).
6. "If this sounds a bit cryptic, think again of words like 'teeny-weeny,' 'un peau,' and 'diminutive,' for which the mouth and lips and pharynx actually become small as if to echo or mime the visual smallness" (Jaynes, 2000, p. 173).
7. Jaynes says the following about the visual-physical metaphor of mind-space: "When in any discussion or even in our thinking we can use spatial terms, as 'locating' a problem or 'situating' a difficulty in an argument, as if everything in existence were spread out like land before us, we seem to get a feeling of clarity. This pseudo-clarity, as it should be called, is because of the spatial nature of consciousness" (p. 454).

8. Dennett (1991) defines materialism as follows, "there is only one sort of stuff, namely matter—the physical stuff of physics, chemistry, and physiology—and the mind is somehow nothing but a physical phenomenon. In short, the mind is the brain" (p. 33). The opposing view, which is idealism, considers reality, or matter, to be the product of mind, and does not exist outside of it.
9. Mysterianism is a term in philosophy that posits that human beings do not have the mental ability to understand consciousness on a scientific level.
10. Like Jaynes, Broks highlights the fact that "it" signifies a thing; consciousness as an object is a metaphor, it is not a "thing" to be located, says Broks, but closer to a function or process whose elements still cannot be said to be located in some region of the brain.
11. I make these generalizations based on autistic narratives (autie-biographies), which will be discussed in Chapter Five.
12. See V.S. Ramachandran's (2011) mirror theory as one of the possible causes of autism, in *The Tell Tale-Brain: A Neuroscientist's Quest For What Makes Us Human.*

REFERENCES

Belmonte, M. K. (2008). Human, but more so: What the autistic brain tells us about the process of narrative. In M. Osteen (Ed.), *Autism and representation* (pp. 166–179). New York, NY: Routledge.

Broks, P. (2003). *Into the silent land: Travels in neuropsychology*. London, England: Atlantic Books.

Broks, P. (2006, November 18). The big questions: What is consciousness? *New Scientist*. Retrieved from: http://www.mintinnovation.com/links/docs/Mind_and_consciousness/Big%20Questions%20-%20what%20is%20consciousness.pdf

Broks, P. (2007, May 26). *Writing the brain: Part I-Into the silent land with Paul Broks*. Australian Broadcasting Corporation. All in the Mind. Retrieved from: http://www.abc.net.au/radionational/programs/allinthemind/writing-the-brain-part-1—-into-the-silent-land/3248810

Broks, P. (2010a, May 24). *Neuropsychology*. Retrieved from: http://www.abc.net.au/radionational/programs/allinthemind/writing-the-brain-part-1—-into-the-silent-land/3248810#transcript http://www.youtube.com/watch?v=m0K-4ElPYsw

Broks, P. (2010b, July 3). *Into the silent land*. Retrieved from: http://www.youtube.com/watch?v=E-CbMuqWdq0

Broks, P. (2012). *The rest is silence*. Plymouth University. Retrieved from: http://vimeo.com/45242445

Damasio, A. (1999). *The feeling of what happens: Body and emotion in the making of consciousness*. New York, NY: Mariner Books.

Dennett, D. C. (1986). The self as a center of narrative gravity. In F. Kessel, P. Cole, and D. Johnson (Eds.), *Self and consciousness: Multiple perspectives*. Hillsdale, NJ: Lawrence Erlbaum. Retrieved from: http://ase.tufts.edu/cogstud/papers/selfctr.htm

Dennett, D. C. (1991). *Consciousness explained*. New York, NY: Back Bay Books/Little Brown.

Descartes, R. (1637). *Discourse on method of rightly conducting one's reason and of seeking truth in the sciences*. Leiden, The Netherlands.

Glover, J. (1989). *I: The philosophy and psychology of personal identity*. London, England: Penguin.

Glynn, I. (1999). *An anatomy of thought: The origin and machinery of the mind*. New York, NY and Oxford, England: Oxford University Press.

Hofstasdter, (2007). *I am a strange loop*. New York, NY: Perseus Books Group.
Hume, D. (1978) *A treatise on human nature* (2nd ed.). England: Oxford University Press.
Jaynes, J. (2000). *The origin of consciousness in the breakdown of the bicameral mind* (3rd ed.). New York, NY: Mariner.
Luria, A. (1966). *Human brain and psychological processes*. New York, NY: Harper and Row.
Marcus, E. (1998). *On almost becoming a person*. Institute on Communication and Inclusion Conference. Syracuse University, NY. Retrieved from: http://soeweb.syr.edu/media/documents/2010/7/on_almost_becoming_a_personmarcus.pdf.
Nagel, T. (1986). *The view from nowhere*. New York, NY and Oxford, England: Oxford University Press.
Nazeer, K. (2006). *Send in the idiots: Stories from the other side of autism*. New York, NY and London, England: Bloomsbury.
Parfit, D. (1984). *Reasons and persons*. Oxford, England: Claredon.
Pike, N. (1967). Hume's bundle theory of the self: A limited defense. *American Philosophical Quarterly, 4*(2), 159–165.
Ramachandran, V. S. (2011). *The tell-tale brain: A neuroscientist's quest for what makes us human*. New York, NY: W.W. Norton.
Ridley, M. (2003). *Nature via nurture: Genes, experience and what makes us human*. London, England: Fourth Estate.
Ryle, G. (1949). *The Concept of mind*. London, England and New York, NY: Hutchinson's University Library.
Sacks, O. (1995). *An anthropologist on mars: Seven paradoxical tales*. New York, NY: Vintage.
Shildrick, M. (2012). *Dangerous discourses of disability, subjectivity and sexuality*. London, England: Palgrave Macmillan.
Yu, J. (1996) (Director). *Breathing lessons. The life and work of Mark O'Brien*. [Motion picture]. U.S.: Fanlight Productions.

2 Constructing Autism Narratives

Leo Kanner (1943) in the United States and Hans Asperger (1944) in Austria are the well-known researchers who coined the term "autism" and its diagnosis. They described their subjects' sensory perceptions as "abnormal," "odd," or "bizarre." Lorna Wing brought Asperger's study to the attention of researchers in the United States in 1981 with her paper "Asperger's Syndrome: A Clinical Account" in the *Psychological Medicine* journal. In this paper, Wing changed Asperger's original diagnostic term *autistic psychopathy* to the more neutral *Asperger's syndrome*. She reported in her findings that the condition Asperger designated for his subjects had similar attributes to Kanner's autism. Their differences, however, lay in the lack of linguistic skills in the Kanner-type autism, the majority of whom were then considered "mentally retarded."

From the neurotypical perspective, the "odd" responses to sensory stimuli were conceived by Simon Baron Cohen, Alan Leslie, and Uta Frith (1985), in their article "Does the Autistic Child have a Theory of Mind?," as a lack of theory of mind (ToM) or mindblindness, and by Uta Frith (1989) as a weak central coherence (WCC). Lorna Wing (1981) and her colleagues in cognitive psychology presented autism's core problem as a triad of impairments of social interaction, verbal and nonverbal communication, and play and imagination. The triad suggests that autists have no true concept or feeling for other minds, or ToM, and describes both WCC and ToM as not benefiting the organism and its survival.

> What often appears as a language problem can be better understood as a problem of semantics of mental states. Similarly, what appears as a problem in affective relationships can be understood as a consequence of the inability to realize fully what it means to have a mind and to think, know, and believe and feel differently from others. What often appears as a problem of learning to become socially competent can be understood from exactly the same point of view. (p. 173)

Both central coherence and ToM are the focus of Bruce Mills's (2008) analysis of the prevailing theory proposing the deficiency of imagination in autism, which is measured by a normative standard for the "natural" creative process. Mills points out that the *DSM-IV* implicitly refers to the "ideal" of one sort of imagination that synthesizes and generalizes symbols, and discredits the more personalized and usually heightened discernment of imagery and experience. The narrowed definition, he says, is the legacy of adhering "the process of creation with the act of thought itself," its roots reaching back to the age of Romanticism, particularly in the texts of two transcendentalist writers, Emerson and Coleridge (p. 118). Emerson theorized coherency as the fruit of maturity, the unity of seemingly disparate phenomena.

The drive for coherence and wholeness was therefore the highest achievement of the imagination and artistic production, according to the Transcendentalists. Coupled with the new scientism of the nineteenth century, the imagination was firmly situated in the mind and body and obeyed its physical laws. During this period, the imagination promised to redeem and unify what appeared to be the unredeemable aspects of existence, particularly its disharmony and disconnection (Mills, 2008).

Mills theorizes the contemporary concepts of central and local coherence, explained by Uta Frith (1989), as echoes of nineteenth century notions of primary imagination and fancy. The former seeks coherence and wholeness while the latter is an inferior mnemonic imagination that fails to provide unifying coherence and instead finds meaning in isolated perceptions. ToM achieves imaginative coherence in individuals as the adaptive advantage to interpret the environment, and to theorize how interior causes create exterior effects and prepare for change (Mills, 2008). Both central coherence and ToM, reasons Mills, are the modern interpretation of the nineteenth century theories of mind and imagination.

The deficit narratives above were at least partly responsible for laying the groundwork for the central role of the doctor/therapist/health practitioner who must "cure" the patient. The autist is not an agent of his or her destiny, but must submit to the moral order (Frank, as cited in Osteen, 2009). Nineteenth century positivist scientific assumptions, writes Majia Nadesan (2009), set the stage on which detached empirical inquiry leveraged the study of a new subjective self along with the Cartesian mind/body binary that located disease in the body. She emphasizes the cultural and economic conditions that, perceived within a social dynamic, developed and changed in the 1940s. Until then, only in extreme cases, or for the economically privileged, were children's psychology and development attended to. A diagnostic condition such as autism before the twentieth century would be "unthinkable."

As new medical categories are introduced, they eventually become susceptible to what Ian Hacking (1999) calls the "looping effect" of "interactive kinds," which are, for example, autists who read what the medical profession writes about their diagnosis and are therefore affected by it. Their changed behavior then alters and influences the classification. Parents also affect the dynamic of autism, as do new therapy programs and theories of causation. Bettelheim's "refrigerator mother," which affected parents and their families for decades, is an example of a cultural and biolooping effect. The introduction of alternative and augmentative communication devices is another example that has broken the silence of the autistic population. With the assistance of these technologies, autists who were thought to be "mentally retarded" reveal their rich interior lives in blogs, websites, and autobiographies (see Chapter Five, this volume).

Mark Osteen (2009) points to the recent ambiguous diagnostic category of pervasive developmental disorder not otherwise specified (PDD-NOS) as illustrative of autism's shifting ground. Nadeson theorizes that while classic autism is a condition of the early twentieth century, the so-called "high-functioning" conditions of Asperger's and PDD-NOS reflect the culture and psychology of the late twentieth and early twenty-first centuries. The concept of a mild autism was contingent on such conditions as "the invention of intensive mothering, the standardization of benchmarks of developmental normality, and widespread pediatric surveillance of very young children" (p. 84). The mystique of the profound interests and intellectual gifts of "high functioning" autists, which are both feared and applauded, awaited computer technology in the latter half of the twentieth century. So much has the popular imagination identified "high functioning" (geeks) with computer technology and artificial intelligence that autistic intelligence is often described as machine-like, robotic, mechanical, and modular.

The twentieth century modernist notion of *self* is theorized as an additional stimulus for identifying autistic categories, particularly in post-war literature, in which many characters are ontologically insecure and existentially alienated (McDonagh, 2009). The reconstruction of self and identity was reflected in and informed by a psychologically altered literary protagonist made possible by such early experimental linguist forerunners as James Joyce, Gertrude Stein, and Virginia Woolf. McDonagh notes that Hans Asperger's (1991) description of his subjects as "egocentric in the extreme . . . following their own wishes, interests and spontaneous impulses" might also be an apt character analysis of a number of modernist novels (p. 81). "Thus the stage was being set. The opening decades of the twentieth century saw the growth of a sociocultural environment in which a condition like autism could seem possible" (McDonagh, 2009, p. 110). A space was designated for an autistic subjective experience of isolation and otherness, which made possible, suggests McDonagh, the diagnostic conditions that Kanner and Asperger designated for their patients. In hindsight, autistic people have existed throughout time,[1] but only by the alienation, destabilization, and fragmentation felt in modernism could autism as such be defined.

BOUNDARIES OF THE BODY-SELF: EMBEDDED IN THE WORLD

Paying attention to Mukhopadhyay's body challenges—with proprioception, sensory processing, over- and under-inclusion of details in his

> *apprehension of the environment, word finding, a drive to associate, a persistent animism, and synesthesia—it suggests that he is a cross-cultural, cross-sensorial migrant: a neuro-cosmopolitan armed with metaphor in a world that is often quite hostile to the neurological other.*
> (Savarese, 2010a, p. 273)

I begin this section with this rich quotation by Ralph Savarese in his paper, "Toward a Postcolonial Neurology: Autism, Tito Mukhopadhyay, and a New Geo-poetics of the Body," because of a sharp paradigm shift into metaphors of autism with terminology such as colonization,[2] neuro-cosmopolitanism,[3] and "migrantcy." These are refreshing metaphors that attempt to replace the deficit metaphors of the mainstream/medical narrative of autism. Savarese points out that the anthropologist trope, benignly used by Oliver Sacks (1996) in *Anthropologist on Mars*, belies the colonizing impulse of medical practitioners and the perpetuation of the unequal power relationship between doctor and autistic client. While heeding the critique of the wholesale use of postcolonialism as a metaphor, a postcolonial neurology would nevertheless disrupt this old binary by allowing "us to see the current struggle for self-determination being waged by autistics as a kind of neuro-nationalist uprising" (p. 274). Savarese propels the metaphor further by pointing out that autists are meant to rely heavily on the right hemisphere, often to the exclusion of the left. That western culture favors the left hemisphere as the loci of logic and reason sets the autist in a location further removed and further oppressed.

Western philosophy and culture, it has been argued (Lakoff & Johnson, 1999; Pallasmaa, 2009), project a separation of mind and body by valuing the mind and colonizing the body. The mind as embodied in physical existence has long been devalued and ignored in the traditional western narrative. The body is relegated to the arts, to dance, to work, writes Pallasmaa, but rarely to our primary interaction and integration with the world. Given the preference for the disembodied mind over the senses, visualization, and non-verbal language, the ways of autistic knowing are devalued. Poetry, however, crosses boundaries by its use of metaphor, which is inseparable with the sensing body.

Tito Mukhopadhyay is a young Indian man with what most health professionals would label severe autism. He is also a poet with three published books (2003, 2005, 2011) who learned to read and write by an augmentative communication system devised by his mother Soma called the rapid prompting method. He does not use speech, but reports his life through synesthesia-rich metaphors. He is not only a geographical migrant, but also a cultural migrant who enriches the neurotypical world with his vivid stories and poems from his lively atypical sensorium. Ironically, Mukhopadhyay was brought to the United States by Cure Autism Now (CAN),[4] which has quickly become a flash point for two combative ideologies: cure versus quality of life. The "pathologizing impulse" of doctors (Savarese, 2010a,

p. 273), particularly Simon Baron Cohen's (1985, 1997) theory of mind (ToM) and the empathizing-systematizing (E-S) theory, which are discussed more fully later in the chapter, is the groundwork for defining autism in catastrophic terminology, and therefore requiring a cure. Many autists—even those labeled "severely autistic"—suggest that their identities are inseparable from autism and therefore to cure autism would mean the annihilation of personhood. Soma, as an advocate for her son, later distanced herself from CAN (Savarese, 2010a).

The hyper-sensorium of the autist is well presented in Mukhopadhyay's description of his proprioceptive awareness of body in space, a recurring theme of *The Mind Tree*. As a poet, Savarese (2010a) is particularly drawn to the radical otherness of Mukhopadhyay's metaphors, animism, associations, embodiment, proprioception, and sensory processing. In the language of the majority, Mukhopadhyay inserts his fully aware poetics. "The subaltern has learned to speak, and he has most certainly learned to write in the master's tongue" (p. 276). In *The Mind Tree*, Mukhopadhyay (2003) describes his nascent writing.

> The problem was seen. He was unable to copy and mother was throwing up a tantrum. She was not ready to give up.
>
> "Let me hold your shoulder like I used to when you started pointing and communicating," she said, trying to find a way.
>
> This time it was easy for the boy to write, as he could feel the presence of the hand, his own hand linked to his body, at the shoulder point, where his mother was holding him.
>
> I have concrete proof that to start with any new activity, it is important for the autistics like the boy, to be held at that part of the body, which does the work as the 'relating' ability develops slowly through practice. Then it can be faded out as the person gets the habit of that particular work. (p. 48)

Mukhopadhyay was eight years old when he wrote the first version of *The Mind Tree*, originally titled *The Voice of Silence*. In the passage above, Mukhopadhyay writes instructively, with unusual self-awareness for his age. Always referring to himself in the third-person,[5] he loses himself to the language of ecstasy to describe what Savarese calls his intense animism and relation to objects, his synesthesic envelopment in sound, light, touch, and, above all, movement and rhythm.[6] Mukhopadhyay moves his body ecstatically to hold it together.

> He got the idea of spinning from the fan as he saw that its blades that were otherwise separate joined together to a complete circle, when they turned in speed.
>
> The boy went to an ecstasy as he rotated himself faster and faster.
>
> If anybody tried to stop him he felt scattered again. . . .

> The helplessness of a scattered self was to taunt him for years together—even as I write this page. (p. 28)

Spinning his body also harmonizes his mind, and the faster he spins, the more the black thoughts disappear. When every "last speck of black" is gone then he will spin in the opposite direction to let the blue thoughts in (p. 150). He controls the amount of blue thoughts by the velocity of his spins. His mother's objection to his spinning and other forms of perseveration looked to Mukhopadhyay like "sick blue sighs" (p. 158).

The ultimate metaphor, and Mukhopadhyay's adopted identity—a banyan tree—in the last section of *The Mind Tree* is a fully formed poetic vision. Mukhopadhyay (2005) begins *The Crow Feeder* as follows.

> I wish I knew how I looked like. The more I wonder the more I get my mind exhausted with the never-ending guesses of mine. It is true that my branches spread far from my main trunk and my leaves are broad. It is also true that I give shadow to people. So the hot afternoons of my life are never lonely. . . . My concerns and worries are trapped within me somewhere in my depths may be in my roots, may be in my bark or may be all around my radius. (p. 169)

Savarese (2010a) highlights how Mukhopadhyay uses *around* in "all around my radius." He says, "By analogy, Tito's mind is not localized in his head; his sensory dislocations seem to facilitate a kind of extraordinary diffusion of thought and feeling" (p. 281). He uses the preposition *around* with great frequency, indicating an embodied presence, a communion that is the cause and the effect of a dynamic, sensory relationship with the world. The diffusion of the autistic body in space is described often by autists, most notably by Donna Williams in her several texts, and by Amanda Baggs in her video *In My Language*, discussed later in the chapter. Mukhopadhyay speaks as the tree, which suits his penchant as an observing narrator of self, and self merging with the world. On the other hand, writes Savarese (2010a), *Around* indicates "a deterittorialized, postcolonial space, at once mapped and unmapped. . . . A very different understanding of language—of what ought to be its purpose and political effects" (pp. 282–283). Savarese proposes a political signification of proprioception, or a political and ethical relationship to one's own body in space and one's body in relationship to others that, with Mukhopadhyay's empathetic imagination, challenges and rearranges a neurotypical hierarchy of power. Mukhopadhyay, like Donna Williams and Amanda Baggs, declassifies and decategorizes the world, undoing the standards by which discursive language invites valorization and devalorization. For example, in *How Can I Talk if My Lips Don't Move*, Mukhopadhyay redefines autism to mean an "extreme connection" with the world, "a term that re-orders the world, dismantling the privilege that attends to one entity or group" (Savarese, 2010a, pp. 284, 285).

The prepositions *about and around* also appear in Mukhopadhyay's (2011) Author's Note in *How Can I Talk if My Lips Don't Move* as he describes the many ways a story might be inspired.

> There are times in everyone's life when there is a need to tell a story. It can be any story. It can be a story *about* a hairpin you were fascinated by. . . . A story can be *about* the shadow of a beggar woman on some street in Bagalore. . . . A story can be *about* the mask of a tribal dancer, who is proud of being the last representative of his dying race because of cultural diffusion and global tendencies toward modernization, as he claimed. Or a story could grow *around* a hat. (p. xv, emphasis added)

His relationship with people and things is associative, they *grow around* his being, enveloping it and becoming it rather than mastering the other. The relationship between the signifier and signified is more porous and bendable in this interaction.[7]

Mukhopadhyay and Williams invert the meaning of autism and neurotypicality such that neurotypicals are stuck inside their privileged position of superiority, immune to other forms of alterity, which include nonhuman species. Dawn Prince-Hughes and Lucy Blackman are sensitive to inter-species communication and question the superiority of a conceptual construction of the world and its bifurcation of the sensual being in the world.

> What is speech? I laugh to myself when the scientific community privileges our interaction over [that of] the animals. . . . How can we say a sardine doesn't know the meaning of life? They don't necessarily become part of a silver flowing school by chance. To suggest that a cat doesn't know what death is would seem to be downright totally unobservant. But we big brained apes, because so much else is going on in our heads, have to work so hard at this, using different social construction to do so. (Blackman, 2005, p. 153)

The western predilection for the left hemisphere of the brain is the way science, says Blackman, pathologizes the extreme sensory, non-verbal connection with the world, characteristic of autism. Savarese (2010a) theorizes that neurological devalorization functions as "the forces of history [that] have moved inside the brain, and their impact is so much more significant than any simple social constructionism" (p. 285).

Later Mukhopadhyay asks where the earth keeps its mind. The earth also listens—he can feel it run through his roots. Savarese (2010a) writes about these passages as follows.

> If the head has been dethroned by autism, or if in the terms of this conceit neither a tree nor the earth has a head, and if the autistic body

> cannot be said to be conventionally discrete, at least in the way that it makes itself known, then mind is an entity linking all things. (p. 281)

From his immovable position as the tree, Mukhopadhyay (2003) narrates a most sensitive and empathetic story of a burning village, a calf, and its mother. He exhibits here the kind of relational empathy that over-identifies with and becomes the other, which many autists report having and their parents have witnessed.

> Yes I have sensed it getting hurt. When a fire had broken one night, on that sleepy village and when the fire had spread into the houses, when a calf which was newly born could not keep pace with its running mother and got burnt before her helpless eyes, when she had called out to the calf for the last time, I had sensed the earth sigh with great pain. Otherwise, why should my leaves and branches shake when there was no wind?
>
> I had sighed too, as I could smell the fire even from here. It was a moment I had wished that I had no mind at all. I was as helpless as the earth. A little chick in its nest somewhere on my branches woke up when I had sighed. I promised myself to be gentle next time. (p. 175)

Erin Manning's (2009) metaphor of a self that leaks through its skin-container is an embodied description of Mukhopadhyay's extreme sensory, non-verbal connection with the world. In her essay, "What if it Didn't All Begin and End with Containment?," she calls into question the concept of unified self. Manning draws a picture of an alternative view of self as porous, permeable, and ambiguous, in contrast to psychoanalytic theory that suggests that strict boundaries of the self are necessary for coherency and self-self interaction. But Manning asks, "What if the skin were not a container? What if the skin were not a limit at which self begins and ends?" (p. 34). She suggests that *relation* might be replaced by self-self interaction as central to development. Physical and sensory relation creates a third space in experience—being with the world—that is more than the sum of its parts, much like Paul Broks's theory of unstable and multiple selves contained within one body, and a multi-dimensional theory of self in which self is conceived as plural—the self in relationship. Manning calls *feeling with the world* "a body-world that is always tending, attending to the world" (p. 35), dynamic, and not fully contained. In other words, action is located neither in the subject nor object, but in their relation, always dynamic and moving to a momentary destination. According to this theory, earlier selves are contained and present in a constantly emerging self. This relational potential is most active in infancy, yet it remains as the primary experience in autistic adults. Manning cites Amanda Baggs's *In My Language* as an example of hyper-relational, synesthetic connection to the environment. Like Donna Williams, Baggs explains in her written/spoken role in the video that talking creates the illusion of a self-contained static self, differentiated from the environment.

DECONSTRUCTING SENSORY RESPONSE

In *Autism and the Edges of the Known World,* Olga Bogdashina (2010) traces the misunderstanding, negation, and indifference to the sensory experiences of autists. Autists live in alternative perceptual worlds, which Mukhopadhyay and others experience as expansion and diffusion, translating into one-of-a-kind experiences with things rather than discrete categories within which things are apprehended. In pathological terms, damage in the sensory motor region in which categorical thinking is grounded alters the signals that the brain interprets, disrupting the conceptual processing of categories (Damasio, 1999). However, Bogdashina reinforces time and again that the normative ordering of the brain, which can conceive categories, is a limited, albeit serviceable, one, particularly in comparison with other non-human species.[8] In order to turn chaotic stimuli into cohesive categories that help make conceptual sense of the world, the neurotypical brain has learned to be selective. Bogdashina asks the same question posed in Chapter One (this volume): "Is the 'normal' interpretation necessarily the 'correct' one?" (p. 26). Rather than perceiving things as one-of-a-kind, with age and experience, neurotypicals tend to leave out more, perceiving what is expected rather than what is there. "As a result, the final picture is inevitably distorted, without us even realizing that our perceived world is not a true copy of the real one. Thus, there is always something of *us* in our interpretation of stimuli. Our response is not objective" (p. 26).

The filtering of extraneous stimuli is not available to autists, sensory-overload being one of the most frequently discussed experiences in self-reports. This unavailability is typically described as a deficit, but it may also be, as Bogdashina calls it, a "superability" that brings with it frustration and anxiety. The common designation of "high" and "low functioning" is an artifact of this superability, and the less able one is to manage incoming stimuli—an impaired selective attention or sensory gating deficit—the more he or she will be perceived as "low functioning."

Blackman, Mukhopadhyay, Baggs, and Williams, among others, describe what Bogdashina calls "Gestalt perception," the perception of things in the world not as functional objects, but as patterns and rhythms of sensory stimuli. Henry and Kamila Markram and Tania Rinaldi (2007) proposed a hypothesis called *The Intense World Syndrome* to explain the cause of hyper-functioning (which includes hyper-attention, hyper-perception, and hyper-memory) in affected brain regions. They claim that this model unifies the very divergent traits of autism, for example, from slow or no speech to hyper-linguism, and from minor stereotyping to complex rituals.

> The vast autism spectrum could be explained by the specific degree to which this hyper-functional molecular syndrome is active in different brain areas, which could depend on the precise stage of development that the brain is exposed to a triggering insult, the type of toxic insult,

> and the presence of any predisposing genes. (Markram, Rinaldi, & Markram, 2007, p. 3)

Research in the smallest unit of mental information processing, called minicolumns, supports The Intense World Syndrome (Bogdashina, 2010). In comparative studies, the smaller and more numerous columns are not structured in a way by which stimuli can be contained within them, as they are in non-autistics, but instead are amplified by overflowing into nearby units. Autists have a higher ability to process information in the microcircuits that produce hyper-perception of sensory stimuli. The combination of sensory overload and a faulty filtering system causes withdrawal, notably described by Donna Williams (2003) in her text, *Exposure Anxiety—The Invisible Cage*.

Aversive and repetitive behaviors of autists, upon which they are judged abnormal, are explained by The Intense World Syndrome as a way to contain the amplifying effect of stimuli, which squares with autist self-reports. Williams (2003) calls "Exposure Anxiety" the mechanism that protects her from both external and internal invasion.

> It was less than a year later [three years old] that I first remember "the big black nothingness" coming to eat me. I know this now as sensory flooding triggering such a degree of information overload as to cause an epilepsy-like total shut down on the processing of incoming information. (p. 43)

Markram, Rinaldi, and Markram (2007) shift the paradigm from deficiency of cognition to excessive cognitive functioning, or over-performing, and therefore invite the re-examination of treatments that have been based on the deficiency model. For example, Bob Morris reported at the Autism99 Internet Conference:

> If you were being FOREVER forced (at times none too patiently) to do upsetting functions or at times acutely painful ones, just because everybody else does it with no discomfort, AND expects you to be the same; would that make you outgoing, and a party personality? *Or*, would you turn away from your tormentors, acting as if you were uncomfortable or afraid or possibly frustrated with them? (as cited in Bogdashina, 2010, p. 61)

The misunderstanding of the underlying effects in behavior modification therapies, says Williams (2003), is due to its temporary success in increasing socialization skills. Bogdashina (2010) points out the social consequences of aversion behaviors in the loss of shared experiences. Because submitting to behavior therapy is an act of compliance rather than empowerment, autists will not find "the internal connection to the action" (Williams, 2003,

p. 102). The direct and confrontational interaction of behavior modification caused aversion behavior and "seething rage" beneath Williams's compliance (p. 195).

Along with a greater degree of intensity, autists experience a cognitively different kind of perception of the world. Williams, Mukhopadhyay, and other autists report that words are heard or seen in patterns and rhythms without discursive meaning until later in life. Early in life, Mukhopadhyay (2011) interpreted words as color rather than sound. "I am not sure whether or not I had to put any kind of effort toward hearing because I was too young and uninformed in science to analyze the sensory battle that was taking place within my nervous system" (p. 6). Bogdashina calls this way of perceiving in "sensory abstractions" a primary experience that is verbally untranslatable, which has not been fully apprehended in autism research, and tends to be conceived as less complex than conceptual thinking. Rather than developing separately, Bogdashina theorizes that non-verbal and verbal knowing develop in parallel as "two interactive systems, according to different sets of rules" (p. 69). This theory is supported by Williams (1998), who explains how experience is stored as an impression without interpretation, but still felt as experience, sensation, and emotion.

Grandin, Mukhopadhyay, and Williams describe the conscious effort of mapping and visualizing to form alternate routes to reach conceptual thought. Mukhopadhyay's mother taught him the symbolic meaning of numbers by introducing each one as a name, like his own, "You are Tito and this is one" (2005, p. 129). He learned by the "touch method," in which his mother mapped onto his body everything from bringing food to his mouth to passing a ball. Grandin (1995) is well known for her vivid descriptions of compensating for delayed language and the ways she learned to conform to neurotypical thinking.

> Words are like a second language to me. . . . When I read, I translate written words into color movies or I simply store a photo of the written page to be read later. When I retrieve the material, I see a photocopy of the page in my imagination. I can then read it like a Teleprompter. (p. 1)

Grandin's (2014) own research has led her to re-conceptualize autism with three subtypes: sensory seeking, sensory overrepsonsiveness, and sensory underresponsiveness, the latter two being caused by sensory overload. Health professionals who rush to fix the social behavior first would do well to understand the reasons for resistance or underresponsiveness. She observes that in the majority of cases the problem is not indifference to others, as the behavior might suggest, but rather intolerance to the environment. Opportunities for socialization are therefore minimized and this results in a looping of cause and effect.

The problem with the data is its interpretation, Grandin says, which relies on caregiver testimonies, while the conclusions of the study rely on the methodology of the researchers, who are usually neurotypical. The problem is also that studies are ontological and experiential in nature. "If researchers want to know what it's like to be one of the many, many people who live in an alternate sensory reality, they're going to have to ask them" (Grandin, 2014, p. 76). Ironically, researchers do not validate self-reports because they are subjective, but *that*, Grandin says, is exactly the point. Not only are the views of autists subjective, but they are also unconventional, and therefore presumed "defective." Overcoming this bias would mean the inclusion of typed reports from autists considered "low functioning" and non-verbal, which would also challenge the scientific community's suspicion of augmentative and alternative communication, particularly facilitated communication.

Like many autists, Mukhopadhyay observes more than one self; he describes his reality as divided between a "thinking self" and "acting self." Grandin (2014) witnessed both behaviors when she met him at a San Francisco library in a carefully modulated environment for their visit (e.g., absent of fluorescent lighting and visual and auditory distractions). She asked him three questions in succession. After each he ran around the room flapping his arms. Although the questions and his typed answers were brief, they took much psychic effort. "What I had witnessed, I realize now, is Tito's acting self in action, the self that the outside world sees: a spinning, flailing, flapping boy. . . . The thinking self observes the acting self running around a library flapping his arms" (p. 79). His "acting self" keeps his body intact, which he perceives as parts that become unhinged from the whole. Biklen (2005) urges the observer of such behavior to presume competence, or in Mukhopadhyay's words, the inhabitance of a "thinking self." Mental retardation, he says, "is the most disgraceful label" that autists have endured; he was labeled as such at three because he didn't respond to the psychologist's directions (p. 136). "I was not able to apply my knowledge although I could understand perfectly well what was being asked" (p. 136). The existence of the thinking self in "low functioning" autists has also been substantiated by Donna Williams, who reports similar survival responses to sensory overload and, while involuntarily doing so, is nevertheless carefully observed by her thinking self.

Grandin's point is that the autist's internal observer is as astute as a parent, health professional, or researcher, with the exception that autists can interpret accurately the meaning and *feeling* of the overwhelmed "thinking self" and the survival response of the "acting self's" involuntary actions and behaviors. The misinterpretation of aversion behavior redefined by Williams and Grandin invites further doubt about the accuracy of theory of mind (ToM). If hyper- and hypo-activity are linked to the same cause—such as in the Intense World Theory of sensory overload affecting the amygdala and therefore emotional responses—then rather than a lack of empathy, autists feel too much.

DECONSTRUCTING THEORY OF MIND

> *In many respects, to be autistic is to be conditioned—conditioned into believing that your words are idiosyncratic, self-focused, ephemeral. There exist entire anthologies dedicated to this very idea.*
>
> (Yergeau, 2013, p. 7)

In her "autie-biography" titled "Clinically Significant Disturbance: On Theorists Who Theorize Theory of Mind," Melanie Yergeau (2013) discusses the ironies, injustices, contradictions, and paradoxes of life as a "high functioning Aspie" academic. During her second week as a new faculty member, she was involuntarily committed to the university psych ward. This painful and humiliating experience crystallized her position as the receiver of the cultural assumption about the internal life, capacities, and limitations of people on the spectrum, which she calls "neurological determinism." It was the moment she says that "their ventriloquism started" (p. 2). Institutional commitment meant forfeiting one's own judgment, self-knowledge, integrity, and humanity. From that moment she could not speak for herself. "Suddenly, the experts claimed, *I* wasn't talking. God, no. 'That's your depression talking,' they explained. 'That's your autism talking. That's your anxiety talking. Really, it's anything *but* you talking'" (p. 2). As a rhetorician, Yergeau found that autism is alarmingly devoid of rhetoric because rhetoric is about audience, and according to research, autists do not participate as audience or, in other words, participate in a universal theory of mind. "And so, I've had to get used to not existing, rhetorically speaking" (p. 2).

> I am bombarded by representations of autistic people as non-rhetors—as non-rhetors who cannot emote (goodbye *pathos*), as non-rhetors who cannot recognize the mental states nor visualize the needs of the people around them (goodbye *ethos*), as non-rhetors whose logics are so mechanistic and rigid that their only comparable non-rhetor analogues are robots and chimpanzees (goodbye, *logos*). (p. 5)

With their 1985 article, "Does the Autistic Child Have a Theory of Mind?," Simon Baron-Cohen, Alan Leslie, and Uta Frith established theory of mind as the marker of the superiority of the human species—of humanity itself. The theory has been resonating across disciplines[9] "as a binary between the humans who have it and those distant Others who do not" (Yergeau, 2013, p. 3). As the intellectual version of ultimate *othering*, Baron-Cohen writes, "A theory of mind remains one of the quintessential abilities that makes us human. . . . The theory of mind difficulties seem to be universal among such [autistic] individuals. . . . The gulf between mindreaders[10] and the mindblind must be vast" (as cited in Yergeau, 2013, p. 3).

Yegeau asks, "Without a theory of mind, then, what is a body? What is an *autistic* body?" (p. 4). Autism, she writes, is an embodied experience and therefore penetrates every muscle, movement, and gesture of the body. "If the body is where theory is actualized, and autistics lack a ToM—under whose domain must our embodiment fall?" (p. 4). Referring to Adrienne Rich's (1985) essay, "Notes Toward a Politics of Location," writing one's body is to bring one back to a specific location, to bring attention to theories and abstractions as integral to physical location and their inevitable reflection of race, gender, class, and ability. Without acknowledging the body as such, ToM researchers clinically theorize autists by their lack in an abstract location.

> When is autism speaking? And, when autism speaks, where is the body? Where is personhood located? Do autistic people, as Roger Gottlieb (2002) so asks, represent moral subjects? Whose corporeality is reflected—and deflected—by the discursive construct of autism? In other words: Where does my autism end, and where do I begin? Am I my mind? (Yergeau, 2013, p. 6)

The skepticism that non-autistic researchers have for the validity of autistic narration permeates and defines Yergeau's life as an academic. Most disturbing, she says, is that we are asking these questions now; ToM is pervasive, accepted by scholars, teachers, and students without question. There are several reasons for the tenacity of the term. It has history (30 years) and therefore a significant amount of scholarship has been invested in this theory. It is also a useful and efficient category that may stand for a number of deficiencies in empathy, cognition, and intentionality. But its neatness belies a fundamental logic, as Yergeau and others (Pinchevski, 2005; Ryan, 2010) have discovered. It is a self-reflexive, epistemologically bounded, reductionist term that Yergeau theorizes cannot exist without the autistic construct. We only know it exists because we have determined that in 2% of humanity it does *not* exist.

The Validity of Autistic Writing

Returning to the premise of this book, therefore, neurotypicals are not equipped to understand the minds of autists because their organization of reality does not include those who do not have the filter of the "I" to organize phenomena. Williams (1998) compares the neurotypical mind to a reformatted new computer that can't read old disks. Mills (2008) suggests that rather than supposing an absence of ToM, we might make room in the vast possibilities of human knowing for a different *kind* of ToM. Behavior is unreliable; what appears to be ritualistic rather than symbolic might instead be acts of defense against an onslaught of sensory stimulation that require different forms of unification.

ToM promoters have discredited autie-biography on a vast scale, most notably, Francesca Happe (1991) in her essay "The Autobiographical Writings of Three Asperger Syndrome Adults." The three adults (which include Temple Grandin, whose diagnosis is not Asperger's syndrome), are widely divergent in age, academic achievement, interests, and employment. She compares the published work of Grandin with personal letters of the male subject and the unpublished autobiography of the female subject. But Happe did not foresee that the variables might affect the reliability or merit of her study.

Happe begins her essay with the question, "How far can autistic children go in matters of social adaptation?" (p. 107). Her use of autobiographical writing by these adult autists reinforces the credibility of the triad of impairment: social, imaginative, and communicative skills. The significance and, indeed, the question, set up the study as a proof of autistic impairments that appear in autistic life writing and, therefore, what shortly follows in her next paragraph is the question of their validity.

One of the highlights of Happe's analysis of Grandin's writing comes after her surprising first impression of its normality. Grandin's writing is so normal, in fact, that it challenges what is presumed to be autistic. "For example, there are accounts of friendships and imaginative games which are surprising coming from an autistic child" (p. 208). The contribution of the non-autistic co-author/editor, Margaret Scariano, is the only plausible reason that an autistic child might appear to experience life in a way that does not fit into ToM. Happe cites a passage in *Emergence: Labeled Autistic* in which Grandin exhibits the ability for pretend play. "This is an extraordinary thing to be told of an autistic child doing, and it is very hard to know what to make of it . . . but if true it shows a very good understanding of others' minds" (pp. 208–209). Happe underscores another passage in which Grandin shows not only an understanding of another person's beliefs and emotions, but also how to manipulate them. Happe invalidates this possibility on two counts. First, the authenticity of the writing is suspect given the non-autistic co-author. This suspicion has been voiced regarding the publication of Grandin's book as well as of other autistic autobiographies, writes Oliver Sacks (1995). Sacks also questioned Grandin's authorship until he read her academic papers and found "a detail and consistency, a directness, that changed my mind" (p. 253). Like Happe, however, Sacks found the abrupt change of subject, lack of background information, and narrative gaps to be consistent with the autists' failure "to realize their own or their readers' states of mind" (p. 253). Ambiguous authorship, along with suspected "parroting," or the co-opting of neurotypical language, "may lead us to believe the autistic writer is more socially adept than is the case," rendering autie-biography misleading and suspect at best (Happe, 1991, p. 222).

Second, in a footnote Happe back steps with the following assumption: "Interestingly, Temple's account of this incident also shows a *lack* of understanding of her reader's probable reaction. She does not temper such candour with excuses or claims of guilt or regret" (p. 209). Later Happe misinterprets Grandin's ability to put herself in the position of livestock in order to understand them as lack of empathy. Happe compares Grandin's search for the animal's point of view with the conventions of human empathy. "When we empathize with another person we generally mean that we *feel with* them, despite the fact that we are not actually *suffering with* them" (p. 210). Grandin's notorious empathy for animals, which could be argued surpasses others in the field, has led her to become one of the foremost consultants in the cattle industry.

Ultimately, "These problems mean that the writings of able autistic people must be viewed with caution if used as evidence for more than an appraisal of that one individual" (p. 223). To offset this possibility, Happe used a control group that included a schizophrenic female author she thought a good match for Grandin because of their similar age and, most importantly, their self-designated oddness, "almost from birth" (p. 224). These clinically sanctioned studies, which are legion, do potential damage to the credibility and livelihood of autists (Cohen-Rottenburg, 2011). ToM researchers fail to acknowledge the mental states unique to autists, who do in fact "read" the intentions of other autists (Baggs, 2010; Cohen-Rottenburg, 2011; Sinclair, 1992). They also fail to recognize the social use of language[11] that binds discourse communities together with their own brand of conventions. Thus, the writers that Happe offers as models must be understood not only in their specificity, but also as outsiders entering an unfamiliar discourse community. As Amanda Baggs (2010) writes, non-verbal autists in particular are never fully initiated into the language of the stratified and political academic discourse community.

In Amanda Baggs's (2003) rejoinder to Happe's essay, entitled "The Validity of Autistic Opinions," she presents several problems with Happe's research; first is the non-autistic researcher herself who claims to have more insight into the motivations of autistic people than autistic people do. The result is that the researcher studies autism as a collection of impairments, which are often more of an effect of the autistic condition than its cause. What is really happening, says Baggs, is a "difficulty in translation between two or more species" (para. 6). Baggs's explanation for what Happe found to be Grandin's lack of information about her *oddities* is that, like neurotypicals, she writes about her interests. Baggs writes ironically, "Why would an autistic possibly want to write something that showed who she was, not what her symptoms were? Why, above all, would an autistic want to write something that *did not* totally fit the expert opinions . . . ?"(para. 10). Since autistic writers have begun blogging, such rhetorical questions have invited autism researchers to reflect on possible answers.

Rachel Cohen-Rottenberg in Conversation with Simon Baron-Cohen

In 2009, Rachel Cohen-Rottenberg, blogger and web editor of *Autism and Empathy*, wrote a critique of Baron-Cohen's (2009a) article, "Autism: The Empathizing-Systematizing (E-S) Theory." What soon followed was an invitation from Baron-Cohen to respond in her blog on the website Science 2.0.[12] Baron-Cohen's first response to Cohen-Rottenberg's argument was that theory of mind is a misleading notion and, rather, autists have the opposing problem of an excess of empathy.[13] Scientific evidence from international studies and tests and self-reports (E-S and EQ-Empathy Quotient), writes Baron-Cohen (2009b), is difficult to ignore. "So whilst some people believe that theory of mind and empathy difficulties in autism are mythical, the results of many independent scientific studies suggest otherwise" (para. 2). Cohen-Rottenberg then challenged Baron-Cohen's statement that children with Asperger's syndrome do not know when and if they hurt others. Evidence comes from the Faux Pas Test,[14] in which a group of older children with AS scored lower than a younger group without AS. She also challenged Baron-Cohen's assertion that people on the spectrum do not respond empathetically to another's distress. He writes, "In particular, Rachel says, 'once someone tells me how he or she feels, I don't usually have a problem with an empathetic response.' This is exactly the point. For most people, they don't need to be told by the other person 'I am upset.'" Baron-Cohen makes a distinction between cognitive and affective empathy, the former being the inability to read visual cues, which he claims is lacking in autists. Finally, Cohen-Rottenberg argued that "stimming"[15] does not indicate a need to systemize but, rather, is a form of calming oneself. Baron-Cohen did not consider the two interpretations to be incompatible, since "stimming" creates order through patterns from chaotic stimuli.

I will not cover all of Baron-Cohen's ten points but rather continue on to Cohen-Rottenberg's (2011) response to his response, which she found troubling. She found that Baron-Cohen was selective about addressing her concerns, most importantly the bias and flawed test instruments of the E-S and EQ test that she suggests cannot measure the complexity of the autistic experience. He also failed to recognize that the 30-year-old false belief test, which assesses ToM, depends on verbal responses and language processing, a failure that has been documented in several papers by Morton Ann Gernsbacher (2005) and her colleagues.[16] Cohen-Rottenberg also determined that the term "cognitive empathy" was misleading. In other writings, Baron-Cohen conflated ToM and cognitive empathy, the latter depending upon the former, and both subject to the ability to decode non-verbal signals. Using the example of a blind person who must depend on spoken language to interpret emotion, she says, "It's my contention that calling a physical inability to see and to interpret nonverbal signals a failure of any kind of empathy is to make an unmerited interpretive leap" (para. 7). What Baron-Cohen has in effect done, she writes, is to make a processing disability an empathy disability, since "if I can't separate the signals, the net effect is that I can't see them as signals" (para. 8). Finally, she takes issue with Baron-Cohen's evasion of the real problem, which is the damage caused by ill-conceived definitions and conclusions. The following paragraphs shift to the historical context of the term *theory of mind* as it was used to describe primate behavior. The transfer from primate to autistic human is in itself a troubling relationship that would potentially cause ill-conceived definitions and conclusions.

Autists and Apes

In 1978, David Premack and Guy Woodruff coined the term *theory of mind* in their article "Does the Chimpanzee Have a Theory of Mind?" In their study, the authors found that chimpanzees had the ability to ascribe mental states and understand human goals (Tomasello & Call, 2008), which they called a theory of mind.[17] Psychologists have borrowed this term as a way of describing its absence in autism. In more recent research, a penchant to group primates and autists together has appeared among scientists and researchers (Pinker, 2003; Tomasello, 2005, 2008). In "Understanding and Sharing Intentions: The Origins of Cultural Cognition," Michael Tomasello et al. (2005) argue that evidence shows that great apes and some autistic children might understand intentional action, but they do not participate in activities that require shared intentionality. They outline three stages of intentionality: acting animatedly,[18] understanding the pursuit of goals, and understanding the choice of plans. It has been shown that nonhuman primates and autistic children accomplish the first phase and elements of the second, but the complexity of shared intentions, which means to share the same goals and internalize the plans to achieve those goals, is not available to them. "But they [nonhuman primates and to some degree, children with autism] do not thereby engage socially and culturally with others in the ways that human children do" (pp. 675–676). Therefore, the bar must be raised, and to be fully human an additional ability is needed beyond understanding the intentions of others: cooperative communication is theorized as the lynch pin of Homo sapiens. Tomasello (2008) makes a distinction between individual and shared intentionality, evidenced by the known fact that "children with autism point imperatively but not declaratively as do some apes when interacting with humans" (p. 122).

Cultural learning, the authors write, is what humans do best. They have evolved to transmit culture across generations and throughout time by shared linguistic symbols and social institutions. What underlies this developing ability in children to participate in the collective of human cognition is not only the understanding of human intentions, goals, and perception, but also the "*motivation* to share these things in interactions with others—and perhaps special forms of dialogic cognitive representations for doing so" (p. 676, emphasis added). Their concern is primarily with the ontological question, where and how does this ability to understand others' intentions emerge?

After 14 months of age, an age at which infants typically understand intentional actions, the way is made for rational imitation and cultural and social learning. At this stage, shared learning of complex goals is possible, which the authors say is truly collaborative, containing both self and other. Each must internalize the other's role in achieving the goal as well as the differentiation of each role. The dyadic relationship becomes triadic engagement, in which the infant and carer collaborate on a task or an external entity. Thus begins not only cultural learning but also cultural creation, including the construction of "generalized social norms (e.g. truth) that make possible the conceptualization of individual beliefs and, moreover, to share those beliefs" (p. 684).

The authors explain what nonhuman primates can and cannot do. They do understand both trying and accidents that do not achieve results, following gazes to external targets, and some intentional action and perception. They are not able to engage in the planning and decision making of intentional action or cultural learning, shared psychological states, and triadic behaviors. They do not point to, show, or offer objects. Needless to say, they do not share what the authors consider the pinnacle of human behavior: the motivation to share emotions, experience, and activities. But what happens to autistic children in adulthood the authors do not make clear. What they can do is reach the animate stage and show *some* signs of understanding others' goals with mixed results in cultural learning, such as imitating styles. They do not share psychological states and triadic engagement is lacking, which the authors remind the reader is one of the diagnostic criteria of autism. Collaborative activities are rare and there is a lack of evidence of role reversal or supporting others' roles. It is also well-known that lack of linguistic collaborative communication may be traced back to early problems with emotional relatedness. And finally, they propose that "although there may be a few unusual individuals, the vast majority of children with autism do not participate in the cultural and symbolic activities around them in anything like the normal way" (p. 686).

To summarize, the authors observe that both nonhuman primates and children with autism are not entirely without intention and reading skills. And contrary to previous conclusions, both species do *appear* to understand goal-directed action. "This means that both of them show some skills of social learning though not as powerful or pervasive as those of human 1- and 2-year-olds" (pp. 686–687). Ultimately, they indicate that neither primates nor children with autism are on the same social pathway as neurotypical humans, since they do not share in dyadic, triadic, or collaborative engagements with joint intentions and attention necessary for cultural creation.

The Tomasello et al. online article includes open peer commentary by invited scholars in the related fields, Jerome Bruner among them. In a most respectful review, after noting how not one classic evolutionary writer appears in the bibliography (including Darwin), Bruner writes:

> Reading it leads me to a rather odd conjecture. May it not be the case that the unique result of human evolution—our newly acquired reliance upon conventionalized or institutionalized procedures for relating to

> each other and to the social world in general—that this is what makes ours the first and only "unspecies-like" species in the animal kingdom? I mean that in the sense that *unless* one human being has come to appreciate the "rules" of the cultural setting of those with whom he is interacting, he is unable to proceed collaboratively. (p. 694)

Bruner continues by recognizing that our species has become more localized than any other extant species, which he does not attribute to the diversity of languages. "The paradox, rather, is that *Homo sapiens* has become 'localized' by having to depend upon learned, *culture*-specific modes of interacting," which often "*misguides* inter-cultural perceptions," at times with catastrophic results (p. 694). The costs of local culture are high, including misunderstandings and conflicts. Our species has developed, Bruner points out, in an atypical way that belies the notion of species specificity. For example, the additional result of developing written language was the leaving out of intersubjective cues, inevitably leading to the misreading of other minds. Finally, Bruner brings home his point:

> The universal-one-species dogma has, of course, been the dogma of colonialism in all its guises—that everybody everywhere *could* be the same if they were given the same cultural opportunities, the ones *we* have on offer. Beneath the compassionate surface of this ancient dogma lies the belief that *Homo sapiens* everywhere is capable of reading and appreciating what others in the human species have in mind—a dogma given a new lease on life by what's now called evolutionary psychology. (p. 694)

We are capable of such exquisite local sensitivity and intersubjectivity, yet fail at our intercultural readings of the intentions of others, which makes way for the stratification of social class and human value. In Bruner's powerful yet tempered writing, he justifies autists like Amanda Baggs, James Sinclair, Donna Williams, and many others, who ask to be met half way, to take the time to be understood, to allow the voices of autists to speak for themselves as a cultural group and as individuals.

NOTES

1. People such as Peter the Wild Boy, found in the woods of Hanover, England in 1725, and The Wild Boy of Aveyron, France, found in the woods in 1799. Both boys were assumed to be about 12 years old, both were without speech, and both were studied extensively at the time and until the present, and now are considered to have been on the spectrum.
2. I use the term *colonized* in the context of disability as it is defined by Arthur Frank (1997) in *The Wounded Storyteller: Body, Illness, and Ethics*. In western medicine, the patient's story is told by the professional. The reversal, a

post-colonial narrative, would mean that the patient/autist speaks for himself/herself.

3. Ralph Savarese (2013) coined the term *Neurocosmopolitanism* to mean the notion of equal participation beyond accommodation, or the meeting "half way" between neurotypicals and autists.
4. CAN merged with Autism Speaks in 2006. See Chapter Five for more about this organization.
5. Savarese suggests that Tito's use of the third-person is an intentional mockery of the theory of mind paradigm.
6. In an interview with Mukhopadhyay for the *Disability Studies Quarterly*, Savarese (2010b) asks him to explain why he diverges from discursive writing to poetic fragments. Savarese interprets this stylistic change as an intentional emphasis on his alienation from humans and stronger connection to nature. Mukhopadhyay explains that he gets bored by the intensity and thickness of a paragraph and seeks out free verse. "So instead of being gravitated towards the core, the reader can stay and watch the exterior. And that is where beauty lies!" (p. 2).
7. Henri Bergson (1912/1999) describes the non-verbal knowing of an object as not depending on a particular point of view or symbol.
8. For example, Bogdashina offers the example of whales and dolphins, which experience the curvature of the earth because of their three-dimensional sonar representation.
9. For example, see philosopher Daniel Dennett's (1998) *The Intentional Stance*. Dennett theorizes that empathy developed in human beings from spoken language. He coined the phrase "the Intentional Stance" as an alternative to theory of mind because he objects to the use of the word *theory* in this context.
10. Baron-Cohen calls *mindreaders* anyone (the majority of humanity) who has a theory of mind.
11. The communication between Baron-Cohen and Cohen-Rottenberg was reprinted on Autism Blogs Directory. Also, see Patricia Bizzell's (1997) *Cognition, Convention, and Certainty*.
12. The reprint appeared on Autism Blogs Directory Saturday, September 10, 2011, at http://autismblogsdirectory.blogspot.com/2011/09/simon-baron-cohen-replies-to-rachel.html
13. Donna Williams (2003), in her book *Exposure Anxiety—The Invisible Cage*, outlines several reasons for this misconception. One is the direct acknowledgment of self in social interactions and personal relationships "that puts one in the social—emotional world of *with*. Exposure Anxiety is allergic to that because *with* equals *invasion* which equals *overload* which equals *loss of control* which equals *survival response*" (p. 98).
14. The Faux Pas Recognition Test was created in 1999 by Simon Baron-Cohen, Michelle O'Riordan, Rosie Jones, Valerie Stone, and Kate Plaisted. The purpose is to test social sensitivity in normal children and children with Asperger's syndrome. The experimenter reads the child a set of stories and then asks questions such as, "In the story did someone say something that they should not have said?" (p. 1).
15. *Stimming*, which means self-stimulating behavior, is a term preferred by the autistic community.
16. See for example, Gernsbacher, M.A. and Frymiare, J.L., "Does the Autistic Brain Lack Core Modules?" (2005). The authors question the empirical evidence for theory of mind based on the Salley-Anne/false belief test. "We illustrate that successful performance on theory of mind tasks depends on linguistic ability; therefore, it is not surprising that autistics are more likely to

fail theory of mind tasks because a qualitative impairment in communications is one of the primary diagnostic criteria for autism" (p. 3). For example, the use of the phrases "look at" and "look for" are far more complex than they seem and suppose that the child has a sophisticated understanding of syntax.

17. The conclusions of this study have been debated ever since. In their 30th anniversary review of Premack and Woodruff's article, the authors write, "The answer will not be a simple yes or no, however, because part of the progress that has been made in recent years is the recognition that there are many different ways in which organisms might understand the psychological functioning of others" (p. 187).
18. Tomasello et al. (2005) define "acting animatedly" as follows: "An observer perceives that the actor has generated his motion autonomously; that is, she distinguishes animate *self-produced* action from inanimate, caused motion. There is no understanding that the actor has a goal, and so means and ends are not distinguished, nor are successful and unsuccessful actions" (p. 678).

REFERENCES

Asperger, H. (1944/1991). 'Autistic psychopathy' in childhood. In U. Frith (Ed.), *Autism and Asperger syndrome* (pp. 37–92). Cambridge, England: Cambridge University Press.

Baggs, A. (2003). *The validity of autistic opinions*. Retrieved from: http://archive.autistics.org/library/autopin.html

Baggs, A. (2010). Up in the clouds and down in the valley: My richness and yours. *Disability Studies Quarterly, 30*(1). Retrieved from http://dsq-sds.org/issue/view/43

Baron-Cohen, S. (1997). *Mindblindness: An essay on autism and theory of mind*. Boston, MA: MIT Press.

Baron-Cohen, S. (2009a). Autism: The empathizing-systematizing [E-S] theory. *The Year in Cognitive Neuroscience*, 68–80. Retrieved from: http://www.autismtruths.org/pdf/Autism-The%20emphathizing-systemizing%20es%20theory_SBC_ARC.pdf

Baron-Cohen, S. (2009b). A reply to Rachel Cohen-Rottenberg's (July 7th 2009) critique of the empathizing-sytemizing [E-S] theory of autism. Retrieved from: http://autismblogsdirectory.blogspot.com/2011/09/simon-baron-cohen-replies-to-rachel.html

Baron-Cohen, S., Leslie, A. M., & Frith, U. (1985). Does the autistic child have a theory of mind? *Cognition, 21*, 37–46.

Baron-Cohen, S., O'Riordan, M., Jones, R., Stone, V. E., & Plaisted, K. (1999). A new test of social sensitivity: Detection of faux pas in normal children and children with Asperger syndrome. *Journal of Autism and Developmental Disorders, 29*, 407–418.

Bergson, H. (1912/1999). *An introduction to metaphysics*. Cambridge, MA: Hackett Publishing.

Bizell, P. (1997). Cognition, convention, and certainty: What we need to know about writing. In V. Villanueva (Ed.), *Cross-talk in comp studies* (pp. 387–411). Urbana, IL: NCTE.

Blackman, L. (2005). Reflections on language. In D. Biklen (Ed.), *Autism and the myth of the person alone: Qualitative studies in psychology* (pp. 146–167). New York, NY: New York University Press.

Bogdashina, O. (2010). *Autism and the edges of the known world: Sensitivities, language and constructed reality*. London, England: Jessica Kingsley.

Cohen-Rottenburg, R. (2011). Unwarranted conclusions and the potential for harm: My reply to Simon Baron-Cohen. Retrieved from: http://autismblogsdirectory.blogspot.com/2011/09/unwarranted-conclusions-and-potential.html

Damasio, A. (1999). *The feeling of what happens: Body and emotion in the making of consciousness*. New York, NY: Harcourt Brace.

Dennett, D. (1998). *The intentional stance*. Cambridge, MA: MIT University Press.

Frank, A. W. (1997). *The wounded storyteller: Body, illness, and ethics*. Chicago, IL: The University of Chicago Press.

Frith, U. (1989). *Autism: Explaining the enigma*. Malden, MA and Oxford, England: Blackwell.

Gernsbacher, M. A., & Frymiare, J. L. (2005). Does the autistic brain lack core modules? *DLD Journal*. Retrieved from: http://gernsbacherlab.org/wp-content/uploads/papers/1/Gernsbacher_autistic_modules.pdf

Grandin, T. (1995). *Thinking in pictures: And other reports from my life with autism*. New York, NY: First Vintage Books.

Grandin, T. (2014). *The autistic brain: Helping different kinds of minds succeed*. New York, NY: Mariner Books.

Hacking, I. (1999). *The social construction of what?* Cambridge, MA: Harvard University Press.

Happe, F. (1991). The autobiographical writings of three Asperger syndrome adults: Problems of interpretation and implications for theory. In U. Frith (Ed.), *Autism and Asperger Syndrome* (pp. 207–242). Cambridge, England: Cambridge University Press.

Kanner, L. (1943). Autistic disturbances of affective contact, *Nervous Child, 2*, 217–250. Retrieved from: http://neurodiversity.com/library_kanner_1943.pdf

Lakoff, G., & Johnson, M. (1999). *Philosophy in the flesh: The embodied mind and its challenges to western thought*. New York, NY: Basic Books.

Manning, E. (2009). What if it didn't all begin and end with containment? Toward a leaky sense of self. *Body and Society, 15*(33), 33–45.

Markram, H., Rinaldi, T., & Markram, K. (2007). The intense world syndrome—An alternative hypothesis for autism. *Frontiers in Neuroscience, 1*(1), 77–96. Retrieved from: http://www.ncbi.nlm.nih.gov/pmc/articles/PMC2518049/

McDonagh, P. (2009). *Idiocy: A cultural history*. Liverpool, England: Liverpool University Press.

Mills, B. (2008). Autism and the imagination. In M. Osteen (Ed.), *Autism and representation*. (pp. 117–132). New York, NY and London, England: Routledge.

Mukhopadhyay, T. (2003). *The mind tree*. New York, NY: National Autistic Society.

Mukhopadhyay, T. (2005). *The gold of the sunbeams*. New York, NY: Arcade.

Mukhopadhyay, T. (2011). *How can I talk if my lips don't move?: Inside my autistic mind*. New York, NY: Arcade.

Nadesan, M. H. (2009). Constructing autism: A brief genealogy. In M. Osteen (Ed.), *Autism and representation* (pp. 78–95). New York, NY: Routledge.

Osteen, M. (Ed.) (2009). *Autism and representation*. New York, NY: Routledge.

Pallasmaa, J. (2009). *The thinking hand: Existential and embodied wisdom in architecture*. Chichester, England: John Wiley & Sons.

Pinchevski, A. (2005). Displacing incommunicability: Autism as an epistemological boundary. *Communication and Critical/Cultural Studies, 2*(2), 163–184.

Pinker, S. (2003). *The blank slate: The modern denial of human nature*. New York, NY: Penguin Books.

Premack, D., & Woodruff, G. (1978). Does the chimpanzee have a theory of mind? *Behavioral and Brain Sciences, 1*(4), 515–526.

Rich, A. (1985). Notes toward a politics of location. In M. D. Diocaretz & I. M. Zavala (Eds.), *Feminist identity and society in the 1980s: Selected papers* (pp. 7–22). Philadelphia, PA: John Benjamin Press.

Ryan, M. (2010). Narratology and cognitive science: A problematic relation. *Style, 44*(4), 469–495.

Sacks, O. (1995). *An anthropologist on mars: Seven paradoxical tales.* New York, NY: Vintage.

Savarese, R. J. (2010a). Toward a postcolonial neurology: Autism, Tito Mukhopadhyay, and a new geo-poetics of the body. *Journal of literary & cultural disability studies, 4*(3), 273–290. Retrieved from: http://www.ralphsavarese.com/wp-/uploads/2011/08/PostColonialNeurologyPDFsavarese.pdf

Savarese, R. (2010b). More than a thing to ignore: An interview with Tito Rajarshi Mukhopadhyay. *Disability Studies Quarterly, 30*(1). Retrieved from: http://dsq-sds.org/article/view/1056/1235

Savarese, R. J. (2013). From neurodiverstiy to neurocosmopolitanism: Beyond mere acceptance and inclusion. In C. D. Herrera & A. Perry (Eds.), *Ethics and nuerodiversity* (pp. 191–205). Cambridge, MA: Cambridge Scholars Press.

Tomasello, M. (2008). *Origins of human communication.* Cambridge, MA: MIT Press.Tomasello, M., & Call, J. (2008). Does the chimpanzee have a theory of mind? 30 years later. *Cell Press.* Retrieved from: http://email.eva.mpg.de/~tomas/pdf/TICS30.pdf

Tomasello, M., Carpenter, M., Call, J., Behne, T., & Moll, H. (2005). Understanding and sharing intentions: The origins of cultural cognition. *Behavioral and Brain Sciences, 28,* 675–735. Retrieved from: http://email.eva.mpg.de/~tomas/pdf/BBS_Final.pdf

Williams, D. (1998). *Autism and sensing: The unlost instinct.* New York, NY: Jessica Kingsley.

Williams, D. (2003). *Exposure Anxiety—the invisible cage: An exploration of self-protection responses in autism spectrum and beyond.* New York, NY: Jessica Kingsley.

Wing, L. (1981). “Asperger syndrome: A clinical account. *Psychological Medicine, 11,* 115–129. Retrieved from: http://www.mugsy.org/wing2.htm

Yergeau, M. (2013). Clinically significant disturbance: On theorists who theorize theory of mind. *Disability Studies Quarterly, 33*(4). Retrieved from: http://dsq-sds.org/article/view/3876

3 On Language and Autism

LANGUAGE AND SYMBOLISM

> *Can [we] ever truly share subjective experiences, as opposed to simply imagining that we do?*
>
> (Deacon, 1998, p. 461)

Very generally, three concepts of language in the past century have been at odds: language as purely theoretical, language as innate, and language as inseparable from the development of human physiology and culture. In *The Symbolic Species: The Co-evolution of Language and the Brain*, Terence Deacon (1998) references the renowned linguist Ferdinand de Saussure (1916/1969) only once, most likely because Deacon is essentially a pragmatic scientist concerned with the evolution of language, while Saussure is the founder of theoretical linguistics. Deacon conceives of language as somewhat autonomous, the cause of human evolution rather than its effect or a self-invention. Saussure, on the other hand, suspects this notion to be illusory. He proposes that to be a science, linguistics would need to be exclusively a concrete object of *language alone*, or *language as such*, in which linguistic units exist in arbitrary but concrete relationships to others; arbitrary because "the object is not given in advance of the viewpoint . . . it is the viewpoint adopted which creates the object" (Saussure, as cited in Harpham, 2013, p. 33). Noam Chomsky (1966, 1972, 1975, 1980, 1987), who wrote forty years after Saussure's 1916 *Course in General Linguistics*, upended Saussure's theories of arbitrariness, construction, and sign, instead arguing for necessity, innateness, and universal grammar.

Chomsky's Cartesian theory of language separates and frees humans "from the beast machine" (Chomsky, 1987, p. 145), and cites language as "the essential difference between man and animal" (1966, p. 3). According to Chomsky, at some inconclusive point in history, humans achieved a power of complexity for language that essentially produced a new kind of organism. The universal grammar (UG) theory, with adherents such as Steven Pinker (1995), is at the root of the notion that language equals intelligence, since according to this theory, superior intelligence is required to grasp the complexity of language. "It requires rapid and efficient learning, demands immense memory storage, takes advantage of almost supernatural rates of articulation and auditory analysis, and poses an analytic problem that is worthy of a linguistic Einstein" (Deacon, 1998, p. 39). The problem with the UG theory is that these savant-like skills would demand adequate external support to achieve them in the critical stages of childhood, which Deacon argues, we do not have.

If complexity is not the distinctive attribute of language, which Deacon argues it is not (i.e., the evolution of language from simple to complex), then UG and superior intelligence theories lose their veracity. According to Deacon, human language is separate and different from non-human communication, although the latter can be equally as complex. Additionally, the evolving complexity of the human brain over many millions of years is not the cause of human language, although it has affected it. Deacon's fundamental thesis is that language complexity is a secondary effect of the primary mental adaptation of symbolism.[1]

Rather than complexity as the defining difference that sets the language limits between human and non-human species, Deacon suggests that the distinguishing feature of language is its symbolic references and the logical system of relationships that support it. According to his definition of language, it is unlikely that "simple language" exists outside of our species. The justification for UG cannot hold within this frame; lower intelligence is not the reason why other species do not have language.

Other Chomsky opponents, such as Edward Sapir (1949) and his student Benjamin Whorf (1956), hypothesized language as a cultural convention built upon specific linguistic group habits. These language groups created distinct worlds, "as no languages are sufficiently similar to be considered as representing the same social reality" (Bogdashina, 2010, p. 94). Whorf, who proposed the theory of linguistic relativity, theorized that the perceptions of the cultural groups he studied matched their grammatical categories. Not only does language organize our sensory perception, but Newtonian space and time are also artifacts of the way language organizes the world of the speaker.

> Just as it is possible to have any number of geometries other than the Euclidean which give an equally perfect account of space configurations, so it is possible to have descriptions of the universe, all equally valid, that do not contain our familiar contrasts of time and space. (Whorf, as cited in Bogdashina, 2010, p. 97)

Deacon admits that the UG theory is an understandable explanation of how the complex task of language can be executed with so little external support. Nevertheless, it is a sweeping generality that makes assumptions about the evolution of the brain, since language evolution is many times more rapid than brain evolution. Neither UG nor the social theory of language learning provides a sufficient explanation because the answer is neither inside the brain nor in the external support of parents and teachers. Rather, Deacon proposes that the answer lies within language itself.

If the complexity versus simplicity theory is discarded, the significance of human language becomes the "everyday miracle of word meaning and reference" (Deacon, 1998, p. 43). The ability to symbolically represent experience marks a mysterious boundary between non-human and human species in evolution. The threshold that Deacon says only our ancestors were able to cross is the difference between symbolic and non-symbolic reference, even though human non-symbolic forms of communication remain.[2] In well-structured contexts, primates have learned signs and symbols, yet they will probably never capture symbolic references with the ease and expanse that humans do.[3] How and why symbolic reference has appeared has been an ongoing mystery, which Deacon sets out to explain.

Deacon supposes that language is its own cause, setting off an array of adaptations—the evolutionary pressure of semiotic innovation, which was the cause of language complexity.[4] These early adaptations of symbol systems introduced a unique form of information transmission. In order to accommodate a symbol system, the brain needed to be re-engineered to support complex behavior as well as the selective pressure to re-introduce symbols into subsequent generations.

Language, as an unprecedented skill in evolution, requires a unique learning structure. Deacon suggests that one of the reasons it is so difficult for primates to learn is that they are not predisposed to the way the human brain has been honed by evolution. The learning required might even be *opposed* to typical ways the brain was originally designed. The *kind* of referent is what distinguishes language from other forms of communication, since animal calls have referents such as predators, food, and other events. Part of the mystery is that we still cannot imagine how words became invested with referential meanings, and how and what mental and neural processes were used to arrive at this most ordinary experience. Paradoxically, the only means we have to understand words and meanings is through language.[5]

The linguistic-reference relationship is determined by an interpretive response, a "mediator that brings the sign and its referent together" (Deacon, 1998, p. 64).[6] Deacon borrows Charles Sanders Pierce's (1978) semiotic theory of a hierarchal three-level system of referents—icon, index, and symbol, which describes representation as a dynamic process among relationships.[7] He delineates them as follows:

> [I]cons are mediated by a similarity between sign and object, indices are mediated by some physical or temporal connection between sign and object, and symbols are mediated by some formal or merely agreed-upon link irrespective of any physical characteristics of either sign or object. (Deacon 1998, p. 70)

These categories are based solely on interpretation rather than intrinsic qualities of objects and events, and the interpretation of categories is dependent on context, existing in an ascending hierarchy of complexity. Unlike icons and indices, symbols form more than a pairing with something in the world, and therefore are stable and independent of these correlations.

The association between words and their complex iconic, indexical, and symbolic relationships is based not on the probability of future correlations, but the internal relationships among symbols. This complex set of relationships, according to Deacon, invites both a learning and an unlearning problem, since "learning is, at its foundation, a function of the probability of correlations between things, from the synaptic level to the behavioral level" upon which indexical reference is based (p. 83). Therefore, symbolic learning means a seismic shift away from conditioned associative learning. Herein lies the reason that primates, who learn language at the iconic and indexical levels, can rarely make the shift to symbolic communication[8] that makes categorical generalizations possible. This shift into highly ordered structures and associations freed the working memory of redundancy, enhancing the possibilities of representation, or *re*-presentation, as well as implicit knowledge. This new mnemonic strategy re-codes information from the bottom up (indexically) as well as from the top down (symbolically). The most striking difference between indexical (pre-symbolic) and symbolic thinking is the transition from the pairing with concrete objects or events in the world to a system of interdependent associations that only indirectly refer to them. At some time in the evolution of language, a new kind of relationship between indexical associations had to be established in order to arrive at symbolic insight. What appears to be nearly universal in language is produced by what Deacon calls "tiny perceptual biases," which include not only mental biases, but also "biases from our visual-manual-dominated primitive heritage," evident in our universal use of visual and manipulative metaphors (p. 120).[9]

How most children are able to step into this world of recoded information is the critical question that will be raised concerning autism. Deacon suggests that language became "user friendly" to adapt to children's ways of knowing,[10] and because children transmit language, it would be beneficial if it were to fit children's minds. A theory of adaptability to language would make an innate language structure unnecessary. Deacon's rebuttal to Chomsky's universal grammar lies in the premise that the specific attributes needed to acquire language are uniquely located in infancy. This argument also has significant implications for the late appearance—or complete absence—of language and speech in non-verbal autists. The learning of symbolic relationships is unlike other typical learning processes and, therefore, potentially out of reach for children whose ways of learning are not linked to the structure of language, which correlates to the typical decline of language learning skills once children with classic autism are beyond infancy. Paradoxically, because of other features of early childhood—most importantly separating the variability of details from the logic of language—most children are able to capture the patterns of language, while autists do not have this "biased head start" (p. 135). Deacon explains that:

> Only by shifting attention away from the details of word-object relationships is one likely to notice the existence of superordinate patterns of combinatorial relationships between symbols, and only if these are sufficiently salient is one likely to recognize the buried logic of indirect correlations and shift from a direct indexical mnemonic strategy to an indirect symbolic one. (p. 136)

Therefore, it is not a language instinct that non-verbal autists are missing, which will be discussed subsequently, but a language-learning bias, the "top-down global-to-specific" decoding of symbolic reference (Deacon, 1998, p. 139). Olga Bogdashina (2010) suggests that because autists develop language in an atypical way, their view of the world might be more "accurate" because they engage in it with an abstract-less, concept-less immediacy, which makes possible "savant-like" memory. With both immediacy and memory, awareness is highly tuned to the physical world of details (local coherence). However, this way of thinking conflicts with the linguistic construction of the world.

Deacon describes language evolution in Baldwinian terminology, a modification of Darwinian evolution that suggests that non-genetic learning and behavior can change the course of natural selection, as opposed to genetic selection, which maintains continuity across generations. What makes symbolic association difficult to learn, says Deacon, also prevents it from being genetically assimilated and therefore it must be relearned for each individual.[11] What sort of adaptive pressure could have initiated the radical shift to this never-before-needed mode of learning? Deacon theorizes that it is symbolic use itself that motivated the shift in the overdevelopment of the prefrontal brain rather than the other way around. Our cultural evolution indicates that more than any other species, our biological evolution has been determined by behavioral adaptations.[12]

An additional mystery of language is the preference for speech as the primary medium of symbolic communication and the way it is passed on to each generation of children. But speech might not have always been dominant; rather, multiple modes of gestural and visual communication, which remain within speech today, point to the theory that gesture competed with and then co-evolved alongside speech, beginning as early as two million years ago.[13] Speech is processed automatically and below the level of conscious awareness, which makes the conscious learning of language additionally difficult for autists who are not predisposed to this complex system.

AUTISTIC MODES OF LANGUAGE

The impact of symbolic communication co-evolving with social and cultural evolution established new modes of interaction that Deacon calls "a mode of extrabiological inheritance" (p. 409). This theory indicates the conundrum neurotypicals have understanding autistic minds. Symbolic abilities have affected our social and behavioral experiences, such as our pragmatic ability to consider alternative choices without the immediacy of stimulus-driven responses. The indexical thinking of autism, sometimes called local coherence, has been well-documented in autie-biography. For example, Kamram Nazeer (2006), author of *Send in the Idiots: Stories From the Other Side of Autism*, describes in poetic detail his dependency on an alligator clip he kept in his pocket as a salve for complex social events.

> I opened the clip and I closed it. I opened it and held it open. I put a finger between its jaws and let go its sides. I released my finger and placed the clip briefly in the palm of my hand. The alligator clip provided what I described before as local coherence. I could focus on what I was doing with the clip, and other matters could become just a backdrop. . . . I could take a break and worry about the clip instead . . . a simpler thing to understand and manipulate. (p. 122)

Resistance to "stimulus-driven immediacy" is quite low for autists, often because of past indexical associations that are stimulated by events and objects active in the present (Deacon, 1998, p. 415). In another example, Lucy Blackman (2005) associates the inevitable entanglement of the omnipresent "M" of McDonalds with the generic word, "lunch." Her indexical associations preprogram her to unintentionally and unconsciously ask to stop at McDonalds.

> I learned this was involuntary the day we were standing on a pedestrian crossing in sight of the big gold M. We were talking about where we would have lunch, and I typed, "PLEASE DON'T LET ME MAKE YOU GO TO 'MCDONAL'!!" while physically tugging at my bewildered companion so forcibly that we ended through the sliding doors . . . before she could begin to analyse her own responses. (p. 166)

The inability to repress overwhelming impulses, such as Blackman's, prohibits intentional choices: thus the contradiction between thought and action in autists. Deacon suggests that classic autists have a bias in modes of ability other than language that are sometimes savant-like. On the other hand, neurotypicals have an exaggerated savant-like prefrontal bias for language, applying "one favored cognitive style" to the exclusion of all else, rendering neurotypical responses to sensory stimuli differently than all other species

(p. 416).[14] Neurotypicals are comforted when the world fits into symbolic categories and discomforted when they see its lack, which has a cascading effect in the way they perceive and live in the world. Language-users have a difficult time conceiving an alternative to a world constructed by language, and thus distort the reality of other minds while "not recognizing the oddities of our own" (p. 417). Bogdashina suggests that once linguistic patterns are projected onto the world, we see them whether they are there or not. Our perceptions, she says, are sorted into concepts ready to be labeled; whatever is not sorted and labeled in language is invisible. We have made the world adaptable to dominant, relatively similar, sensory perceptions. The way neurotypicals organize and label sensory perception is vastly different from autists, who have an acute and sometimes fragmented sensorium. For example, some autists have reported separating out blended colors, such as blues and reds, instead of seeing the dominant shade of purple. Names and objects for autists, according to Bogdashina, are not always aligned, and are made complex by associative or indexical thinking. Tito Mukhopadhyay does not recognize the things in his world as unified, but in partial perceptions, mentally filing each characteristic such as shape, color, texture, and sound in his mind until he can classify them under one appropriate identity.

LANGUAGE AND EMPATHY

The abstract representations of the world made possible by symbolic thought re-structured the human neural system, which was originally programmed to adapt only to concrete experiences. The neural system was re-serviced to accommodate "an alien world and recode its input in more familiar forms" (Deacon, 1998, p. 423). The results, says Deacon, "are both marvelous and horrendous" because we have direct knowledge of ourselves, but only indirect knowledge of other minds, and sometimes we don't even know ourselves (p. 423). According to this argument, theory of mind (ToM) is a relative, if not illusory notion. "In other words, if our mental experiences are mediated by representation all the way down, then there is no direct knowledge" (pp. 424–425). The problem of knowing ourselves and others lies in subjective representational experience, and depends on our interpretive abilities. The majority of our information about each other is bound and organized by social habit. Conceiving the subjective experience of others is not inborn, but rather learned within the cultural group. The autist, not always privy to social conventions, will not share the same assumptions. Deacon asks, other than proposing "an innate 'theory of mind module,' how could such a mental representation be produced?" (p. 426). It would require a symbolic leap since the subjective experiences of others have their roots in indexical association. It would also require that one maintain indexical awareness while experiencing the perspective of the other, "a complicated double-negative referential relationship" (p. 427).[15] Deacon likens this phenomenon to novelists who invent characters whose experiences are reconstructed by the reader according to his or her indexical representation. Therefore, if symbolic reference is "interpreter-independent," it is not a pre-requisite for empathy "because each interpreter independently symbolizes the nonsymbolic ground for it" (p. 427).[16] Language might even be less effective in sharing emotions than non-verbal communication, the latter evolving specifically for this purpose, and perhaps makes us less skilled than our pets at interpreting emotion in others. He concludes that not only has language contributed little to empathetic ability, but it might also have, to some extent, obstructed it. In addition, our lack of ability to closely read non-symbolic vocalizations in favor of language, and the ability to respond emotionally with symbolic constructions, put humans in the unique position among all other species to experience simultaneous and conflicting emotions.

More problematic is our predisposition to project symbolic patterns and meanings onto the world, or globalizing information in excess of what might actually be there. While an autist with local coherence sees the trees, the neurotypical with global coherence sees the forest. Our symbolic perception of the world not only ensures that our image is reflected in everyone and everything we encounter, but we are also compelled to turn them into symbols. In other words, we not only interpret our world, but the world itself becomes a symbol. The autist is not caught in the web of the prefrontal cortex, which consumes experience by recoding it into representational meaning. Ultimately, much of this compulsion is to make sense of death and loss, primarily with our ubiquitous religious symbolism. Deacon concludes that this tendency has the potential to be both the most noble and pathological of human behaviors, since although ideology serves to protect us with symbolic meaning, cultural groups with opposing ideologies can be perceived as a threat to our existence, and we act accordingly.

SYMBOLS, CONSCIOUSNESS, SELF, AND OTHER

The central question of this book is whether a perceptual hierarchy is illusory, an artificial scaffold inseparable from the linguistic structure that formed consciousness. Deacon's theory poses the additional question of how icons, indices, and symbols are linked to create a conscious representation of the world. As Daniel Dennett (1991) proposed, the conscious self is not an observer in a Cartesian theater. Similarly, Deacon theorizes that subjective experience is the product of neural signals modulated by events in the world that cascade into further patterns in a causal chain of neural activity, "each re-presenting some formal aspect of the initial interaction in an additional neural context" (p. 448).[17] The brain that Deacon describes is spontaneously and automatically adapting, fitting, and anticipating the environment with new patterned information.

Any change in how information is represented in the brain will determine the nature of consciousness, depending on whether it is the product of iconic, indexical, or symbolic representation. Temple Grandin (2013), probably more than any other autist, has investigated the nature of neurotypical and autistic consciousness. In 2006, she co-participated in a diffusion tensor imaging (DTI) study, a form of MRI technology that measures white-fiber tracts in the brain. It found what she had suspected earlier, an over-connection in two white fiber tracts. Grandin often uses computer metaphors, which ironically is similar to neuroscience terminology of over-connectedness, such as the description of her "savant-like" visual memory as the over-connection of "an internet trunk line . . . into the visual cortex" (p. 28). While her visual tract is 400 percent higher than a control subject's, her auditory system is 1 percent of a control subject's. Walter Schneider, senior scientist at University of Pittsburgh, suspects that during the verbal and motor babbling activity (hand-waving actions) in infancy, brain connections are made as infants engage with the world. Between the first and second years, children are able to verbalize single words as fibers form an interconnection between the two systems of hearing/speaking and seeing/doing in the brain. Schneider's tentative hypothesis is that during the single-word phase, Grandin did not make connections between seeing and doing. To compensate, new fibers were grown in the visual cortex. At this period, between the first and second year, many parents of autists report that their children's language declines. Other complications occur for autists as they try to simultaneously interpret visual and aural cues. Grandin explains that her visual cortex defers to the auditory system of the brain while listening to sound cues. MRI studies showed that when autists listen, their visual and auditory cortices are active at equal levels. This evidence would corroborate the many self-reports by autists about the problem of eye-contact while engaged in listening.

Lev Vygotsky (1978) also theorized that language plays a central role in consciousness as an internalized social process—the ability to self-reflect. According to this theory, early socialization is essential in forming the mental links between one's own experiences and others'. Language is fundamentally a shared code that functions as a translating device for sharing otherwise idiosyncratic memory and images. Autists must learn these shared social symbols later in life, as Donna Williams (2003) attests, and many of the ways she perceives the world remain untranslatable. Nazeer (2006) ponders that although language is complex, it is its variability that is the problem for autists:

> the same word may mean two different things. The more rules and structures there are, the less an autistic individual has to rely on intuition and context to get the meaning of someone else's utterance. One meaning, one word would be the ideal. That's manageable. (p. 22)

Nazeer notes that artificial language can be easily fabricated to match speech patterns, but it is not easy to generate code that is sensitive to context.

Later, deliberating about the nuance of implicit codes in conversation, he realized that the purpose of conversation is to entertain, which requires it to be insincere and indifferent to truth. "It should circle, it should break off, it should recommence at an entirely different point. . . . These juxtapositions musn't be aimed at establishing a particular collective point—they may do so, but that musn't be the reason for them" (p. 28).

Nazeer's perception of language as insincere and indifferent to truth has a ring of validity considering its instability, particularly when used in the symbolic representation of self in the alternating contexts of past and future. A self begins from early social-symbolic experiences of childhood in a "network of [language] users extended in space and time" (Deacon, 1998, p. 452). These symbols are not eternally the same, but variable and effervescent, coming and going. While maintaining continuity, the references for symbols exist only within the current social system. Individuals are dependent on the system, and each is dependent on the other's consciousness as represented through these symbols that have the power to affect every way we live in the world.

> The self that is the source of one's experience of intentionality, the self that is judged by itself as well as by others for its moral choices, the self that worries about its impending departure from the world, this self is a symbolic self. It is a final irony that it is the virtual, not actual, reference that symbols provide, which gives rise to this experience of self. This most undeniably real experience is a *virtual* reality. (p. 452)

The virtual/symbolic representation of self is grounded in indexical representation. Symbols condense these simpler representational relationships, allowing the ability to project oneself into possibility, unbounded from the constraints of the present. The totalizing symbolic-social order of neurotypical thinking, however, renders non-symbolic ways of representing the world inconceivable. Autists do not develop in a network of symbol users and, therefore, they experience the world in its immediate present. Each has its advantages and losses, but the prevailing symbolic thought imagined and constructed the world.

THE DYS-/DISARTICULATE

According to James Berger (2014), the system of knowledge, representation, and language has been the model for symbolic order since the Enlightenment. In *The Disarticulate: Language, Disability, and the Narratives of Modernity*, he uses the neologism "dys-/disarticulate" to describe "the figure of cognitive or linguistic impairment: the figure outside the linguistic loop" (p. 1).[18] Berger is ambivalent about his invention of this semi-fictitious figure, since terminology for trauma is inevitably beyond language. The dys-/

disarticulate emerges from the social-symbolic world as a counter-narrative, embodying the failure of articulation, a "modern radical other, concerned specifically as other to symbolization" (p. 55). If the *modern* can be characterized as the conflation of knowledge, representation and language—a failed attempt at capturing a coherent whole—then the dys-/disarticulate is a recognition of incoherency and alterity beyond knowledge, representation, and language. The self-referential system that makes language appear to be stable is revised by postmodern linguists, such as Valentin Voloshinov (1973) and Jean Jacques Lecercle (1990), as an opened rather than closed system, a dynamic process that is socially alive. This conceptual shift also indicates an opening of the boundaries that separates the articulate from the disarticulate.

> In these views of language, the conflation of dys-/disarticulation can be disentangled. One is not irretrievably trapped in a structured totality of representation, knowledge, production, and administration; and an external, radical other is conceptually unnecessary, for otherness is always present in language and subjectivity. (Berger, 2014, p. 59)

The incoherency, resistance, instability, and contradiction in language belies its totalizing system, and calls for, says Berger, greater attempts at recognizing others as capable of representing themselves, rather than classified, fixed, and labeled. To be part of the social-symbolic system is the privilege of representing oneself in a more favorable way than the public images and stereotypes that obfuscate the identity of people with disabilities. Without self-representation, communication is done about you and without you.

Narrative is the defense, according to Berger, from totalizing language, models, and labels because of its open and dynamic, permeable and porous, unpredictable and ambiguous use of language from which new social meanings can emerge. "One needs story because the world is imperfect. One needs story because there is no goal. And one needs story because things do not fit" (Morson, as cited in Berger, p. 188). Storytellers resist the conservative status quo, control and order, preferring possibility, unpredictability, and new meanings. Many authors of postmodern narratives about disability avoid labeling, preferring ambiguity and our shared otherness. Story is the perfect way to describe the ambiguity of self and other.

Christopher Boone

In Mark Haddon's (2003) *Curious Incident of the Dog in the Night-time*, Christopher Boone, the protagonist and narrator, tells his own story that reveals the entangled connections between language, knowledge, and the social community. Haddon recognizes that Christopher's location on the autistic spectrum is one in which "all people are neighbors" (p. 191). He composes a mise en scene where all characters are at some time disarticulate, albeit with different levels of skills in their encounters with unpredictability, each with their own communicative limitations and conceptions of the Other. Rather than overtly designating a label for Christopher, Haddon uses a metaphor for his protagonist's search for *communication without lies*. Berger calls to mind Donald Davidson's (1984) essay, in which he says metaphor is not an alternative to language but rather "a literal use of language and is, literally, a lie" (as cited in Berger, 2014, p. 191). For Christopher, metaphor is in the same category as a lie because of its inherent ambiguity, and he abhors both metaphors and lies. With his indexical thinking, he associates the thing for the word, its "transient embodiment," rather than the word standing for the thing (p. 195). Christopher prefers maps and diagrams because they are stable, unlike the shifting meanings of words or the unpredictability of time; they stabilize Christopher and ground him in a closer connection with the world of things.

Berger's primary thesis is that within the impulse to perfect language is the desire to return to a perfect correspondence with things, the impulse to do away with the social-symbolic order and reclaim indexical thinking, which is the apocalyptic impulse of Berger's dys-/disarticulate. As Deacon explains, indexical thinking still lingers in our neural responses, more fully revealed in thinkers on the spectrum. The infinite number of details, for which there are not enough symbolic signs, is a source of frustration for Christopher. Rather than a disorder, autism may be conceived as a manifestation of the linguistic conflict that Berger outlines above.

Berger notes that the mystery novel that Christopher writes—enfolded within Haddon's novel—is closer to the algorithm, model, and map.[19] Christopher's indexical thinking is easily appropriated in the detective persona, and the mystery genre serves as a critique, revealing the underbelly of the social order. Underlying his investigations, ostensibly about a murder of a dog, is an examination of social-symbolic relationships. The double entendre of Christopher as an autist with a detective persona is twice removed from the normative social order, although the social order itself is disarticulate and on the spectrum.

A distinct linguistic breakdown occurs at the climax of the drama, which also serves as the *real* discovery. Christopher finds letters from his mother he thought dead because of a convenient lie his father told him. His mother's non-symbolic response at this revelation is a protracted cry. "She had been banished by a symbolic act of betrayal. . . . Her wailing is her first utterance on returning to the social and symbolic realms" (Berger, 2014, p. 207). Deacon hypothesizes that sobbing and laughing in humans are distinctive from other species, although sobbing has counterparts in non-human animals. Human sorrow, however, is an exaggerated emotion extended by symbolic thinking and mental representation. That they are the first two social vocalizations that continue across the lifetime indicates that they have been important for social cohesion and identity in hominid evolution. Particularly because they are independent of speech systems, they appear to have been influential in bridging the periods between non-symbolic and symbolic thinking. Yet, the non-symbolic urge to disconnect from the social order is still present, and highly visible in autists whose impulse to disconnect is at odds with their desire for communion. With the revelation of this shared cognitive disruption, Haddon delivers the notion of the relativity of otherness.

METAPHOR AND LARRY BISSONNETTE

> *A painful, traumatic event acts as an incision or wound in language. The event, in its temporal-historical occurrence, is unique, singular, and, as such, is unreadable and unrepresentable.*
>
> (Berger, 2014, p. 219)

Berger (2014) examines metaphor in poetry and prose as disruption in the sense of Paul Ricouer's (1978) meaning of metaphor as a semantic innovation from which new meanings materialize. Berger proposes that metaphor constructs new combinations of language and perception, or in Mark Turner's (1996) words, "an 'assault' on conventional symbolic practice" (as cited in Berger, 2014, p. 215). Metaphor alters meaning with its syntaxical use of words, creating an unstable form of meaning (Trimble, 2007), rising "out of the ruins of the literal sense shattered by semantic incompatibility" (Rocouer, as cited in Berger, 2014, p. 216). Metaphor is compatible with Derrida's *catachresis*, an expressive form standing in for trauma, albeit less sufficiently, and the breakdown of the symbolic order. Metaphor as apocalyptic is the emergence of a radical alterity. In this view, metaphor becomes an uncontrollable tic in the symbolic order, which reestablishes itself, but with a trace of the wound remaining (Derrida, 1986). Once trauma becomes a word, it is normalized; "the metaphor of the wound, the wound as language" (p. 220). With these notions of metaphor we turn to Larry Bissonnette, a painter and poet without speech. As a foreigner to language, Bissonnette's metaphors, which he uses in abundance, shatter semantics, signs, and symbols, making way for a new catachresis.

In "Gobs and Gobs of Metaphor," Ralph Savarese (2012) contrasts two typed messages from Bissonnette. One describes his tactile encounter with paint, "Creation of dramatic painting starts each time in the movement of fingers on sopping, great malleable gobs of paint" (p. 186). The other is a description of his touch on the key board in the construction of symbolic text. "Typing is like letting your finger hit keys with accuracy. . . . Leniency on that is not tolerated" (p. 186). Typing requires precision, Bissonnette says, in counterdistinction to his characteristic "gobbing" of paint with his hands.

Bissonnette paints at the Grass Roots Art and Community Effort (GRACE) in the Northeast Kingdom of Vermont and, like the Creative Growth Art

Center in Oakland, California, it does not produce the typical outsider stereotype (see Chapter Six, this volume), but rather artists who are situated in a community of making. In an astonishing self-reflexive statement, he reveals an accurate awareness of his position in the art world, uncharacteristic of the label "outsider artist:"

> Others would say serious art is made creatively holding paint brushes nicely in a proper art school way. Scrap that approach. Work like Larry on letting your hands take off on the large paper without dealing with orderly way of premeditating every stroke. (Bissonnette, as cited in Savarese, 2012, p. 187)

Under the Outsider brand, artists would not know they were making art if it were not for the clever curators and collectors who "discover" them. Even when found, they might never know the social and cultural meaning of art.

Many of Bissonnette's paintings are dominated by the empty-of-people "letterless" walls of his former institution, Brandon Training School, on which he now writes his new present. "It's ever so easy to paper walls with ambitious words but the real difference in clearing Larry's needs has been the wonderful, caring people who support him everyday" (p. 191). The community involvement in his nascent literacy, and thus apparent intelligence, has propelled him on a mission to not only let the world know that he *is* intelligent, but also that other non-verbal autists have been drastically underestimated.[20]

Among its many purposes, such as communicating political, aesthetic, and philosophical statements like those above, typing has enabled Bissonnette to write about his artwork and how it reduces his stress. Savarese scaffolds this idea by introducing the word *massage* to serve as both a homonym for *message* and a metaphor, not only for stress reduction, but also the necessary bodily involvement in symbol making. Stress reduction, says Savarese, means that Bissonnette is able to self-organize the disconnected sensory system of autism.

In a lucid and instructive statement, Bissonnette says that the "role of art is to prepare thoughts visually in a way that language clearly can't articulate" (p. 193). Savarese suggests that for Bissonnette, metaphor is like painting in language. Bissonnette writes, "Scrap the grammar and syntax, and let go like Larry" (p. 187). As Savarese notes, accuracy implies the possibility of inaccuracy, and intolerance to leniency implies the tolerance of leniency. "He wants 'splashing language,' repaired relation through metaphor" (p. 187). What happens, though, when the alphabet crumbles? "Not only words but also letters lose their distinctions" (p. 187). Bisonnette's narratives are considered poetry (sometimes they are intentionally written as poetry) because of their associative comingling of words, images, and ideas. Savarese's own poetics embellish even more the Baroqueness of Bissonnette's texts, "where language, particularly metaphor, is a typed massage (and/or typed message)," a *corporeal alliance* preserving "the tactile prompt that makes multi-sensorial delight" (p. 188). Savarese notes the consonant sounds and alliteration that Bissonnette must relish, luxuriating in a textural language as rich in touch as his artwork; for example, "Powered print treats painted images well as long as colors Larry selects match. Larry loves pink and purpose because pressured painter gets to lighten stroke" (p. 190).

With their sense of smell and touch to compensate for other sensory limitations, autists perform tricks of coherency and coordinated thought through the interconnectivity of metaphor. If atypical sensory processing produces a "leaky self," according to Erin Manning (2009), then metaphor is the "self's leaky language" (Savarese, 2012, p. 188). Two kinds of touch are active in facilitated communication (FC):[21] the typist's touch of the keyboard and the light touch of the facilitator on the body of the typist. Like the touch of paint, touch during typing organizes the body, initiating organized language, as Bissonnette indicates when he says, "Ladle of doing language meaningfully is lost in the soup of disabled map of autism so I need potholder of touch to grab it" (p. 189). Savarese imagines the metaphorical "pot" to be proprioception, the ladling is typing, and the potholder is the tactile encounter that "rescues the heated instrument of linguistic expression from the mesmerizing murk of autism" (p. 189).

In a study by Koshino et al. (2005), the use of MRI technology showed evidence that autists favor the right hemisphere of the brain, whereas most neurotypicals rely on the left hemisphere. The underconnectivity between the hemispheres in the autistic brain, often cited in medical studies, including Temple Grandin's (2013) qualitative research, causes hyper-perception and attention to detail. Given that visual processing is located in the right hemisphere, it was not a surprise that their autistic participants remembered letters as visual shapes. Savarese asks, "What if . . . Bissonnette has somehow achieved the greater connectivity required for higher order thinking but has retained atypical cerebral dominance and activation patterns?" (p. 194). Then, Bissonnette's words would be more similar to calligraphy than text, "a pleasing design that also did symbolic work," as well as ticking off details as they are registered in his visual memory (p. 194).

Bissonnette makes continuous references to his language development, particularly in the titles of and commentary about his work. Savarese analyzes the words in the title of the painting, *Seeing-eye Friend Felicia in Gathering of My Very Canned Together Speech*, such as the verb *to gather*, which Bissonnette uses here to evoke the feeling of proprioception as a muscular effort to organize his thoughts and words into intelligible "speech." Bissonnette's (2005) commentary on the painting continues as follows, "Larry's somewhat bastardization of English language puts friends in the role of interpreters extraordinaire" (p. 175). Savarese points out that Bissonnette needs Felicia—as a presumed neurotypical—to interpret his idiosyncratic language, the way a seeing person might guide a non-seeing person through space. This synesthetic trope, says Savarese, highlights the extreme interrelationship of Bissonnette's sensorium, the transaction between the senses that occurs when one sense needs to be accommodated by another. The result is an often heightened visual perception. Smell and touch are sometimes the more reliable senses, and are used to augment visual perception. In Brian Massumi's (2002) terminology, "mesoperception" is the location in which all five senses can converge together, particularly in proprioception, where the most salient of senses—touch—envelops the world. This dynamic relationship among the senses allows us to feel comfortable inside and outside our skin. The neurotypical takes this relationship for granted, forgetting how the sensing body is dependent on the physical world (Savarese, 2012). All systems must be working together cooperatively in order to enjoy this unfettered state. The co-functioning of our senses then explains the tenuous physicality of many autists, their atypical movement and their recalcitrant muscles.

THE ROLE OF TOUCH IN LANGUAGE PRODUCTION

The autistic body's fragmentation might also serve to explain why autists are sometimes only able to focus on one sensory modality at a time. Tito Mukhopadhyay (2003) and Donna Williams (2003) use the term Monoprocessing[22] to describe how their perceptions are expressed with such hypersensitivity. Mukhopadhyay (2003) writes, for example, that it is not the water he fears, "but it is losing my senses in the new situation" (p. 67). Narrating in the third person, as he often does, he continues, "He felt stiff and saw himself as a rock, very strong and heavy" (p. 67). In "the next experiment," his mother Soma took him to the gymnasium:

> Although the place was an ideal place for children to develop their muscles, bones, and whatever, like flexibility. Yet this very noisy environment made him deaf. He on the other hand shouted louder to make others deaf. . . . His shout was so sudden that the boys left their place, and surrounded him in a ring—the so-called happy children in a world that is perfect filled with laughter and friendship! (p. 68)

To live in such a body would probably mean that little energy is left for symbolic interpretation (Savarese, 2012). Mukhopadhyay describes above what has been called "movement lapses," which the occupational/physical/speech therapist or communication facilitator attempts to shore up. In the following chapter, I inquire in greater detail about facilitated communication. For the purposes of this chapter, I explore the role of the facilitator as a synthetic organizer of the structure and order of language. In this deepened relationship, the facilitator behaves as a social partner and a prosthesis, doing the neural work that is required to connect the index to the symbol, which is not necessary when Bissonnette constructs visual images. For this "higher-order" connection to the world, he still needs intermittent facilitation.

Bissonnette describes how movement lapses impede typing, the facilitator serving as a counter-resistance to an unruly body. "Sock sand racing into vast beach of expression is not totally accident free" (as cited in Savarese, 2012, p. 204). The metaphor of resistant sand on socked-feet is made cooperative by the facilitator. In a passage about Mukhopadhyay's (2003) introduction to speech, Soma acts as an aggressive facilitator, literally forcing out her son's speech:

> The idea came to mother like a battery charged in a torch. She told him to relax and asked him to sit with a loose body. Then she did "it" with all her suddenness. She gave him a push from the back on his chest. The boy was not prepared for the push, and he gave a sound "uh!" as air pushed out of his mouth due to the reflex action of the push. "There! Your voice is found! Now with each push, you will find it," she told him. Then for the next 10 minutes, they did the voice finding process. (pp. 81–82)

Bissonnette uses the phrase "a potholder of touch" as a metaphor for a mediator that grabs onto a forbidding language. Savarese points out that touch, here, like Temple Grandin's squeeze machine,[23] applies deep pressure to control the disorganized body's connection to language. Gerald Edelman (2006) calls "basal syntax" the product of an interaction of the basal ganglia with motor, sensory, and prefrontal areas of the cortex. Basal syntax supports the theory that the touch of typing and the more aggressive forms of physical facilitation, such as strategies used by Soma, initiate symbolic learning, writing, and speech. Basal syntax, therefore, suggests that the participation in bodily movement is necessary in the early acquisition of language, as it is throughout life.

METAPHOR AND METONYMY

Olga Bogdashina (2011), like Savarese, explains how autists produce poetic-like narratives as a function of translating their mental images into the abstraction of language. Therefore, they employ concrete, sensory, and rhythmic words, "a cognitive preference [that] nicely matches up with poetry's own aversion to unmediated abstraction" (Savarese, 2012, p. 209). Bogdashina and Savarese conceive of this matching process as the common ground of sensory knowing and symbolization. Erin Manning (2009) describes the fitting of rhythm, meter, pulse, and movement to the neurotypical world of symbols as a "rhythmical re-invention" (as cited in Savarese, 2012, p. 214), capitalizing on poetry's relational features. "Metaphor is that reconciliation.

It is perceptual language in-the-making: the eye, ear, nose, skin, and proprioception gone marching, quite literally on the move" (Savarese, 2012, p. 211). Savarese suggests that in Bissonnette we can witness an "earlier" thought process impelled by the transitional, overlapping aspect of metaphor between index and symbol, thing and idea, the "figurative origins" that languages have lost (p. 212). In the same way, predominant denotative language contains within it its affective experiential beginnings. Savarese asks how appropriate and fitting the metaphors are within the context of Bissonnette's messages. Rather than "far-fetched," Savarese says we might think them "far fetching," piecing the world together from its ripped condition, remaking it vitally new and engaging (p. 214).

Mark Turner (1996) theorizes that the parabolic projection of one story onto another—or the projection of an image schematic structure of a spatial bodily experience onto an abstract concept—is the origin of language and developing consciousness. Turner's theory of parable shares many similarities with Julian Jaynes's (2000) theory of metaphor. Metaphor, like parable, projects human qualities onto objects and events, and both scholars argue that language arises from metaphorical associations. Metaphor, says Jaynes, stretches out the limited set of terms in language and creates new realities in its expansion. As discussed in Chapter One (this volume), the language that we use to talk about consciousness is inescapably metaphorical; even the notion that consciousness *does* something is to project onto it a human ability. Doing something also requires a spatial existence, an additional metaphor projected onto consciousness, but which does not exist in physical space. Jaynes theorizes that we project spatial qualities onto all entities, even those without spatial qualities, such as time, or we would not be conscious of them.

In Turner's parabolic thinking, image schemas (patterns of sensory and motor experience as the foundation of spatial concepts) construct story from complex connections among bodily, mental, and temporal experience. Like Jaynes, Turner argues that thinking and telling stories is essential to human consciousness. Literary thinking is not the exceptional talent we might suppose, but rather a necessity in making meaning of unrelated events. Spatial concepts are translated into the language categories of prepositions, such as *in*, *out*, and *through*, and these categories, Turner says, share a skeletal image schema of dynamic interactions between subjects and objects, the foundation of parable. The projection of image schemas—one onto another—must be without contradiction in order to make sense. Thus, it seems natural to project such common bodily movement as holding, grasping, grabbing, and having, onto non-human objects.

According to Turner, human mental activities are based upon the sequential nature of projecting spatial experience onto abstract thought and speech. This nature, however, is not shared with autists, evident in their atypical visual/motor control and coordination. For example, Bissonnette's and Mukhopadhyay's syntax and sequencing of events are idiosyncratic, in which causation and origination of action are not clearly defined. According to Turner's definition of image schemas as a complex coordination of neural patterns at various sites, Bissonnette, Mukhopadhyay, and probably other autists, might not share the same unity of neurons that are automatically available to neurotypicals. This possibility might explain why their non-linear and idiosyncratic sensory associations read more like poetry than prose.

Jaynes (2000) calls the mental activity of sequencing spatial experiences "excerption," a representation of an event to which memory adheres. Jaynes suggests that we retrieve memory from a file of successive excerpts, or Turner's image schemas. As discussed in Chapter One (this volume), the actor who tells the narrative is the metaphorical self, the imagined *I*, or the narrator. The function of the protagonist and narrator of the story in the neurotypical mind is to fill in missing pieces of information, insuring that continuity of self is sustained. Thus, language and narrator are inseparable in the construction of neurotypical consciousness. The consequence of delayed or absent language in the development of self-representation will continue to be examined throughout this book.

Kristina Chew (2008) suggests that we read autistic language as we would poetry, presuming that there is meaning and intention beneath seemingly arbitrary juxtaposed words. She theorizes that the idiosyncratic language of autists is grounded in the concrete associations of metonymy, a close relative of metaphor, in which one entity stands for another, or the bleeding of index and symbol. Chew distinguishes metaphor from metonymy by the former's linkage of two entities based on similarity, while the latter's association of two entities is its contiguity, occurring in close succession with each other. Metaphor is contingent on agreed upon symbols relating to so-called natural experiences (Lakoff & Johnson, 2003), while metonymy pertains to indexical associations. The use of metaphor is not "natural" or automatic for autists, who learn the vicissitudes of language through convention and repetition. Without the cultural agreement that makes symbols and metaphors legible, their associations appear arbitrary. Lucy Blackman (2005) reflects on her laborious introduction to language in adulthood, and her involuntary utterances rooted in childhood associations.

> That's why I would chant "Just Jeans" again and again. I could link my mouth movement to a sound that I understood, and that related to a strong positive emotion. That is because I adored denim. As a child I could make patterns with the diagonal weave, and the stitching on the pockets and hems was totally symmetrical. Denim was constant, calming and demanding. I loved it. (p. 165)

Similarly, "Bertie" was the default word for a variety of emotions associated with childhood events surrounding a long-haired dachshund. "Bertie" might mean anger at her mother, which was linked to what she thought to be her mother's neglect of the dog's eczema and eventual death. "Bertie" is also a generic word for canine, and sometimes a "slightly built, dark-haired man with horn-rimmed glasses" who looks like her father (p. 157).

Metonyms represent essential relationships for autists who hold onto language with a metaphorical potholder, tentatively reconstructing the world by inventing signifiers to represent indexical relationships and associations among objects and events. They represent, in a hybrid language, their version of the universe, "the person's own private cosmos" (p 142).

As a non-speaking autist, Amanda Baggs (2010) discursively uses language to meet non-autistic needs, but also for the purpose of disavowing neurotypicals of their stereotypical notions about autism. As Chew notes, to do this neurotypicals need to not only translate, but also interpret the perceptions of autists in their various forms of communication. Baggs's (2010) first language is color, sound, texture, flavor, smell, shape, and tone. The long and deep experience she has had with sensations led to maps, patterns, and connections without symbolic meaning. "Each experience is like a new rainbow for every sense, and each thing fits in a pattern such that I can perceive everything else around it" (p. 5). She makes a distinction between these linked, purely sensory, impressions and the symbolic categories upon which language is based:

> If I were merely a speaker of a foreign language, then I might be able to find ways to translate between my system of patterns and another's categories, but as far as language goes, I am something closer to a speaker with a foreign brain. (p. 3)

This form of communication, the arranging of and interacting with objects and actions according to interest and time, are the roots of autistic metonymy as Chew describes, and the translation of indexical relationships into symbolic thought and language. Some information, however, will not translate, says Baggs, into poetry, metaphor, symbol, or abstraction, all of which "take[s] place in the sky" (p. 4). She considers these arrangements, interactions, and patterns of objects and actions to be thoughts. These soundless, speechless thoughts are quieter than symbolic and cognitive thinking. She wants neurotypicals to know that she is not living a pale copy of their lives, but rather that hers is filled with its own kind of richness.

NOTES

1. Deacon (1998) clarifies this statement as follows: "If language complexity is a secondary development with respect to this more primary cognitive adaptation, then most theories have inverted the evolutionary cause and effect relationships that have driven human mental evolution. They have placed the cart (brain evolution) before the horse (language evolution)" (p. 44).
2. Non-symbolic forms remain in speech as, most obviously, laughing and sobbing, which will be discussed later in the chapter.

3. Many linguists and anthropologists have weighed in, such as the researchers and opponents of human uniqueness, Sue Savage-Rumbaugh and Roger Lewin (1994). Their subject, the bonobo chimp Kanzi, learned over 300 signs and lexigrams. They suggest that Kanzi grasps syntactic structures, a "cognitive substrate" to language or "proto-grammar" that "existed in a common ancestor" (as cited in Harpham, 2013, p. 228).
4. Deacon (1998) writes that "though simple languages exist in no society found today, they almost certainly existed at some point in our prehistory. These simple languages were superseded by modern complex languages, and the brains that originally struggled to support simple languages were replaced by brains better suited to this awkward adaptation" (pp. 44–45).
5. In *Language, Thought, and Reality*, Whorf wrote that "science's long and heroic effort to be strictly factual has at last brought it into entanglement with the unsuspected facts of the linguistic order" (as cited in Harpham, 2013, p. 46). Most prominent is that thinking in a language inhibits or obstructs our ability to perceive language. "Moreover, the limitations of any given language ensure that we will have only a very partial and imperfect view of anything higher, anything universal" (p. 46).
6. French linguist Ferdinand de Saussure was the originator of the notion of "one-to-one mapping of words onto objects and vice versa" (Deacon, 1998, p. 69).
7. The semiotician Pierce was most successful at specifying differences in references, and distinguishing "different forms of referential relationships" (Deacon, 1998, p. 70).
8. Deacon (1998) does not believe that his interpretation of indexical to symbolic communication is at odds with Savage-Rumbaugh's. He says that although Kanzi's and Lana's use of lexigrams was symbolic, "they had learned the individual associations but failed to learn the system of relationships of which these correlations were a part" (p. 85).
9. The visceral basis of language is supported by many researchers who subscribe to a theory of co-evolution of the hand with the development of symbolic language. For example, neurologist Frank Wilson (1999) characterizes bodily movement and the brain as interdependent, the hand being extensively represented throughout the brain. The emergence of tool use approximately three million years ago is also thought to correlate to subjective and intentional thought and meaning, that perhaps pre-language was primarily a way of thinking in tools or mechanics (Pallasmaa, 2009).
10. Deacon (1998) goes on to say that "if we could study children in 'the wild' to discover their natural tendencies, we could then design the perfect language that took advantage of what kids do spontaneously. Learning this artificial language would then be more like trying on new clothes and discovering that they just happened to fit, as opposed to going on a diet in order to fit into clothes that don't" (p. 109).
11. According to Deacon (1998), the grammar that must be encoded in words, and the logical rules that govern relationships, make the most universal attributes of language structure the most variable in their representation, "and poorly localizable within the brain between individuals or even within individuals. Therefore, they are the *least* likely features of language to have evolved specific neural supports" (p. 333). Deacon later goes on to disprove UG with this theory, arguing that the aspects of language that one would suppose to be universal are not eligible. "Whatever learning predispositions are responsible for the unprecedented human facility with language, they specifically cannot depend on innate *symbolic* information. No innate rules, no innate general principles, no innate symbolic categories can be built in by evolution" (p. 339).

12. Most notably is the use of stone tools. But almost every aspect of social life, says Deacon, can be perceived as a selection pressure. Theories mostly differ in their focus, such as the cooperation between mother and child, hunting and foraging, attracting mates, and defense from outside groups.
13. "Pointing might be the exception that proves the rule. This universal gesture exhibits many features which suggest that its production and interpretation are subject to innate predispositions. The fact that it appears prior to language as a powerful form of social communication in children (but not in other primates), and subsequently plays a very powerful role in children's language development, is particularly relevant evidence that it traced a complementary evolutionary path with the evolution of speech" (Deacon, 1998, p. 362). Pointing is also relevant to autism, since most infant autists do not have the inclination to point. This theory, which connects pointing and speech, might elucidate the late or lack of speech for classic autists.
14. Deacon (1998) also calls typical human behavior savant-like in the ability to perceive the world only "in symbolic categorical terms, dividing up according to opposed features, organizing our lives according to themes and narratives . . . we see not just a receptivity to symbolic relationships but a propensity to employ the biases that make symbols possible" (p. 416).
15. Deacon (1998) theorizes that "because of a difficulty in perspective shifting, they [autists] may only develop knowledge of another's predispositions to behave by virtue of attention on physical behaviors as indices" (p. 427). He makes a distinction between forming a general representation of another's mind and his or her disposition, the former requiring symbolic thinking.
16. Deacon (1998) goes on to say that "the problem of empathy is not necessarily a problem of representing another mind; rather it is a problem of arriving at an emotional state that is the same as, or parallel with, that of another" (p. 428).
17. Deacon (1998) here uses the color of an object as an example. "The color does not inhere in the object alone, nor is it merely a mental phantom. Something intrinsic to the object is re-presented in the pattern of light waves and again re-presented in the pattern of neural signals" (p. 448).
18. Berger (2014) clarifies his use of "dys-" with "disarticulate" as situated in language and modernity. "It is always language we are concerned with, even when we study discourses of its limits, failures, or exclusions. The dys-/disarticulate is the figure for the outside of language figured in language. But he is also a representation of a human being living as an individual subject in a social world. And as a person perceived and figured as 'other,' he becomes the focus of ethical considerations" (p. 2). Berger later says that "if the forces of modernity are conceived as systemic and all-pervasive, then the critique of modernity must be total as well. The dys-/disarticulate other must embody some radical, unaccountable alterity in relation to the social-symbolic order; must occupy some utopian apocalyptic, purely negative position and detach itself from any practical political program" (p. 9).
19. Berger (2014) compares the identity of the detective, and his or her position and impact in society, with the autist, in which the former shares few components in society and, therefore, is beyond society, beyond reason. "But these same traits that isolate the detective are the traits that enable him to see and think more clearly. And only in his isolation can the detective preserve the social order" (p. 199).
20. Larry Bissonnette, along with Tracy Thresher, have become well known in Gerardine Wurzburg's (2012) documentary *Wretches and Jabberers*, in which they are on a global quest to change the way people perceive autism. Episodic scenes of empathy and humor between Bissonnette and Thresher remake the label of autism.

21. FC will be discussed in detail in Chapter four (this volume).
22. In *Exposure Anxiety, The Invisible Cage,* Williams (2003) explains that "being mono" (p. 51) can express itself in many ways. The most obvious is that sensory channels are not integrated. Another way of being mono is not integrating information, each piece unrelated to the others.
23. In Grandin and Scariano (1986), Grandin famously described how she invented her squeeze machine in *Emergence: Labeled Autistic,* which was inspired by cattle squeeze chutes. She wrote, "The effect was both stimulating and relaxing at the same time. But most importantly for an autistic person, I was in control—unlike being swallowed by an over-affectionate relative" (p. 87).

REFERENCES

Baggs, A. (2010). Up in the clouds and down in the valley: My richness and yours. *Disability Studies Quarterly, 30*(1). Retrieved from http://dsq-sds.org/issue/view/43

Bally, C. & Sechehaye, A. (1916). *Course in general linguistics.* London: Duckworth.

Berger, J. (2014). *The disarticulate: Language, disability, and the narratives of modernity.* New York, NY: New York University Press.

Bissonnette, L. (2005). Letters ordered through typing produce the story of an artist stranded on the island of autism. In. D. Biklen (Ed.), *Autism and the myth of the person alone* (pp. 172–182). New York, NY: New York University Press.

Blackman, L. (2005). Reflections on language. In D. Biklen (Ed.), *Autism and the myth of the person alone: Qualitative studies in psychology* (pp. 146–167). New York: New York University Press.

Bogdashina, O. (2011). *Autism and the edges of the known world: Sensitivities, language, and constructed reality.* London, England: Jessica Kingsley.

Chew, K. (2008). Fractured idiom: Metonymy and language of autism. In M. Osteen (Ed.), *Autism and representation* (pp. 133–144). New York, NY: Routledge.

Chomsky, N. (1966). *Cartesian linguistics: A chapter in the history of rationalist thought.* Lanham, MD: University Press of America.

Chomsky, N. (1972). *Language and mind.* New York, NY: Harcourt Brace Jovanovich.

Chomsky, N. (1975). *Reflections on language.* New York, NY: Pantheon.

Chomsky, N. (1980). *Rules and representations.* New York, NY: Columbia University Press.

Chomsky, N. (1987). Language and freedom. In J. Peck (Ed.), *The Chomsky reader* (pp. 139–155). New York, NY: Pantheon Books.

Davidson, D. (1984). *Inquiries into truth and interpretation.* New York, NY: Oxford University Press.

Deacon, T.W. (1998). *The symbolic species: The co-evolution of language and the brain.* New York, NY and London, England: W.W. Norton.

Dennett, D. C. (1991). *Consciousness explained.* New York, NY: Back Bay Books/Little Brown.

Derrida. J. (1986). Shibboleth. In G. H. Hartman & S. Bidick (Eds.), *Midrash and literature* (pp. 307–347). New Haven: Yale University Press.

Edelman, G. (2006). *Second nature: Brain, science and human knowledge.* New Haven, CT: Yale University Press.

Grandin, T. (2013). *The autistic brain: Helping different kinds of minds succeed.* New York, NY: Houghton Mifflin Harcourt.

Grandin, T., & Scariano, M.M. (1986). *Emergence: Labeled autistic.* New York, NY: Warner Books.

Haddon, M. (2003). *The curious incident of the dog in the night-time*. New York, NY: Doubleday.

Harpham, G. G. (2013). *Language alone: The critical fetish of modernity*. New York, NY and Oxford, England: Routledge.

Jaynes, J. (2000). *The origin of consciousness in the breakdown of the bicameral mind* (3rd ed.). New York, NY: Houghton Mifflin.

Koshino, H., Carpenter, P. A., Minshew, N. J., Cherkassky, V. L., Keller, T. A., & Just, M. A. (2005). Functioned connectivity in an fMRI working memory task in high functioning autism. *Neuroimage, 2*, 810–821.

Lakoff, G., & Johnson, M. (2003). *Metaphors we live by*. Chicago, IL: Chicago University Press.

Lecercle, J. J. (1990). *The violence of language*. London, England: Routledge.

Manning, E. (2009). What if it didn't all begin and end with containment? Toward a leaky sense of self. *Body and Society, 15*(3), 33–45. Retrieved from: http://bod.sagepub.com

Massumi, B. (2002) *Parables for the virtual: Movement, affect, sensation*. Durham, NC: Duke University Press.

Mukhopadhyay, T. R. (2003). *The mind tree: A miraculous child breaks the silence of autism*. New York, NY: Arcade.

Nazeer, K. (2006). *Send in the idiots: Stories from the other side of autism*. New York, NY: Bloomsbury.

Pallasmaa, J. (2009). *The thinking hand*. London, England: John Wiley & Sons.

Pierce, C. S. (1978). *Collected papers. Volume II*. C. Hartshorne & P. Weiss (Eds.). Cambridge, MA: Belknap.

Pinker, S. (1995). *The language instinct*. New York, NY: HarperPerennial.

Ricouer, P. (1978). The metaphorical process as cognition, imagination and feeling. In S. Sacks (Ed.), *On metaphor* (pp. 141–157). Chicago, IL: The University of Chicago Press.

Savarese, R. (2012). Gobs and gobs of metaphor: Dynamic relation and a classical autist's typed massage. Retrieved from: http://www.inflexions.org/n5_t_Savarese.pdf

Sapir, E. (1949). *Selected writings in language, culture, and personality* (D. G. Mandelbaum, Ed.). Berkeley, CA: University of California Press.

Saussure, F. de. (1969). *Course in general linguistics* (C. Bally & A. Sechehaye, Eds., W. Baskin, Trans.). New York, NY: McGraw-Hill.

Savage-Rumbaugh, S., & Lewin, R. (1994). *Kanzi: The ape at the brink of the human mind*. New York, NY: John Wiley.

Trimble, M. R. (2007). *Soul in the brain: The cerebral basis of language, art, and belief*. Baltimore, MD: Johns Hopkins University Press.

Turner, M. (1996). *The literary mind: The origins of thoughts and language*. New York, NY and Oxford, England: Oxford University Press.

Voloshinov, V. N. (1973). *Marxism and the philosophy of language* (L. Matejka & I. R. Trans.), Titunik. New York: Seminar Press.

Vygotsky, L. S. (1978). *Mind and society*. Cambridge, MA: Harvard University Press.

Whorf, B. L. (1956). *Language, thought and reality: Selected writings of Benjamin Lee Whorf* (J. B. Carroll, Ed.). Cambridge, MA: M.I.T. Press.

Williams, D. (2003). *Exposure anxiety: The invisible cage*. London, England and New York, NY: Jessica Kingsley.

Wilson, F. (1999). *The hand: How its use shapes the brain, language, and human culture*. New York, NY: Pantheon Books.

Wurzburg, G. (Director). (2012). *Wretches & jabberers* [Motion picture]. New York: Institute of Community and Inclusion, Syracuse University.

4 Augmentative and Alternative Communication

I've only got one life and I don't want to spend it all proving I exist.
(McDonald, as cited in Crossley, 1997, p. 23)

Rosemary Crossley (1997) met Anne McDonald[1] in 1974 at St. Nicholas Hospital in Melbourne, Australia, where she was a patient with severe cerebral palsy. Crossley was hired to lead play-groups for the 160 young residents. Most of the children, assessed as profoundly retarded, lived and often died at the hospital. Those who survived were transferred to other institutions; none had re-entered the community. The overwhelmed and understaffed therapists hardly had time to work with the children, none of whom received academic training. Crossley found in McDonald's file that she had received physical therapy for three months in the 1960s. Because of her unusual bodily degeneration, she was unable to sit in a chair, and she lay on her side until bedtime at 4:30 when the children returned to their cribs. McDonald was then thirteen years old and the size of a four-year-old, expected to die within six months.

Crossley relieved the boredom by taking the children to the park and other activities that passed the bureaucracy of the hospital. She also formed a weekly play-group with McDonald and nine other socially responsive children. At these sessions, Crossley worked out a yes/no communication with McDonald using her involuntary tongue thrusting by clamping her tongue in her teeth as a yes signal and holding it back as no. For three years, McDonald existed within this limited communication until she became Crossley's subject in a study of a communication system she developed to pass a graduate teaching certification. Her responsiveness led Crossley to believe that she could teach McDonald to "talk" by pointing. McDonald lay on her side as Crossley presented an array of objects that she asked McDonald to point to and name while she supported McDonald's arm. She soon graduated to playing-card-sized pictures and a simple menu of words for drinks she had seen before.

> What Anne and I were doing in 1977 later came to be called "facilitated communication." At that time, though, I was simply trying to adapt

> an ordinary nonspeech communication method to a very particular set of disabilities. I didn't know whether this would work on Anne, and certainly I wasn't looking at it as something that could ever be applied to anyone else. It was (and is) simply a way to help improve someone's ability to point. (p. 8)

Crossley was satisfied with the results of her study and thought she had reached the limits of McDonald's ability, given her severe mental retardation. It was the intervention of a colleague, however, that changed Crossley's mind. Because he hadn't worked with severe disabilities, he didn't have preconceived notions about what McDonald could or could not do. Was it possible that she could recognize words? At the next session Crossley added more nouns and verbs to see if she might form sentences. "On May 2 she constructed her first sentences: 'Annie likes coffee,' 'Annie likes tea,' and 'Annie likes walks' " (p. 11). A week later she formed a command, " 'I want a book please' " (p. 11). McDonald released an internalized language by pointing.

The difference between what is now known as facilitated communication (FC) and previous strategies is that the client could not choose the content she wanted; it was embedded in the program. To move forward, then, McDonald would need to learn how to spell. Children who live at home have text-rich environments, such as mail, books, newspapers, magazines, children's games, and television education programs. The deprived hospital environment would be a challenge. Crossley papered the walls with posters rich with text and hung photocopied pages from books on McDonald's crib.

Not everyone was enthusiastic about McDonald's sudden communication, particularly the doctors at St. Nicholas hospital who had, after all, labeled her as profoundly retarded and thus justified her placement in the hospital. "In a reaction which was to become all too familiar, they first declared that Anne could not be spelling, and then refused to come and see what she was doing on the grounds that there was nothing to see" (p. 16). This "nothing to see" response, along with the allegation that the support of a wrist, hand, or arm caused the client to strike the letters, became ubiquitous among the harsh criticism and categorical disbelief of facilitated communication, discussed subsequently in more detail. The Mental Health Authority (MHA) tested McDonald's reading comprehension while Crossley left the room. A statement by Dr. Murphy read, "I have observed her [Anne] working with the magnetic letter board both as the person supporting her and the person who was asking the questions. I am satisfied in both instances that she did indeed answer the questions and in each case had read the material and the questions" (p. 17). The St. Nicholas hospital pediatrician, however, conducted another test in which he found that McDonald, now seventeen, had the potential of a twelve-month-old. The "test" comprised dangling a plastic ring in front of McDonald as she lay in her crib. He made his assessment based on her lack of effort to reach for it. Needless to say, McDonald's life in the hospital did not change as a result. The following week Crossley was asked to resign her position.

In January 1979, McDonald turned eighteen. She was the first of the hospital residents to file for a release at the Supreme Court of Victoria and succeed on the basis of habeas corpus. The hospital's proof of McDonald's retardation was based on her small stature (of a five-year-old) and lack of evidence that she was, in fact, communicating on her own. The Health Commission's report was mysteriously absent from her files, and under oath the hospital superintendent denied its existence. Under pressure and with evidence to the contrary, he blurted out that he didn't believe the report any more than he believed Crossley. Nevertheless, McDonald won her case and left the hospital to live with Crossley and her partner. *Annie's Coming Out*, authored by McDonald and Crossley, was published in 1980, and by 1981 the government closed St. Nicholas, re-housing its residents in the community. McDonald passed a high school exam, entered college, and completed her bachelor's degree in 1993.

THE BEGINNING OF DEAL

To learn speech, writes Crossley, is the most complex of human endeavors. As discussed in Chapter Three (this volume), it is the product of a network of people, relationships, events, and opportunities in the infant's environment. By comparison, most normatively developing infants are prompted and cued by their carers, who are full of expectation for meaning in every verbalization. The child with atypical, delayed, or absent speech eventually leads to passivity in carers who have been advised not to expect meaningful communication with such paltry evidence. The expectation of listeners, therefore, essentially determines the success of communication. During these early vocalizations, the typical infant enters the social world while learning the subtleties of speech. Without speaking skills, children will bypass the induction into family and culture, the connectedness that comes with our dominant ways of communicating. Crossley emphasizes that this disadvantage is exacerbated by the child's lack of a social identity, which would protect his or her boundaries. "Infants spend a lot of time saying 'no,' rejecting assaults on their persons or their egos. Children who can't say 'no' and who may not be able to move away from unwanted attention . . . can either tantrum or accept whatever comes" (p. 93). Tantrum behavior is less acceptable as children become adolescents and adults, but the alternative is terminal passivity.

Historically, children without speech are assumed to be intellectually inferior, and with their civil rights abandoned, their lives are governed by the state in its various institutionalized forms (Foucault, 1988, 2009). The assumption that children must speak before they read,[2] and that speechlessness equals "mental retardation," has persisted, and only with recent computerized augmented alternative communication (AAC) has this assumption come under question (Biklen, 1993; Biklen & Cardinal, 1997; Cartwright, 2008; Crossley, 1997; Duchan, 1993). In 1977, The Canon Communicator became the first computerized and portable device made available for a large number of non-verbal children and adults.

Dignity, Education, Advocacy and Language (DEAL) was conceived by Crossley while still working at St. Nicholas; she developed it in earnest after she was dismissed in 1980. In 1985, Crossley received funding from the Australian government to establish the first center for the enhancement of communication of non-speakers. With funding she was able to hire therapists and purchase communication equipment. Before the opening of DEAL in 1986, Crossley had limited contact with autistic clients. Her interest in the autism community was looked upon as a disjunction of its established theories, particularly because alternative forms of communication were not yet on the radar. In 1987, she wrote to Margot Prior, a respected academic and psychologist who was part of the IQ testing movement that concluded that most autistic children were "mentally retarded," despite the few anecdotal reports of developmental growth from caretakers. Crossley detailed her surprisingly unprecedented results in establishing reliable written communication, and the nascent theory that neurological disorder might be developmental dyspraxia, which meant the disruption between intentional neurological messages and the ability to physically carry out commands. This theory would explain automatic (perseverative) and involuntary movement, two manifestations of autism. The facilitator appeared to act as the substitute for the children's lack of an external motor "inhibitor." This was thought to be the critical part of the process in FC in which the facilitator is able to help override reflexive movement, impulses, and unwanted messages that prohibit muscular control. DEAL facilitators focused on interrupting the pattern of involuntary movement by introducing an unrelated action. For example, the facilitator might pull back the client's arm between striking keys, or the client might independently disrupt the pattern by touching the table between striking keys. This interference, whether through the facilitator or client, disrupted the flow of unrelated letters and words that cluttered communication.

Crossley received the following reply from Prior.

> I view with some concern your venturing into the field of autism since autistic children suffer from such severe and global cognitive problems which have been amply documented over the years in a veritable explosion of research. (as cited in Crossley, 1997, p. 129)

This letter was the first of many confrontational correspondences from the holders of official autism theory and praxis. A group called the Inter-Disciplinary Working Party on Issues in Severe Communication Impairment was formed for the primary purpose of closing down DEAL because the communication outcomes were "inconsistent with informed expectations . . . in terms of established psychological, medical, or educational theory" (p. 129). It appeared to this group that DEAL's intrusion into the field ruptured the hard and realistic work of professionals while encouraging what might be the false hope of families. Thus, long before observation, testing, and qualitative research of FC (detailed later in this chapter), a decisive response was made in the medical community.

The Government of Victoria enlisted the Intellectual Disability Review Panel (IDRP) to determine the validity of DEAL's methods. The panelists tested six clients in two types of testing strategies, one quite clinical (headphones and prerecorded questions), and the second in a natural conversational style. Only one of the three clients passed the first test, while all three passed the second. It is also important to note that the panelists spent time with the clients in the second test, brought them small gifts, and in one case took one young man, Marco, to a shopping center for coffee and chocolate. Marco was asked to communicate by typing independently what he had been given. Early independent typing often highlights word-finding problems, now well documented by FC users and facilitators, such as Eugene Marcus and Mayer Shevin (1997). Crossley demonstrated how Marco might find the correct category of things, but needed prompting with further questions to arrive at the correct answer.

The panel's final report was positive and secured DEAL's funding. It said in part:

> Most of the clients who participated in the studies had their communication and intellectual functioning doubled by others over a long period. Three of the four clients whose communication was validated are currently attending regular schools, whereas they had been previously assessed as suitable for Special Schools or Special Developmental Schools. . . . It appears that the use of the "assisted communication technique" has greatly contributed to their progress in regular schools. (Crossley, 1997, p. 133)

The question of client authorship and facilitator influence had yet to be reckoned with, which has since become the most contested issue surrounding FC. Jill, a clever and resistant fourteen-year-old diagnosed as autistic and intellectually impaired, introduced Crossley to this problem. In her communication, Jill described what Donna Williams (2003) calls "Exposure Anxiety," which is the involuntary aggression and opposition to external intrusion into one's world, even though intrusion might be desired. In one communication Jill typed:

> The prisoner in me was going to be defeated, but not without a fight that would be bitter and cruel. I used every trick I knew to resist having to communicate. I drove my family to the point of despair and made life hell for my poor teacher. (as cited in Crossley, 1997, p. 213)

Jill had word-finding and perseverative problems, but facilitation eventually lessened to a hand on the knee for emotional support. Her typing and speech improved so that at fifteen she was admitted to a regular secondary school. After completing ninth grade, her facilitators left her in fear that she was telepathic. Crossley observed that Jill picked up her facilitator's subtle unconscious cueing. Crossley likened this "mind-reading" effect to a story in physicist Richard Feynman's (1985) book *Surely You're Joking, Mr. Feynman*, in which a carnival "mind-reader" finds a hidden five-dollar bill simply by lightly holding the hand of the man who has hidden it and walking to the hiding place. Feynman explains the method as follows:

> You hold on to their hands, loosely, and as you move, you jiggle a bit. You come to an intersection, where you can go forward, to the left, or to the right. You jiggle a bit to the left, and if it's incorrect, you feel a certain amount of resistance, because they don't expect you to move that way. But when you move in the right direction, because they think you might be able to do it, they give way more easily, and there's no resistance. (as cited in Crossley, 1997, p. 220)

Crossley realized that in order for this subtle system to work, Jill had to be a willing participant. Her hunch was that Jill was picking up her facilitator's unconscious cues, checking and acting on her guesses based on the predictability and redundancy of the English language and the pressure of the facilitator's touch. Crossley's hypothesis turned out to be correct, which implies that first, Jill must be highly sensitive and intuitive to others, a characteristic that did not escape Crossley as being unfeasible under the prevailing theory of autism. Second, she *was*, in a sense, "mind-reading," or possibly, as befits Feynman's example, "body-reading."[3] If true, her hyper-sensitivity to another's thoughts, and the intelligence to decode both verbal and body language, contradicts the prevailing notions about autism and reinforces its unknowability. But even more curious is *why* Jill wanted her facilitators to believe she was telepathic. Crossley's final and astute analysis of this scenario suggests that she enjoyed it. The pleasure of controlling another's behavior was most likely satisfying for someone who had so little effect on others. And as someone who had been devalued, she was given savant status with hyper-human powers. Nevertheless, her performance, or pretend play, was of such a high level that I think she deserved her new status. But more importantly, this event sets the stage for the bigger question of facilitator influence. The tenuous sensitivity between the client and facilitator can as easily be broken down as it can be elevated. If broken during the pressure of testing, particularly during the testing of the FC by external evaluators, the confidence and trust in the client's answer might be compromised. The following sections will discuss the controversy of testing the authenticity of FC in greater detail.

FACILITATED COMMUNICATION'S BEGINNINGS IN THE UNITED STATES

Facilitated communication was introduced in the United States during a time of intense debates about speech, agency, sexuality, and power (Cartwright, 2008) sustained by the disability rights movement and its influence in the passage of the Americans with Disabilities Act (ADA) of 1990. It was also a time of marketing computerized devices that became essential to the disability community as assistive technologies, and as justification of ideological notions of "accommodation as a human right" (Cartwright, 2008 p. 170). In addition, the deinstitutionalization movement was in full mode in North America as well as in the UK and Australia. Anne McDonald's legal battle with St. Nicholas coincided with the exposure of abuse and shuttering of Willowbrook and other state institutions in the United States in the 1970s. The abuse allegations surrounding FC were to become the medical community's redemption, which they claimed to be the inevitable confusion that followed deinstitutionalization as health care fell into the hands of amateurs.

Founder of the Institute on Communication and Inclusion at Syracuse University in New York, Douglas Biklen, who in 2014 retired as the Dean of Education at Syracuse University, is at the forefront of educational inclusion practices and deinstitutionalization. He heard about DEAL from a report sent by Crossley's partner. Biklen's (1990) article in the *Harvard Educational Review* titled "Communication Unbound: Autism and Praxis," introduced the North American public to FC. Biklen had met Crossley several years earlier and was familiar with *Annie's Coming Out* (Crossley & McDonald, 1980). While Biklen (1993) thought it conceivable that FC could work for a few autists, he was skeptical of its general use, since it contradicted the current understanding of severe autism. He thought no more about it for a year and a half.

Biklen (1993) met clients Jonothan Solaris and David Armbruster during a brief visit to DEAL in December 1988. Both were young adolescents who spoke slightly and unintelligibly. Both displayed the "symptomology" of autism, such as toe walking, peripheral vision, and gazing into a point in space, yet what Biklen was to learn about them "assaulted [his] assumptions about autism" (p. 1). After speaking to Solaris, Armbruster and his mother, and several staff members, Solaris typed "ILIKEDOUGBUTTHHEISMAAD" (p. 1). On further questioning from Crossley he typed, "HETALKSTOMELIKEIMHUMAN" (p. 1). These thoughts and others that revealed humor, sophistication, use of metaphor, and other abstract concepts raised complicated questions for Biklen:

> How, why and with whom does facilitated communication work? Does facilitated communication work anywhere or is it more effective in certain settings, under specific education or social conditions, and with

> certain people more than with others? . . . Did the success of students like David and Jonothan portend a dramatic transformation in how we think about and define autism? (p. 3)

The last question, which has become the most contested in the field, led to the prolonged controversy among established autism experts, programs, and organizations. Others are the questions of authorship, the lack of consistency of results depending on the environment, and the facilitator's touch, or influence. This phenomenon has led to unsuccessful empirical testing and the disbelief in the validity of FC.

Biklen returned to DEAL in July 1989 to study the method more systematically with the majority of its 21clients. All were non-speakers labeled mentally retarded with echolaic expressions. The purpose of the study was to observe without preconceived notions or assumptions FC, autism, and mental retardation, while preparing to recalibrate the autism labels and behaviors as well as presumptions that affect education. Biklen wrote in 1993 that given its broad range of behaviors, the category of autism is not precise, and the literature is not always in agreement and often contentious. But while it was not long ago assumed that 80% of autists were mentally retarded, this notion has since been revised, probably with the influence of the growing and "vocal" FC users.

Biklen (1993) searched for an alternative hypothesis that might explicate the emerging language of FC users. A neurological problem rather than a cognitive one—one of *praxis*, he thought, was an obvious explanation. With this hypothesis he shifted the deficit from intellectual understanding to expression. Nor were other behavioral and sensory "peculiarities" indicators of cognitive deficit. Biklen suggests that Rosalind Oppenheim's (1974) hand-over-hand writing with autistic clients was a precursor to Crossley's typing, and concluded that developmental dyspraxia[4] rather than cognition was the cause of autistic behaviors. This theory was not obvious to many in the field, particularly speech pathologist Diane Twachtman-Cullen (1997), who wrote about her research observations for her dissertation and subsequent book, *A Passion to Believe*, discussed later in the chapter. Typing, writes Biklen (1993), allows the client more freedom than pointing at pictures, symbols, language boards, and other often-used communication devices, because it offers "nonprogrammed, nonpreselected communication symbols . . . thus making communication their own" (p. 20). Proof of authorship, however, is a concern of Biklen's as well as his detractors. While his observations have proved the validity of the method, particularly with independent typers, those who typed with the facilitator's touch were "less ironclad" (p. 28).

By the fall of 1989, Biklen began the FC project in Syracuse at the Jowonio School.[5] Shortly after reviewing the videos of DEAL at a meeting with 50 parents and educators, 21 students were selected by parents and teachers to work with nine graduate students and two faculty members (including Biklen) for a six-month research project of facilitated communication. All the children were non-speakers, or with limited speech and echolalia. Audio recordings of discussions with parents and staff, training sessions, and observations of students in classrooms with and without facilitated communication, became part of the research observation. Videotaped FC sessions were reviewed repeatedly to identify the methods of support, response, and interaction among students and facilitators. While FC opponents claimed that the discarding of traditional assumptions was a flagrant dismissal of the medical and therapeutic fields (Twachtman-Cullen, 1997), Biklen (1993) underscored the importance of proceeding without traditional notions of autism: "if we had assumed that many individuals with autism had receptive and/or processing problems, had specific or global cognitive deficits, and had difficulty analyzing language, then there would have been no reason to believe that facilitated communication would be helpful" (p. 41). Responses to abstract questions and engagement in conversations supported a theory that autists did have internal language and that behavior, appearance, and absence (of speech) does not justify assumptions of cognitive deficit and should not be predictors of potential. Biklen points out that the ideal disposition of an educator is to *expect* children to learn rather than predetermine who can or cannot learn. If we observe a student pointing to words, then we must persist in accessing his or her ability to communicate.

Biklen began research at Jowonio with the hypothesis that autists are capable of communication, that they want to be treated as competent, and that their difficulty is in expression rather than cognitive processing. This ideology ostensibly sowed the seeds for the success of the research project. Success also brought with it complex questions about the nature of disability and communication. Questions such as unconscious cueing with both intensive and less intensive touch, as it influenced verbal and body language, were to become the flashpoint of the FC movement. However, Biklen points out that facilitation is reported by parents (Barron & Barron, 1992; Eastham, 1992; Park, 1982) as a common strategy for supporting many daily motor functions, such as brushing one's teeth, tying shoe laces, or turning on the water faucet. In her biography about her daughter Jessie, Clara Park wrote about many instances of limp muscles that leaped into action when she cupped her hands over Jessie's, always with the goal of decreasing support and increasing independence. The Jowonio study was too early to predict the percentage of children writing independently in the future, but reaching the youngest children was promising, since they might develop the voluntary behaviors that would optimize typed communication.

THE OPPOSITION

Early opposition came from Australia, soon after Biklen's publication in the *Harvard Educational Review*, claiming that FC was untested and therefore had no proof of validity (Cummins & Prior, 1992). The two primary concerns, mentioned earlier, were facilitator influence and the contestation of valid autism research. These and other concerns continue to be voiced by experts, therapists, and parents. "No one that I know of disputes the fact that influence can occur with facilitation; this is why facilitation is not a perfect solution for communication," Biklen wrote in an email to me on May 31, 2014. But he also added that influence occurs in all forms of communication, which might lead to the natural incidence of reading the partner's intentions. "If individuals spend time together, they may pick up on signals of mood or recall experiences they share—married couples do this, family members do this. And we all have seen people who tend to finish other people's sentences" (personal communication, May 31, 2014). He does not, however, believe that FC users display exceptional abilities in detecting clues. To put the specter of facilitator influence to rest, the Institute on Communication and Inclusion stresses physical independence with no or minimal contact, as well as including the use of facilitator speech with, before, or after typing.

Immediate responses to Biklen's article in the *Harvard Educational Review* were enthusiastic, which caused professional suspicion. Within a year, Eric Schopler, the editor of the *Journal of Autism and Developmental Disorders*, accused Biklen of publishing without supportive data and called for double-blind testing. Biklen responded from the disability rights perspective rather than submitting to scientific testing with a rejoinder article titled "Autism Orthodoxy v. Free Speech" (Cartwright, 2008). He insisted that the over-diagnosis of cognitive deficit embraced by the medical profession, and its devaluation of children, disrupted their potential to access appropriate education. FC challenged medical ideology and testing methods. "From the *Harvard Educational Review* exchange forward, both sides of the debate held up the child as the entity it sought to protect and liberate from the other's appropriating claims" (p. 199). For proponents, FC meant liberation from the debilitating beliefs of special education and psychology research. For FC critics, children needed protection from pseudo-scientists "who believed they had the power to bring intellectual ability and voice to the intractably speechless child" (p. 200). From their point of view, the delusion of offering agency to children such as these was nothing less than a human rights violation. Integral to this debate was the scientific backlash to the humanities scholars of the postmodern movement who challenged empirical methods, to which FC proponents were tied. Long held theories of autism, such as theory of mind, were being contested, and FC was well situated within a movement that scientific researchers found to be spurious.

During the Jowonio study, a few parents were also skeptical, such as the father of a child labeled severely mentally retarded. His lack of success typing with his daughter was perplexing because he did not have problems with other types of communication they used daily. The justification that his daughter could communicate with some facilitators and not others seemed to him to be "circular reasoning." The rationale from proponents of FC, he writes,

> is that the child is merely choosing not to produce or give a message because he/she is "afraid," doesn't want to be "found out," doesn't "trust," the facilitator doesn't "believe" strongly enough and the child "senses" this, or for some reason only the child knows. (as cited in Biklen, 1993, p. 120)

I addressed this father's disbelief in correspondence with Biklen in May, 2014; he wrote that the facilitators were probably defensively guessing, and these would not be the words he would have used as explanations. However, anxiety does affect performance, as has been self-reported by Temple Grandin and Donna Williams.

Ultimately, the discrepancy between his daughter's diagnosis and her purported academic output with the use of FC seemed unrealistic and therefore impossible for him to believe. The father encapsulates in a statement the complex issues of disability and its treatment that have been adopted by many FC opponents, particularly Twachtman-Cullen: "Raising false hopes does a disservice . . . by creating the illusion that handicapped people must fit into our scheme of 'normal' instead of [our] accepting and valuing them for who they are" (as cited in Biklen, 1993, p. 118). In this polarized perspective, FC practitioners and their opponents accuse each other of intolerance by enabling and normalizing atypical children. Biklen found this father's disbelief and concern understandable, since his daughter was now redefined as a person of "seemingly normal intelligence rather than as severely retarded" (p. 118).

While Crossley was teaching a course at Syracuse in 1992, she observed the excitement about FC that had taken hold in the United States. Without training, parents improvised at home with their children, often to poor effects. Biklen, in his article in the *Harvard Educational Review*, however, warned of the potential dangers of FC as a deceptively simple method that required careful training. But the haphazard effect of the media phenomenon resulted in incorrect assessment and facilitator influence.[6] Crossley was surprised that FC was embraced without information or knowledge of literacy skills.

Acceptance of FC on faith spurred positive stereotypes and mythologies of autism, such as casting both children and adults as "innocents" and "holy fools," which caused untoward effects by inexperienced facilitators who categorically accepted the client's typing as truth, failing to check for facilitator influence. The extremely unfortunate instances of false statements of abuse sealed the expectation for invalid communication as an unavoidable reality of FC. Crossley points out that the early 1990s in the United States was a critical moment of heightened anxiety about sexual abuse by caregivers, and typed reports intensified the serious finality and legality of the accusation.

One of the adverse outcomes was that blame mostly rested on the facilitator since it was politically incorrect to blame the non-speaker, and thus the categorical self-delusion of the method itself.[7] Lucy Blackman (2001) sheds some light on this tragic side effect, explaining how and why she manufactured an abuse narrative:

> I remembered a conversation about a school where parents had removed their children because one of the men running the programme had done certain things. I had not quite grasped that this kind of professional misconduct had actually taken place. . . . *I simply had no idea that speech and other language did not create a fact.* Also I did not comprehend that there could be appalling consequences from these types of accusations. (p. 102, emphasis added)

Blackman admits that she should have known the consequences of confusing fact with fiction from watching soap operas, but the nascent communicator looked upon her text as somewhat of a script, as near to fact as television. Luckily her mother knew her fourteen-year-old well enough to be skeptical. Blackman's resentment at her sister and frustration with her special school was revealed as the motivation for creating a false drama.

Biklen was blamed for the uncontrolled dissemination of FC although, as Crossley notes, FC could not be controlled by one person in a society that reacts spontaneously and enthusiastically to positive media. The involvement of the legal system also prohibited longitudinal research and tests that would be more appropriate with non-speakers, such as testing with multiple facilitators, a variety of topics and situations and, above all, allowing for practice in developing test-taking skills. The variability of the outcomes with FC, such as the unexplainable success with some facilitators and not others, especially when the facilitator is a parent, causes anxiety and skepticism. Its harshest critics have maligned FC as a cult (Twachtman-Cullen, 1997) because of the so-called deluded persistence of FC practitioners in spite of poor testing results.

THEORIES OF AUTISM REVISITED

> *Mrs. Wong,*
>
> *[Not being able to] achieve any of the things ["retarded" people] can do, even though I really am of normal intelligence, is very difficult. I don't think you understand about autism. Many autistic people just will be unable to work without everyone hassling them a lot.*
>
> (Blackman, 2001, p. 118)

While Crossley and other FC proponents agree that a print-rich environment will stimulate the potential to read, Twachtman-Cullen (1997) cites research that contradicts this theory. She claims that facilitators have confused the function and meaning of literacy with pragmatics;[8] Twachtman-Cullen claims that even literate "high functioning" autists will unavoidably exhibit a lack of skill in pragmatics since it is a "universal" feature of autism. This claim is an example of the discord between new constructions of disability categories as contingent and unstable, and traditional medical notions of disability as essentialist in nature. Twachtman-Cullen cites Linda Miller, the "expert in the area of literacy development":

> Generically speaking, *literacy* refers to the ability to read and write. Even if one were to adopt a more encompassing, interactional view of literacy, clients in this study would, according to their diagnoses and their environmental and educational histories, still be compromised. (p. 122)

Twachtman-Cullen refers to the study for her dissertation and published text that included three facilitators and three clients of various "functioning." From this limited qualitative study, she dismisses the many autists who type independently and have contributed to the research that questions the validity of theory of mind and other "universal" theories of autism such as cognitive impairment (Belmonte, 2009; Gernsbacher, Stevenson, Khandakar & Goldsmith, 2008; Soulieres, Dawson, & Mottron, 2011; Yergeau, 2013). Twachtman-Cullen calls the "caught not taught" theory of literacy "ludicrous at best and irresponsible at worst" (p. 123). Judith Felson Duchan (1993) attempts to locate the controversy between the two sides in the contradictory definitions of communication and autism. She addresses several points that Twachtman-Cullen cites as contrary to autism research, and therefore suggests that new theories are needed. For example, the ability of autistic children to learn from the sidelines, sometimes called parallel play, needs to be accounted for, given their historical isolation. The concept of *Emergent Literacy* (Teal & Sulzby, 1986), in which children learn not only in direct instruction but also within the context of daily experience, broadens the notion of literacy and has given peripheral learning legitimacy. Autists such as Lucy Blackman have disclosed that sidelining arouses a different, sometimes more objective perspective of the world. In her autobiography, Blackman (2001) writes that typing proved to her that she learned, without feedback, to read from observation:

> I was not sure until now that I was really literate in the sense of continuous reading of texts. . . . I was getting a reaction, explaining myself, and trying to make a point that I had been aware of my surroundings for a very long time, all at one hit. (pp. 87–89)

Duchan proposes that a revised theory of autism is needed to explain the apparent dissonance between the client's facial expressions and utterances and the content of the textual messages. FC users such as Lucy Blackman and Tito Mukhopadhyay have warned that their speech and behavior are not reliable and do not reflect their thoughts. In other instances, FC users have written about events that did not exist.[9] Duchan cites an example of a client in her study who said "he couldn't help typing it" (p. 11), a function of automatic messaging. Crossley suggests that atypical use of vocabulary might be one explanation for idiosyncratic narrations.

Distractability, looking away from the keyboard during messaging, has been a primary cause for invalidating authorship during communication. Crossley proposes lack of coordination of eye and hand movement, or eye-on-task problems, to be the reason rather than autistic peripheral vision or an internal vision of the keyboard. This is another instance where the facilitator must intervene with feedback and correction in order to keep the client on task. Duchan (1993) suggests that a positive approach might be to consider autists capable of divided attention, or that gaze aversion makes attention to the main task more focused. Both Crossley and Duchan suggest that visual and physical proximity might not be essential. Unintended bodily acts are related to this phenomenon, and might point to an alternate theory of consciousness in which we do not necessarily experience "the world with a single-focused consciousness," consistent with the underlying theory of this book (p. 12). Many autists, such as Williams and Mukhopadhyay, talk of a second self whose actions are not under the control of the first self, dissociated from one's body, and living in an alternate reality. Whatever the source of the unwanted behaviors, writes Duchan, they need to be considered as part of a theory of autism.

TESTING

> *Research is really useless as its own reward. The only good purpose for research is liberation from our limitations. Research designed to make those limitations more real and more legitimate must be stopped.*
>
> (Marcus, as cited in Marcus & Shevin, 1997, p. 133)

Enthusiasm for FC was quickly followed with measured condescension and then indignity by psychologists who had performed their tests with mixed and often negative results, mostly in the double blind trials (Cabay, 1994; Mullick, Jacobson, & Kobe, 1993; Wheeler, Jacobson, Paglieri, & Schwartz, 1993; Smith & Belcher, 1993), while others produced positive, albeit tenuous, results (Calculator & Singer, 1992; Sheehan & Matuozzi, 1996; Weiss, Wagner, & Bauman,[10] 1996; Vazquez, 1994). These positive results also produced questions about the nature of communication and testing because of erratic performance and the complex and differing features of autism. For example, Sheehan and Matuozzi (1996) concluded that "the developing picture of an individual's validity profile replete with the patterns of required support, inconsistency, language impairment, and strides towards independence may well be the only reasonable evaluation of a validity confidence level" (p. 104).

Crossley (1997) described the tests as decontextualized with maximum interference from screens and earphones. The facilitator was often excluded and instructed not to repeat the client's letter and word selections aloud and therefore unable to correct misunderstandings. This set up the conditions for failure, given the tenuousness of the communicators and the variability of the method:

> The procedures used to test FC rested on a binary model of communication . . . the capacity to send a message, was either present or absent—you either had it consistently or you didn't have it. This model certainly did make testing easier. . . . If they could not communicate under test conditions, then this indicated that they could not communicate at all. (p. 258)

The variables of FC, and human communication itself, require a broader and more nuanced assessment. Some of the variables that need to be considered are the nature of the user, the message, the interaction, the situation, and the facilitator. Additionally, says Crossley, tests have limited predictive value because the experience and training of both the facilitator and client is dynamic and changes over time.

Eugene Marcus, an FC user and research collaborator, and facilitator Mayer Shevin (1997) describe Marcus taking and passing the tests that have been used to disprove the validity of FC. This study, which first appeared in *Facilitated Communication Digest* (Shevin, 1996), was reprinted with Marcus's input in Biklen's and Cardinal's (1997) *Contested Words, Contested Science*. Together they replicated the O.D. Heck study (Wheeler et al., 1993), which became infamous in Frontline's *Prisoners of Silence* (1993). It pitted idealistic facilitators and irrational believers against reasonable scientists and researchers, eliciting confessions from reformed facilitators who had snapped out of the so-called trance of belief. After watching the documentary with Shevin, Marcus announced that he wished to take the identical test. He explains that after attending the research group at Syracuse University, he realized the need for his contribution:

> How it seemed to me was: a group of sincere and dedicated and well-meaning blind men, talking about a well-beloved elephant. The missing piece for this well-deserving group was the piece that can only be supplied by me and my disabled sisters and brothers. (Marcus & Shevin, 1997, p. 117)

Marcus points out in his candid and expressive style that speaking comes easily to most people, which invariably sets up the cause for misunderstanding the nature of non-speaking people. "First, you [speakers] are maddeningly slow much of the time at knowing our most basic wants. We need to hope for a miracle if we are to get anything you didn't think of first" (p. 117). Because neither loudness nor silence will get non-speakers what they need, they have become "masters of creative problem solving" (p. 117). Second, speakers cannot assume that they know who non-speakers are because they usually see them when scared and confused. "You don't see our creative, passionate, spiritual, and laughing sides much" (pp. 117–118). He watched as the evidence against FC grew from testing and mean-spirited documentaries with unjustified and misleading reports. The truth about FC, writes Marcus, cannot be understood under ordinary conditions, but rather requires a suspension of presumptions and judgment of the "Other" about whom so little is known experientially.

To put an end to his own frustration with the perceived failures of FC, which he considered irrelevant by comparison to its advantages, Marcus embarked on a year-long journey with testing "to beat them at their own game" (p. 118). What he did not expect was that he would fail at his first attempt and several attempts thereafter. "I tried to pass the test and was amazed—truly amazed at how hard it was for me" (p. 118). Rather than rectifying a personal indictment with his ease of passing the test, its difficulty proved something possibly more important: the realization that he needed and expected physical and psychological support. He was also reassured by his collaborators that in research, failure is as valuable as success.

The O.D. Heck test was replicated with the help of Dr. Laural Sabin, who was then an assistant professor of special education at Syracuse University. She obtained the test pictures that Marcus would need to identify in the test, and Shevin constructed a cardboard visual barrier that would separate Marcus from the facilitator.[11] The first test was conducted on November 17, 1993, closely following the Wheeler protocols in the published study. Shevin reports that the results were not surprising: the test set up a challenging task for the facilitating partnership. What Shevin did not anticipate was that the test was not simply about facilitator control described by Wheeler et al.; timing became a factor in correctly answering the questions without facilitator assistance (or facilitator's knowledge).[12] Marcus saw a picture of a stove and could not retrieve the word "stove," but circled around it with general descriptions. It was not until after a break 20 minutes later that he was able to find the correct word.

> This was consistent with what Eugene and I had learned many times through our informal conversations during the nearly two years we had known each other; it is not uncommon for him to take quite a long time to remember a word he has been searching for, and he will interrupt what he is currently talking about to insert the elusive word. (Shevin, in Marcus and Shevin, 1997, p. 120)

After the first test, Marcus revised his focus, suggesting a variety of approaches he thought might help FC users master the test, while Shevin and Sabin videotaped the sessions. First, he needed to find a way that Shevin could support him without unconsciously interrupting his stream of thought; "it's like trying to sing 'O Canada' when the band is playing 'The Star Spangled Banner'" (p. 124). The second problem was word finding and ignoring "Mayer's tiny hand movements and other indicators of what he was thinking" (p. 124).[13] The third barrier for Marcus was not submitting to Shevin's speculation while still accepting his physical support. "The tendency I have for getting 'automatic' rather than thoughtful in my typing takes lots of energy for me to overcome without support. I need a facilitator like some people use a guide dog to keep oriented" (p. 124). While FC has for the first time afforded Marcus the possibility of communicating what he wants to say, he still must challenge his assertiveness while being dependent on a facilitator. "Taking charge of my communication means giving up on the comforting feeling that somebody else is my leader and I am just a follower. Keeping in charge requires more self-confidence than I have sometimes" (pp.124–125).

During the next trial, in which Shevin was obstructed from viewing Marcus's test, Marcus did not type until he was confident, and Shevin was instructed to wait until Marcus reached over to touch his hand. Long periods of time were spent on each question, without yielding accurate answers. The following session Marcus described how it felt when they both saw the same picture and when they did not.

> How I wish I could just go ahead with this without the difficulty of having to rely on another's hand and mind for support. . . . How I think it goes together is by having you in my mind, I can calm down because I know I can focus. *However, what I can focus on is determined by you, not me.* (p. 125, emphasis added)

Marcus says that the closest word to describing how he knows what Shevin has in his mind is "intuition," which suggests that even that word misses the mark. Something unusual is happening between them, and perhaps any successful FC relationship. At the risk of implying they have a paranormal relationship, which detractors have made part of their critique, I think that the intersubjectivity of communication, described by Biklen (1993), Cartwright (2008), Duchan (1993), and Sabin and Donnellan (1993), is a phenomenon that has developed with this method, and one that we are just beginning to understand.

After several months of pragmatic exploration, six factors were revealed that contributed to Marcus's success. First, he found that he could identify pictures more easily if they could be picked up for a closer look. Second, pictures of individual objects rather than complex detailed images were easier to decipher. Third, practice before the trials was crucial. Fourth, feedback after each selected item was also essential for Marcus to cultivate confidence. Fifth, he did not explain why the items which both he and Shevin could see were easier but, nevertheless, alternating between the two conditions soothed his nervousness. Finally, Marcus was agitated by what he called Shevin's speculation or "wondering." The times when Shevin was receptive and supportive were more productive.

During the following eight months before resuming the next practice tests, Marcus found help in visual integration therapy and a typing course he took at a community college that emphasized independent copying of text. At Shevin's suggestion, Marcus was able to successfully name objects that he handled. In the third set of trials, Marcus labeled correctly all the pictures that he had reviewed earlier, and had difficulty identifying pictures that he had not reviewed in the final set of trials. Nevertheless, the successes had the secondary effect of finding his interior voice in which he answered the questions with ease. "Easy because I had been discovering my true inner voice as a clear and steady one throughout the past year. . . . Inability to feel that clarity at calm communication had been my handicap, and now it was gone" (Marcus, in Marcus & Shevin, 1997, p. 129).

Marcus passed the second and final O.D. Heck replication test at the beginning of 1995. He answered all questions correctly during the segment in which he alone saw the pictures, and typed without facilitation. His initial failure and subsequent success confirms the notion of the importance of time and the need to prepare for test-taking skills. Marcus defined that skill as focus, particularly with word-finding problems, one of the primary challenges of a non-speaker.

INTERSUBJECTIVE COMMUNICATION

Shevin's and Marcus's study represents a typical experience in FC testing, in which both competency and incompetency occurs because of its multidemensionality, the variability of the social, physical, and verbal contexts, and the active participation of the facilitator (Duchan, 1993). The type of testing is also a large factor,[14] case studies and observation in natural interactions having more positive results than controlled experimental designs, such as double-blind tests in which facilitator participation is minimized. FC will also be looked upon as valid or not depending on what is taken for the relative term "success," usually "the belief system of the observer" (p. 4). Duchan proposes that a third perspective might lie in how we conceive communication. If it is expected to be autonomous, then the controversy continues. Duchan suggests that, rather, it is a collaborative interaction both verbally and non-verbally in which movements are synchronized and facial expressions and posture are responsive, all indicators of the content of the partner's messages. While partner influence is highly contested as invalid, it is nevertheless acknowledged as part of the process by FC proponents, who say that autists are in need of more external support in their nascent efforts at communicative and social exchanges.

Lucy Blackman (2001) makes a distinction between training to point at a symbol that eventually becomes part of a repertoire of automatic responses and her introduction to FC in which pointing was an intentional act of communication. Blackman describes Crossley's hand as a sensitive "pulley" that steadied her adolescent wrist, and a "code breaker" sensitive to her contracting muscles:

> In fact by bypassing these learned responses, I was tapping into my internal, spontaneously acquired visual language, as if I were an exile speaking her mother-tongue after a lifetime of struggling with alien words. The bursts of sensible syllables . . . were unmistakably *not what I had been taught, but what I had learned.* (p. 87, emphasis added)

Blackman's words were undeniably her own despite the hand that guided her. The hand in fact corroborated with her own to prevent automatic stabbing actions or perseverative movements. She describes the event as bringing her mind and hand together, her hand a willing agent of her mind. "I was still reaching, touching and registering in my own consciousness that I was doing what I intended, and this in spite of my trying to break away and squealing" (p. 82). She compares FC to other forms of speech therapy that did not work because her body or hand were moved in a direction that was not her own, or because she was taught speech by modeling words, which created its own confusion and problems. FC worked with Crossley and her mother as partners because she owned the emerging text. But FC did not work with her classroom teacher, Mrs. Wong, because "she did not allow herself to be used as a crutch and a reflection of my movement. She was so much a teacher that I was never in control" (p. 100).

In *Moral Spectatorship*, Lisa Cartwright (2008) theorizes communication as located in empathetic identification, affect, and the intersubjective production of agency. All communication, she writes, exists in a dynamic of power among subjects and technologies, each with different and shifting roles, such as mediator, listener, speaker, and observer. While she is a proponent of FC, she is not concerned with its validation, but inquires how this method produces communication relationships through text. The mix of authority, agency, touch, and the dependency of non-speakers is inherently a political issue when presented with the possibility of autonomous or semi-autonomous speech. Cartwright points out the complexity between both sides of the controversy and the ways each conceive of independence and human rights as understood through the ideal of speech. She theorizes that FC is emotionally charged because it underlines the intersubjectivity and dependency of speech, a problematic theory in a culture that values autonomy as the foundation of democratic citizenship. Shevin (1996) writes that the over-reliance on cue-seeking is ubiquitous in vulnerable and marginalized groups, particularly when entering into an experimental form of communication like FC. Reading another's ideas is not that different from hearing emotion in the voice or in bodily gestures. "Most ideas are not feeling-free, giving off signals through the hands. . . . So if I can pick up feeling, it is frankly easy to capture their associated ideas" (p. 5).

Cartwright builds her theory of intersubjective communication on the work of phenomenologists, such as Emmanual Levinas (1998) and Merleau Ponty (1962), who characterize touch between two people as the vehicle that connects and reciprocally changes the other. Her interpretation of the relationship between facilitator and client is based on this model, in which the facilitator and client are both active and passive, "in a partnership of body and will that most people take for granted" (Blackman, 2001, p. 82). Problems arise with the observer, the witness, or "the moral spectator," who further complicates the opposing notions of intersubjectivity and autonomy. Biklen's relocation of autism's deficit from cognition to expression is especially relevant to Cartwright's theory because the location of expression is neither within the performer or the witness, but somewhere in between. The core of the problem that FC underscores is how the intention of the spoken word, written text, and facial and bodily gesture are understood and perceived by another. The more intrusive hand-over-hand should be used only in the training process, says Biklen, to help isolate the index finger. "Of course many facilitators continue to provide hand level support and do not work on independence; this works against the progress of the person with the communication impairment" (D. Biklen, personal communication, May 31, 2014).

Not surprisingly, in light of abuse allegations, the responsibility has fallen on the affective role of the facilitator far more than on computer technology or the architects of FC. While computers have become mediators of agency and connectivity, the facilitators are a reminder that "human facilitators" have always performed the role of mediators between children and speech. Influence also exists, says Cartwright (2008), in any pedagogical situation in which an adult exerts his or her influence. Caregivers and educators, then, inevitably have influence over what, when, and how children will speak. The real test has been overcoming the unconscious assumptions, in a time of heightened mediated communication, that mediators are neutral.

The central question surrounding FC has been at what point touch ends and influence begins. Cartwright shifts the emphasis of this question to the affective support of the facilitator to produce expression. Marcus has made this explicit in his discussions of Shevin's role in his output, confidence, and autonomy. Marcus (1997) explains this phenomenon when he describes the emergence of his interior voice. "Please understand: facilitated communication is how I got from 'point a' to 'point b.' Readiness for independence starts from deep confidence, not a 'sink-or-swim' mentality" (p. 132). Cartwright theorizes that it is the affective nature of the support rather than the technical need of support that has given skeptics the justification to call FC unreliable. Blackman (2001) writes that excitation of the facilitator, not passivity, taps "the internal language spots [that] could enter my visual processing and motor movements" (p. 107). Cartwright (2008) compares the FC facilitator to the background hiss of tape recordings, "whose unconscious noise, and whose role as moral witness, cannot be erased in the process of bringing the nonverbal autistic child to voice" (p. 199).

The success of the affective relationship versus successful independent speech under the watchful eye of the moral spectator is illustrated by Twachtman-Cullen in her book, *A Passion to Believe*. Cartwright emphasizes how Twachtman-Cullen's subjective observation of three pairs of facilitators and clients influences the outcome. What is at stake, which Twactman-Cullen misses, is not the production of independent speech, but the interaction among client, facilitator, and observer. "Was it shame (no speech), or pride (speech)? For as long as we stick to those two poles, however, the controversy about FC will rage on" (pp. 217–218). What is more important, she says, is the new access to the world through the facilitator, with or without conscious influence. For example, after typing for a few years, Blackman (2001) noticed physical and sensory changes, in part because of the feedback from her hand to her brain. She felt "massive" changes in the way her body moved through space; "my use of language was making me more of a person, with better feedback as to why weird movements did not bring the results that other people achieved" (p. 114).

Bringing the expression of autistic affect into the world is valued only if autists are understood to have a complex subjective inner life. Cartwright points out that in the 1990s, when FC was introduced, the autistic mind was characterized by mechanical and robotic metaphors. In contradiction, many autists, such as Sue Rubin, Tito Mukhopadhyay, and Lucy Blackman, have written how typing organized their sensory impressions into cognitive and affective expression. For example, Blackman (2001) speaks of experiencing a second self when she began typing. "Once I started to see my own sentences as they rose out of the depths of the typewriter I typed visualizing myself as another person talking to Lucy who I had been for so many years" (p. 105). This *second self* gives us some insight into her seemingly sudden "caught not taught" fluency and pragmatic language that critics of FC find inexplicable. "I typed more fluently if I imagined I was sitting above my own body, watching, as another Lucy would, a new character, also called Lucy, going through the motions that all other literate people did" (p 105).

Cartwright credits the facilitator as the vehicle that enabled the transition from what Temple Grandin (2013) interpreted as the "acting self" to the "thinking self," or the involuntary action of one self while the other thinking self is helpless to stop it. The facilitator enables the integration of oppositional forces through the cognition of affective touch. The facilitator's touch is imprinted in the body's structure and memory, which makes possible future affective relationships. The facilitator, then, acts as a mental and emotional prosthesis that makes way for the emergent social being, which includes but supersedes FC's initial purpose of text messaging as physical support is "faded":[15]

> The facilitator thus facilitates the very structure of the order of language, her organizing activities having left a structural change in the way the psyche processes the input and output of feeling rather than simply existing there in the psyche as remembered content of someone who has been there, touching. (Cartwright, 2008, p. 221)

Cartwright suggests that the facilitation in communication serves as the laboratory or rehearsal for empathetic relationships, the same way that Donna Williams (2003) explains in Chapter Two of this volume her need for mimicry as the preliminary to experiencing affect. In the same way, the facilitator mediates the social experience with interpretations, affirmations, and corrections.

FINAL THOUGHTS

> *Maybe if we all communicated with someone literally at our arms, we'd be more inclined to embrace peace. Imagine Arafat and Sharon in the Rose Garden plucking out an accord. Imagine Sharon holding Arafat's arm, trying to offer just the right amount of support.*
>
> (Savarese, 2007, p. 284)

The FC phenomenon is inviting us, if we see the opportunity, to envision communication as collaborative, a heightened need to not only engage the other as a listener, but also as a partner in expression. Ralph Savarese recalls Jeff Powell, a young poet who was interviewed by Diane Sawyer in 1991 for ABCNEWS before *Frontline*'s exposé, and again 11 years later. He can type independently but worries that his "poetic self" will be lost without the relationship with another. Savarese characterizes him as resisting totalizing individuality, the exclusion of the Other as a decisive co-narrator, a self that inhabits more than one entity. Savarese (2007) calls the intimacy of physical touch with communication "arm time" (p. 340), which many FC users describe as an explosion, the elative suddenness of social connectedness. FC has transformed the unknowability of autism into another kind of unknowability in which two minds and bodies have produced a mutuality of being. Savarese describes this condition as hyper-identification, so involved in the other that, for example, his autistic son DJ still believes people can read his mind. I argue throughout this book that with autism we enter new territory in our definitions of selfhood as including more than one narrator, an odd notion in a society committed to hyper-individualism (Savarese, 2007).

The FC phenomenon, I argue, also invites us to examine methods of evaluation. First, our definition and meaning of intelligence as an objective category—particularly as it is closely linked to reliable speech—is called into question. Historically this assumption has been a vehicle of oppression, particularly as embedded in gender, class, and race. The orthodoxy of the sciences has long justified the exclusion of the cognitively impaired in the fullness of a socially functional life. With FC, anecdotal evidence has been raised to a more compelling level, for it is in the aggregate of these islands of communication made possible by FC, where none should have been, that we wrestle with our presumptions about reality. Perhaps we are forced into a poetic rather than scientific analysis of the autism phenomenon, at a location where the medical field admits to reaching unknowable territories. Autistic FC users subtly ask us to examine how we have arrived at our own identities, as each of us are, Savarese (2007) says, "products of normalizing agendas" (p. 285).

The FC phenomenon has given autistic users a political platform and a community of advocates with voices declaring themselves to be part of the disability rights movement. Savarese and DJ found FC accidently, like many users, and then discovered the community; they became "his people" with whom he could direct anger outwardly rather than internalize the deficit narrative of disability. DJ eventually refrained from self-deprecation and instead wrote notes that conveyed his hurt from ongoing insults, such as the assumptions of and testing for mental retardation.

The FC phenomenon, including other forms of augmentative and alternative communication, has also spurred a literacy rights movement that insures all children the accessibility of resources, teachers, environment, and, above all, the expectation that all individuals, no matter the severity of their disability, are literacy learners.[16] The by-law of the United States Society for Augmentative and Alternative Communication (USSAAC) states, "If communication is the essence of human life, then literacy is the essence of a more involved and connected life" (as cited in Savarese, 2007, p. 420). Finally, to return to the statement by Anne McDonald, how much longer must FC users prove that they exist?

NOTES

1. Anne McDonald passed away just before turning 50 in 2010.
2. Crossley (1997) points out that the Deaf community has proven that "the acquisition of written language can be divorced from the acquisition of speech and that visual language can be acquired from exposure in the same way as aural language. . . . Two centuries after the Abbe de l'Epee taught his first deaf students to read, the accepted wisdom is still that speaking must precede reading" (p. 136).
3. Crossley (1997) begins the chapter about Jill with a passage from Conan Doyle's (1893) *The memoirs of Sherlock Holmes*, which she returns to later in the chapter. "I outlined a few scenarios that I thought were about right, and Jill sat there smiling at me. The explanation that she was happiest with . . . was the Sherlock Holmes model, where Holmes tells Watson what Watson's been

thinking about, by putting together what Watson has looked at, where he has been, and what he has done previously; magician's cold readings are done along the same kind of lines" (p. 224).

4. Developmental dyspraxia is a neurological condition that disrupts motor control even though the mental intention is present, which means a surfeit of involuntary or automatic action and difficulty engaging with voluntary action. Biklen (1993) hypothesizes that echolalia is a product of apraxia, "in fact, the thinking abilities of people with apraxia far exceed their capacity for expressive language" (p. 80). He describes a "physical analogue to echolalia" (p. 82) as autists who seem to be capable of a task when not asked, but unresponsive or delayed when asked. Thus, Biklen emphasizes that apraxia does not necessarily indicate cognitive deficit. Biklen (1993) cites Wetherby (1984) as supporting the neurological rather than cognitive defect of autism. "Wetherby (1984) hypothesizes that the person with autism may have insufficient cortical control of the limbic system" (p. 64). Autopsies and MRIs of autists reveal anomalies in the limbic system and not in the cortex.
5. The Jowonio School has served young children with a range of abilities since 1969, when it began as an alternative school with individualized instruction. Since 1975, it has operated as an inclusion school.
6. For example, Diane Sawyer interviewed three FC users in 1992 on ABCNews *Prime Time*: Lucy Harrison, Ben Lehr, and Jeff Powell. FC was described in this program as "a miracle" and an "awakening," and mentioned in *Prisoners of Silence*.
7. Biklen suggests the following protocol for any abuse allegation: "to bring in a facilitator who is naïve to what the FC user had typed and to see if through conversation the person could/would repeat the allegation. If repeated, this would verify the person's authorship of the allegation and the court would then need to assess the factual veracity" (personal communication, January 30, 2015). In addition, Botash et al. (1994) found that abuse allegations made by FC users followed the same outcome as speaking persons: one-third are corroborated, one-third remain undecided, and one-third are without merit.
8. Twatchtman-Cullen (1997) defines pragmatics according to *Webster's College Dictionary* (1991, p. 1059) as "a branch of linguistics dealing with language in its situational context, including the knowledge and beliefs of the speaker, and the relationship and interaction between speaker and listener" (p. 122).
9. See Lucy Blackman (2001), *Lucy's Story: Autism and Other Adventures*.
10. In "A Validated Case Study of Facilitated Communication," by Weiss, Wagner, & Bauman (1996) in *Mental Retardation*, the authors reveal success with a single subject, which invites the question of working for some and not others: "The case of a 13-year-old boy with autism, severe mental retardation, and a seizure disorder who was able to demonstrate valid facilitated communication was described. In three independent trials, short stories were presented to him, followed by validation test procedures with an uninformed facilitator providing physical support to the subject's arm. In trials 1 and 3, several specific answers were provided that clearly indicated that the young man, not the uninformed facilitator, was the source of the information. Moreover, some responses seemed to imply that the subject was employing simple inferential and abstract reasoning. The case study adds to the small, but growing number of demonstrations that facilitated communication can sometimes be a valid method of communication for at least some individuals with developmental disabilities" (*CNN*, Facilitated communication studies, http://www-cgi.cnn.com/CNN/Programs/presents/shows/autism.world/fc/studies.html).
11. An illustration of the set up is in *Mental Retardation*, Wheeler et al., 1993.

12. About the importance of timing, see Matthew K. Belmonte (2009) and Rosemary Crossley (http://www.annemcdonaldcentre.org.au/front-line).
13. So it appears that facilitator unconscious messages through minute gestures are unavoidable. But to me this is also a form of communication, one that needs to be explored. It also does not cancel out the fact that the client knows that the answer is the right one, as Marcus explained.
14. In an email communication on January 30, 2015, Biklen wrote, "I have never resisted the idea of conducting empirical research designed specifically to assess authorship, but realize that coming up with a strategy that itself does not disrupt the communication process can be difficult. The Cardinal et al. study proved authorship for a very large number of subjects probably because it was conducted over a period of weeks and sessions, thus presumably allowing individuals to come to feel the assessments were a somewhat normal phenomenon. Even in that study [Tuzzi] however, despite the fact that overall performance got better and better during the weeks of the study, some individuals did superbly or even perfectly some days and not at all well or even completely failed on other days."
15. "Fading" is a term used in FC to describe the increasing independence of the client and diminishing of facilitator support.
16. See *Literacy Bill of Rights* at http://mtdeafblind.ruralinstitute.umt.edu/LiteracyBillofRights.asp

REFERENCES

Barron, J., & Barron, S. (1992). *There's a boy in here: A mother and her son tell the story of his emergence from autism*. New York, NY: Simon and Shuster.

Belmonte, M. K. (2009). What's the story behind 'theory of mind' and autism? *Journal of Consciousness Studies, 16*(6–7). Retrieved from: http://www.mattababy.org/~belmonte/Publications/Papers/09_Hutto/Reprint/Belmonte_JCS_2009.pdf

Biklen, D. (1990). Autism orthodoxy versus free speech: A reply to Cummins and Prior. *Harvard Educational Review, 62*(2), 242–257.

Biklen, D. (1993). *Communication unbound: How facilitated communication is challenging traditional views of autism and ability/disability*. New York, NY: Teachers College Press.

Biklen, D., & Cardinal, D. (Eds.). (1997). *Contested words, contested science: Unraveling the facilitated communication controversy*. New York, NY: Teachers College Press.

Blackman, L. (2001). *Lucy's story: Autism and other adventures*. London, England and Philadelphia, PA: Jessica Kingsley.

Botash, A., Babuts, D., Mitchell, N., O'Hara, M., Manuel, J., & Lynch, L. (1994). Evaluations of children who have disclosed sexual abuse via facilitated communication. *Archives of Pediatrics and Adolescent Medicine, 148*, 1282–1287.

Cabay, M. (1994). Brief report: A controlled evaluation of facilitated communication using open-ended and fill-in questions. *Journal of Autism and Developmental Disorders, 24*, 517–527.

Calculator, S. N., & Singer, K. M. (1992). Letter to the editor: Preliminary validation of facilitated communication. *Topics in Language Disorders, 12*(4), ix–xvi.

Cartwright, L. (2008). *Moral spectatorship: Technologies of voice and affect in postwar representations of the child*. Durham, NC and London, England: Duke University Press.

Crossley, R. (1997). *Speechless: Facilitating communication for people without voices*. New York, NY: Dutton.

Crossley, R. (n.d.). Facilitated communication training: In the front line. Anne McDonald Centre. Retrieved from: http://www.annemcdonaldcentre.org.au/front-line

Crossley, R., & McDonald, A. (1980). *Annie's coming out*. Victoria, Australia: Penguin Books.

Cummins, R.A., & Prior, M.P. (1992). Autism and assisted communication: A response to Biklen. *Harvard Educational Review, 62*, 228–241.

Doyle, C. (1893). *The adventures of Sherlock Holmes*. London: George Newnes.

Duchan, J. F. (1993). Issues raised by facilitated communication for theorizing and research on autism. *Journal of Speech & Hearing Research, 36*(6), 1108–1119.

Eastham, M. (1992). *Silent words: Forever friends*. Ottawa, Canada: Oliver Pate.

Feynman, R. (1985). *Surely you're joking, Mr. Feynman*. New York, NY: Norton.

Foucault, M. (1988). *Madness and civilization: A history of insanity in the age of reason* (Vintage Books ed.). New York, NY: Random House. (Original work published 1965).

Foucault, M. (2009). *History of madness*. New York, NY: Routledge.

Gernsbacher, M. A., Stevenson, J. L., Khandakar, S., & Goldsmith, H.H. (2008). Autistic's atypical joint attention: Policy implications and empirical nuance. *Child Development Perspectives, 2*(1), 49–52.

Levinas, E. (1998). *Collected philosophical papers* (A. Lingis, trans.). New York, NY: Springer.

Levinas, E. (1999). *Alterity and transcendence*. New York, NY: Columbia University Press.

Marcus, E., & Shevin, M. (1997). Sorting it out under fire: Our journey. In D. Biklen & D. Cardinal (Eds.), *Contested words, contested science: Unraveling the facilitated communication controversy* (pp. 115–134). New York, NY: Teachers College Press.

Merleau Ponty, M. (1962, 2013). *Phenomenology of perception*. (K. Paul, trans.). New York, NY and London, England: Routledge Classics.

Mullick, J. A., Jacobson, J. W., and Kobe, F. H. (1993). Anguished silence and helping hands: Autism and facilitated communication. *Skeptical Inquirer, 17*(3), 270.

Park, C.C. (1982). *The siege: The first eight years of an autistic child*. New York, NY: Little Brown.

Palfreman, J. (1993) (Director). Prisoners of silence. *Frontline*. WGBH Educational Foundation. Transcript retrieved from: http://www.pbs.org/wgbh/pages/frontline/programs/transcripts/1202.html

Sabin, L. A. & Donnellan, A. M. (1993). A qualitative study of the process of facilitated communication. Journal of the Association for Persons with Severe Handicaps, 18(3). 200–211.

Sheehan, C., & Matuozzi, R. (1996). Investigation of the validity of facilitated communication through the disclosure of unknown information. *Mental Retardation, 34*(2), 94–107.

Shevin, M. (1996, December). Understanding and negotiating cue-seeking by facilitated communication users. *Facilitated Communication Digest, 5*(1). Retrieved from: http://soe.syr.edu/media/documents/2010/7/understanding_and_negotiating_cueseekingshevin.pdf

Smith, M. D., & Belcher, R.G. (1993). Facilitated communication with adults with autism. *Journal of Autism and Developmental Disorders, 1*, 175–183.

Soulieres, I., Dawson, M.A., & Mottron, L. (2011). The level and nature of autistic intelligence II: What about Asperger syndrome? *Plos One*. Retrieved from: http://www.plosone.org/article/info%3Adoi%2F10.1371%2Fjournal.pone.0025372

Teal, W., & Sulzby, E. (Eds). (1986). *Emergent literacy: Writing and reading*. Norwood, NJ: Ablex.

Twachtman-Cullen, D. (1997). *A passion to believe: Autism and the facilitated communication phenomenon*. Boulder, CO: Westview.

Vasquez, C. A. (1994). Brief report: A multitask controlled observation of facilitated communication. *Journal of Autism and Developmental Disorders, 24*(3), 369–379.

Weiss, M.J.S., Wagner, S. H., & Bauman, M. L. (1996). A validated case study of facilitated communication. *Mental Retardation, 34*(4), 220–230.

Wetherby, A.M. (1984). Possible neurolinguistic breakdown in autism children. *Topics in Language Disorders,* 27, 364–377.

Wheeler, D. L., Jacobson, J. W., Paglieri, R. A., & Schwartz, A.A. (1993). An experimental assessment of facilitated communication. *Mental Retardation, 31*(1), 49–60.

Williams, D. (2003). *Exposure anxiety: The invisible cage.* London, England and New York, NY: Jessica Kingsley.

Yergeau, M. (2013). Clinically significant disturbance: On theorists who theorize theory of mind. *Disability Studies Quarterly, 33*(4). Retrieved from: http://dsq-sds.org/article/view/3876/3405

Yoder, D. E., Erickson, K.A., & Koppenhaver, D. A. (1997). *Literacy bill of rights.* Chapel Hill, NC: University of North Carolina at Chapel Hill, Center for Literacy and Disability. Retrieved from: http://mtdeafblind.ruralinstitute.umt.edu/LiteracyBillofRights.asp

5 Constructions of the Autism Label and the Autistic Identity

> *What if, however, autism along with those who are autistic, proves to be central to the ways in which we conceive of our fundamental sense of self? How controversial might that be?*
>
> (Murray, 2012, p. 101)

REPRESENTATIONS OF AUTISM

Two autism narratives exist in parallel, one more highly public than the other. The more public narrative is focused on loss and tragedy; it is written by the medical community, filtered into the news and entertainment media, and robustly represented by parents of Autism Speaks. Because autism is narrated as tragic, the content is focused on cause and cure. It is also the source of endless reporting of statistics that suggest a growing epidemic. Stuart Murray (2008) reasons that the "upset" of the non-autistic community indicates that divergence from the norm is itself disruptive. Its unwieldy range, and therefore the difficulty in regulating it, is what makes the debate about autism's causes, cures, and treatments so electric, and a lack of medical and pedagogical consensus so unyielding. Each insight or "discovery" about autism is disavowed by the opposition it invites. Looking for a single cause is somewhat of a fiction, but the lack of uniformity of autism does not go over well as a public image of the condition, and therefore a uniform theory is often manufactured. Autism has also become fetishisized and sensationalized because of the wide controversies that it invites from its constituents: doctors, researchers, teachers, therapists, and parents. The news and entertainment stories then fabricate the heroic what-I-learned-from-autism semi-fictional narratives that permeate television and movie theaters. Barry Levinson's *Rain Man* is one of the earliest and enduring examples in this category.

But it is the unwieldiness of autism that makes for the efficacy of the second kind of narrative as an antidote to the medical deterministic content of the first and its sentimentalized/sensationalized fallout (Murray, 2008). Given the long "silence" of many of its members who come from inside the autistic community, it is a more recent one. The thinkers and writers of the autistic community are widely diverse, many of whom do not speak, but communicate by keyboard or some form of facilitated communication. These narratives are countering the "truthiness" of the endless rounds of news reports that often misinterpret and mislead the pubic.[1] Murray points out, however, that the abundance of these narratives has strangely not changed the public's understanding, but definitely adds to autism's mystique as an abstraction or an idea. Mitchell and Snyder (2000) note that Americans learn more about autism from fiction and films than any other source. But most telling, Murray says, are the stories we tell ourselves. The fictionalized versions of glory and courage have inflected our cultural tropes of autism without the critical analysis that is their due. In great measure this resolves the problem of a depressing and fear-inspiring public dialogue, particularly in the wake of the Measles/Mumps/Rubella (MMR) inoculation debate, which still rages today—albeit with a smaller population of parents as its adherents.[2]

The catastrophe narrative in which parents discover that their child has autism is one of the most ubiquitous in our culture. Hollywood, with its sixth sense of polarized topics, has ushered in a "contemporary moment":

> It is, we might say, the condition of fascination of the moment, occupying a number of cultural locations that reflect a spectrum of wonder and nervousness—the allure of potentially unquantifiable human difference and the nightmare of not somehow being "fully" human. (Murray, 2008, p. 5)

Murray, a father of two sons, one with autism and one with Asperger's, is experienced in shuttling between personal engagement and critical distance—the import of knowing the impossibility of speaking for the spectrum, even with his first-hand knowledge. Murray's thesis, which also belongs to others who are discussed later, is that autism has its own logic and intense presence that can only be understood by a suspension of neurotypical perspectives if new and more accurate notions of autism are to be reached.

Autists are asked to suppress their world view in order to live in the neurotypically designed world, but neurotypicals have yet to meet them half way (Savarese, 2013). The main difference between the neurotypical and autist narrative is that autists usually do not recommend a cure, as this would be antithetical to their being. The search for a cure is a subject mostly among non-autistics, often parents of autistic children and in so-called advocacy communities such as Autism Speaks, which is more a function of fear than of difference (Murray, 2008). As Savarese (2007) points out in *Reasonable People: A Memoir of Autism and Adoption*, autism is not something that one has, like a disease, but rather a subjective state of life integral to the person. Jim Sinclair (1992), in his instructive paper "Bridging the Gaps: An Inside-Out View of Autism (Or Do You know What I Don't Know)," decisively explains how autists and non-autists must take mutual responsibility for the misfiring of communication between them:

> If you would help me, don't try to change me to fit your world. Don't try to confine me to some tiny part of the world that you can change to fit me. Grant me the dignity of meeting me on my own terms—recognize that we are equally alien to each other, that my ways of being are not merely damaged versions of yours. Question your assumptions. Define your terms. Work with me to build more bridges between us. (p. 18)

The debate needs to turn from the medical discussion of the features that autists lack, such as theory of mind (ToM), central coherence, and executive functioning, which Murray depicts as an "abstracted, unsourced, alien phenomenon," toward human worth and quality of life (p. 2). If autism is to be understood as a human condition that has always existed throughout history, then it will need to be situated within a more humanized story. The construction of autism in these polarized locations has revealed more about the non-autistic world than it does the condition, and ultimately the reinforcing of normalcy (Davis, 2013; Murray, 2008). Murray invites us to think about the presence of autistic people as one way to keep humanity in mind and offset the dehumanizing and distorting tropes of popular culture. It is in this climate that we turn to the personal narratives of autists, sometimes called "autoethnography" (Lionnet, 1989) and "autie-biography" by the authors. In this chapter, I will focus on written narratives,[3] with visual narratives to be explored in Part II of this book.

Autistic Presence

Looking beyond the cultural tropes, metaphors, and medical designations, Murray finds the most authentic descriptor to be presence; the undeniable fact that the person and his or her own subjective experience exist. Within the reports of Leo Kanner's (1943) and Hans Asperger's (1944) observations of several children, Murray (2008) discovers a brief sentence of recognition from Kanner and Asperger respectively: "He just is there" and "The autist is only himself" (p. 32). Although the two statements might be interpreted in a variety of ways, they nevertheless acknowledge the *personess* that cannot be disavowed no matter how recalcitrant he or she may be. In the narratives that follow, the personess or "presence" is communicated with so much force that cultural assumptions and meanings attached to the label are called into question. Entry into the subjective and lived experience of the autist is suddenly available, instantly challenging the power relationship between the professional players in the field—doctors, researchers, teachers, therapists—and their silent subjects. In so doing, they wrestle an idea of the normal away from the conception of normalcy as illustrated by Lennard J. Davis (2013), promoting a model of lived experience in contrast to the construction of disability central to normalcy's organizing method.

The shift from understanding autism from the position of normalcy to the autistic perspective impacts the field by locating autism as presence, existence, personhood, and experience rather than from the deficit orientation of the fields of education and medicine. From the latter perspective, the autist is identified as lacking something possessed by the expert, and by extension, all "normal people." Temple Grandin (1986, 1995) and Donna Williams (1992, 1994, 2003), who are considered "high functioning," began these inroads into the public consciousness. But as Douglas Biklen (2005) notes, autists who lived their lives without speech were considered "low functioning," which means with severe intellectual disabilities. The entrance of augmented alternative communication, discussed in the previous chapter, has changed these simplistic notions of functioning. Without communication, says Biklen, we can only presume. Based on behavior alone, Biklen asks if anyone would presume Stephen Hawking—who speaks with a computer by moving his eyes—to be "low functioning"? Researchers such as Oppenheim (1974) and autists such as Jim Sinclair (1992, 1993) argue that expectations to fail produce poor performance, one valid reason for an individual's vacillation of performance in the same subject or activity. Biklen urges us, in the face of insubstantial evidence, to presume competence, which he calls a *precondition* for working with such individuals who lack speech or have disordered speech.

An example of the taken-for-granted, deficit-oriented model is Francesca Happe's (1991) response to Grandin's (1986) ground-breaking book *Emergence: Labeled Autistic*, co-written with Margaret Scariano. Happe's assessment is that Grandin is atypical because what she has produced does not correspond to what experts know as autism, and suggests that it was written by her co-author. Oliver Sacks's encounter with the book is also incredulous. Although not disbelieving or discrediting her, he says she is in counterdistinction to the mainstream belief that autists are incapable of self-reflection since there is no self to reflect upon.

Happe's analysis is derived from a neurotypical model, interpreting the inconsistencies in Grandin's text as a lack of theory of mind. Biklen rightly counters Grandin's inconsistencies as an issue of finessing and editing skills, which all writers develop over time, and none are exempt from failing at times to provide adequate context and background. Melanie Yergeau (2000), an assistant professor with Asperger's at Ohio State University, finds a toehold as an Aspie from which to fire out her intelligence and wit, "dis-abling" the non-autistic world of the academic autism essay. In her recantation of the typical autism essay she writes, "I'm not a big fan or user of transition statements—and I teach college writing, the horror! More strikes?" (p. 2). Yergeau (2009) further discredits Happe's haste in pathologizing Grandin's writing style by promoting her own hypertextual style, which received Honorable Mention for the 2010 Kairos Best Webtext Award for *aut(hored)ism: Computers and Compositions Online* (http://www2.bgsu.edu/departments/english/cconline/dmac/). Presented as a website, the home page menu opens to windows of text, images, and videos that make ludicrous fun of autism tropes, such as ToM, stimming (self-stimulation), and the famous Sally-Anne Test.

The urge to tightly adhere to one's hypotheses and theories is well known in all scientific disciplines. Anomalies are routinely treated as anecdotal, even when they become a noteworthy minority whose similarity of experience is undeniable. Thomas Kuhn notes that although anomalies give scientists pause, they cannot or will not disavow an intensely invested theory even when it has become unsustainable. "They do not, that is, treat anomalies as counter-instances, though in the vocabulary of science that is what they are. . . . They will devise numerous articulations and *ad hoc* modifications of their theory in order to eliminate any apparent conflict" (as cited in Savarese, 2007, p. xii, xviii). The emerging view of autism, says Savarese, has begun to acknowledge anomalies, and is finding a way to account for them within the structure that has been set since Kanner and Asperger.

What Biklen and Savarese make clear is that the correlation that exists between behavior and cognition, or speech and intelligence, is called into question time and again by the distinctive perceptiveness of autistic writers. Dyspraxia, the problem of initiating action, might explain misleading appearances. Although the brain is sending intentional messages to a functioning body, it is unable to respond, as many autists, such as Lucy Blackman (2001) and Tito Mukhopadhyay (2003) have described. In Gerardine Wurzburg's (2012) documentary *Wretches and Jabberers*, Tracy Thresher was asked in an interview what it means to have autism. His answer was, "Poor control of responses, movement, and high pitched grating voices got on my nerves . . . trapped in a body that doesn't work, and not being able to let people know." About the obvious disconnection between behavior and intelligence, Thresher says, "We are the perfect example of intelligence working itself out in a much different way." Biklen (2005) reinforces this notion by explaining that there is a gap between "cannot" and "does not." With cannot we infer incompetence, in "does not" we infer "not yet." Autists have explained the feeling of being trapped in their bodies as an involuntary lag in their responses, their need to take time to think and respond, for which most people do not have patience. Often autists write that they cannot attend to their own perspective and another's at the same time, especially while talking and listening.

Savarese (2012) calls "the syntax of surprise" the wonder, disbelief, and sometimes exuberance of experts at finding the anomaly; but they are usually accompanied with the caveat that the child had promising cognitive abilities or a trained educator as a mother (p. 103). Savarese adopted his son DJ when he was six years old after a life of abandonment, poverty, and physical abuse in foster care. He is testimony, says Savarese, of the false exceptionalism that is hoisted on children who defy the experts' grim odds. Without adopting different assumptions and changing the paradigm of autistic development from exceptionalism to commonplace, we might not know the potential number of instances of unambiguous growth.

Cure or Acceptance?

Valerie Paradiz (2002), the author of *Elijah's Cup*, a book about her son, discovered late in life that she, like her son, had Asperger's syndrome. Elijah[4] was schooled in an early intervention program in a private "special" school, and later in a self-contained classroom at a local public school. All was well until his life fell apart in fifth grade. Friendless, lonely, and depressed, his own social development diverged widely from his peers. He leveraged the popular, visual culture of Disney animation, movies, and comedy as an entry point into the social order of early adolescence. Paradiz (2010) knew that typical school settings would not accommodate his idiosyncrasies, which she wanted to support and allow to grow into "a wonderful power of his own" (para. 12). Removing Elijah from school was a pivotal point that prepared her to envision a school for young people on the autism spectrum. In 2003, Paradiz opened the Autistic Strength, Purpose and Independence in Education (ASPIE) school for middle and high school students with Asperger's.[5] The school capitalized on the students' deep interests, such as video gaming, fantasy, and performance in physical and game-based projects partnered with educators in the theater arts.

Amy Harmon (2004), a journalist from the *New York Times*, stepped into a self-advocacy class at ASPIE in 2004. The 15 tenth graders had just viewed a documentary about the search for an autism cure and they were preparing for a critique. "We don't have a disease, so we can't be cured," one of the boys said (para. 2). Another student objected to the "suffering" terminology. "People don't suffer from Asperger's. They suffer because they're depressed from being left out and beat up all the time" (para. 3). Rather than an apologia for their condition, they studied the syndrome's strengths, such as their expert knowledge of their subjects. Paradiz's philosophy is to educate the students in the popular discourse while countering it by honoring their lived experiences, which includes transforming the discourse from a tragedy in search of a cure to an alternative and valid way of living.

This counter-discourse has been raging for more than a decade as both parents and their children on the spectrum are becoming activists in the disability community. Many, like Jim Sinclair, have turned toward the internet and have established websites, like autistics.org and neurodiversity.com. On the other hand, many autistic and non-autistic parents alike challenge the neurodiversity narrative with what they perceive is a much needed cure and intensive behavioral therapy. The most ubiquitous of these therapies is applied behavioral analysis, or ABA. Therapists suggest 40 hours a week to be the optimal treatment, which opponents believe is counterproductive and potentially abusive. Parents of autistic children who perceive autism as a "crippling condition" needing humane but decisive treatment are speaking out in their own forums about their counter positions. In 2004, a heated dispute between the two sides was made highly visible on the internet. A flashpoint arrived when Canadian families argued for government subsidies for ABA therapy because of its medical *necessity*. Autists countered the statement by questioning not only the treatment's medical necessity, but also its logic and ethics. Behaviors, particularly negative ones, they say, are attempts to communicate painful reactions to environmental structures invisible to neurotypicals. Behaviors need to be understood as messages from autists who cannot communicate in typical ways. At the core of the debate is the ontology of autism. Autists propose that autism is a condition of being, integral to the individual rather than a skin that might be shed.

Jim Sinclair (1992) has been one of the earliest and most vocal activists for the autism movement. In "Bridging the Gaps: An Inside-Out View of Autism (Or, Do You Know What I Don't Know?)," he begins by writing, "In May of 1989 I drove 1200 miles to attend the tenth annual TEACCH[6] conference, where I learned that autistic people can't drive" (p. 1). He clears up the sometimes funny, sad, and infuriating assumptions that neurotypicals have, such as mental retardation, emotional flatness, and lack of empathy. "I understand a lot about not understanding," he says, enough to identify the gaps in understanding between autists and non-autists (p. 3).

Sinclair began speaking at 12 but did not understand that language can communicate subjective experience until he was 25:

> I didn't communicate by talking, not because I was incapable of learning to use language, but because I simply didn't know that that was what talking was for. Learning how to talk follows from knowing *why* to talk—and until I learned that words have meanings, there was no reason to go to the trouble of learning to pronounce them as sounds. (p. 5)

Speech therapy was therefore a useless chore of repetition and compliance, a pointed objection to a behaviorist model that does not extend beyond the illusion of normalcy. Sinclair suggests that neurotypicals question their assumptions given that appearances do not tell the full story. Without mutual communication, we can only *presume*, a caveat of which Biklen (2005) repeatedly reminds readers:

> The results of these assumptions are often subtle, but they're pervasive and pernicious: I am not taken seriously. My credibility is suspect. My understanding of myself is not considered to be valid, and my perceptions of events are not considered to be based on reality. My rationality is questioned because, regardless of intellect, I still appear to be odd. (Sinclair, 1992, p. 19)

Sinclair taught himself to read at 3 but lost his ability at 10 and again at 17, 21, and 26. These repeated gains and losses are commonly heard in autists' writings. Even speech has eluded him, and at the time of writing in 1989, he was not confident he could retrieve all the words in his mind. Yet, he says, he has never lost touch with his core, a suspect autistic quality according to experts. A telling incident at the TEACCH conference, in which four autists met in an unstructured setting, highlights the irreducibility of autistic ways of knowing. "Within a few minutes, one person was rambling without enough focus, one was obsessing on a too-narrow focus, and I was having trouble keeping track of both of them at once" (p. 12). The fourth man, who he called "invisible," was most revealing to Sinclair when a neurotypical person walked in and structured the event by asking questions:

> While I could guess how odd he must have looked and sounded to people who are always connected to their bodies, it was exciting to *see* him putting his verbal mode on-line, to *hear* how far from his voice he was, and to be able to recognize the kinds of bridges he was building, because they were the same kinds of bridges I build myself. (p. 12)

"Pale imitations of normalcy" are not worth the time or effort, writes Sinclair (p. 15). Not knowing how to take people for granted, his interactions with others are uncontextualized, singular moments of intensity. His relationships are born from choice rather than need. Since being alone is not lonely for him, he chooses relationships to make his life better than it already is. His choices of relationships are authentically made rather than, for example, made with the goal of gaining social status.

In *Don't Mourn For Us*, Sinclair (1993) speaks directly to parents about their sadness upon discovering their child's autism diagnosis. He invites parents to suspend their grief by looking at autism from the insider's perspective. He underscores the futility of adhering to expectations of reciprocity in relationships of which the autist is not a part. From this perspective, one's child will only appear incapable of relating. "It only means you're assuming a shared system, a shared understanding of signals and meanings that the child in fact does not share" (p. 2). Mothers and fathers in the subsequent narratives struggle to meet their children half way. Over and again, parents say they learn only so much from therapists and doctors, and find they must map out a path by listening to and learning their child's language. Communication with a child who does not share his or her parent's language is a persistent struggle. And, says Sinclair, autism reaches beyond language and culture, so shared meanings might not be an attainable goal. "You're going to have to give up the certainty that comes of being on your own familiar territory, of knowing you're in charge, and let your child teach you a little of her language, guide you a little way into his world" (p. 2). The alienation that is felt between autistic children and their non-autistic parents might be the heaviest burden. Autistic children are expected to enter this alien territory, and so Sinclair proposes that their parents reciprocate by stepping outside their known reality. "Grieve if you must, for your own lost dreams. But don't mourn for *us*. We are real. And we're here waiting for you" (p. 3).

High Functioning/Low Functioning

High functioning/low functioning is defined by people with the unstable condition of neurotypicality. As an Aspie and a fan of neurological diversity, Yergeau (2000) says she is disqualified from the typical rhetorical, neurotypical autism essay, which perseverates (negatively) on "tired autism tropes" about "autistics-as specimens" (p. 2). The power dynamics of autism discourse, says Yergeau, exempt this counter discourse from the autism essay because it does not align with the rhetoric of families, charities, and researchers. The construct of functioning made by the neurological mainstream, however, is itself unstable, which aligns with the thesis of this book. Because of this "normalized constructedness," Yergeau asks:

> If one is able to speak, is she high-functioning? If one is able to attend college, is she high functioning? . . . If one can speak but can't work, can cook but can't drive, can read existential philosophy but can't add single digits . . . is she high functioning? (p. 16)

The artificial high functioning/low functioning binary has set up a problematic debate in which autists who write in protest of a cure are suspect of being so high functioning that they fall off the autism curve and lose their credibility. In "Circle Wars: Reshaping the Typical Autism Essay," Yergeau (2010) asks for the reader's indulgence as she perseverates on the "circles" in autism discourse that with finite certainty supports theories with graphs, charts, and illustrations. The circle, she says, is the most isolating, and proceeds to fill the page with circles that highlight the passive boundaries between the neurotypical and the autistic, between low functioning and high functioning. In the more complex graphs, she combines all four categories, including circles for "neurodiversity" and "cure," with the predictable arrows and the slight "pity-laden" overlaps, making halfhearted attempts at connection (p. 9).

Quoting Patricia Bizzell (1997), Yergeau writes that these constructions and discourse conventions become so powerful that they take on a life of their own. In order for the circular simplicity to remain intact, the theoretical community is wedged within the graph whether or not the community—in all its diversity—fits:

> Per this logic, I have been passively constructed into autism—by discourse. I have been passively constructed into aspiedom—by discourse. My other autistic commonplaces—all identity markers—have also been shaped or spawned by discourses: stimdom, speechdom,

> lack-of-eye-contactdom, patterndom, take-everything-literally-and-then-somedom. (p. 7)

Former Senior Vice President of Autism Speaks, Alison Tepper Singer, constructs new circles that better reflect the right of many parents, therapists, and medicalists to speak for the most "low functioning." Speaking about her daughter, she writes, "It is hard to consider her 'differently abled' because she is not 'abled'" (as cited in Yergeau, 2013, p. 10). So different are the low functioning from high functioning autists that the counter opinions of the latter are not only disruptive, but also have no merit. In this circular construct, the disabled, differently abled, and the abled overlap equally while the "not abled" is positioned separately. "What Singer does, in addition to creating a whole new-abled suffix, is define low-functioning autism and low-functioning autistics wholly in terms of lack. . . . Singer, in accordance with the typical autism essay, labels neurodiversity as the cranial workings of the high-functioning" (p. 10).

Singer is mistaken, says Yergeau, since many autistic activists and their audience are not "high functioning." The three owners of autistics.org posted a rebuttal to parents who hold this false notion, specifically in response to the now infamous ABA wars that began in Canada with Michelle Dawson's objection to ABA's necessity and therefore government funding. Dawson's (n.d.) paper, *The Misbehaviour of Behaviourists*, was attacked by Kit Weintraub—a parent of a "low functioning" autist—with arguments similar to Singer's. In Weintraub's (n.d.) paper, *A Mother's Perspective*, she begins with objections to the use of autism as a noun, which for the autists who use it as such suggests the personness of the condition, rather than the "having," or "verb" form of the condition. The writers of the rebuttal object that the "person-first" language is in fact an imposed top-down signifier of non-autistics who purport to speak for autistic people. They call this designation "factually inaccurate" since autism cannot be removed (archive.autistics.org/library/dawson.html). Weintraub argues that the intellectual skills of the writers of autistics.org suggest that they are not autistic. In a bold move, they compiled a long list of descriptors and facts of their condition. Among them were significant problems with digestion, voluntary movement, and regressive loss of skills once gained, and the need for adult diapers and augmentative communication devices. They persist to "flap, finger-flick, rock, twist, rub, clap, bounce, squeal, hum, scream, hiss, and tic" daily (pp. 3–4). All the above put them in the low functioning, mental retardation, and non-communicative categories.

Parents, professionals, clinicians, and researchers are responsible for defining the autistic community, writes Phil Schwarz (2009), an Asperger's adult with an autistic son. The unequal power relationship between the two distinct voices of autism activists and the mainstream means unequal access to resources, media, presence, and mindshare. The messages of recovery and cure are therefore pervasive. Autists internalize the negative media without adequate allies to parse out the difference between intrinsic impairments and the consequences of social de-valorization.

A functioning scale is a highly technological metaphor for a community of people. The puzzle, computer, machine, robot metaphors reinforce the de-humanizing rhetoric of autism. In her blog, Yergeau holds a sign that states "People Not Puzzles" with a strike dissecting the well-known puzzle piece brand of Autism Speaks. As an ironic double metaphor, a human puzzle piece is featured on the Autism Speaks website posts, "Compliments of the Sunshine Worldwide School in Goa, India" (https://plus.google.com/+AutismSpeaks/posts).

Self- Representation

Autobiographies for the past few decades have been an antidote to the patronization, marginalization, and misrepresentation that prevail in cultural scripts about disability (Couser, 2000). And yet there still remain roadblocks. A few of those are "having a life, writing a life, and publishing a life" (p. 306). First, many autistic lives are circumscribed in ways that have not been considered worthy to narrate. The public expects what has been called the American conversion narrative—"a record of the quest for a transformed or redeemed self" (Fisher, 2009, p. 51). The temptation in the past, therefore, has been to speak for the autist who cannot speak for himself or herself, at best to interpret and at worst to invent the long-road-to-overcoming-obstacles story, culminating with success.[7] The early self-narratives, such as Grandin's (1986) *Emergence: Labeled Autistic*, re-defined the condition and opened the genre to wider interpretations of autism. They also bypassed Couser's (2000) second obstacle by not necessarily ending in triumph, or what he calls "the tyranny of the comic plot": disability as un-depressing (p. 308). The danger in Grandin's case was that she became to some extent the unofficial spokeswoman for autism.

The most significant of theses narratives came later from autists who could not speak but who could write, and so proved that they indeed had a life to narrate. Thus, they ignored the categorical devaluation of their lives and the prevailing notions about the confining limitations of their condition. The personal narrative has therefore substituted the medical paradigm with a "figural anthropology of the self," ultimately bypassing the narrative itself by expanding the critique of autism (Lionnet, as cited in Couser, 2000, p. 307).

The Conversion Narrative

The conversion narrative is defined by Mark Osteen (2009) as the cure or recovery story that dominates the media. Often inaccurately conceived as a "disorder of selfhood," autism is visualized as the puzzle piece, the human who cannot fulfill his or her humanity by way of narration. This is the story that all other humans are capable of telling: the fictional self of their consciousness. The conversion narrative, "a record of the quest for a transformed or redeemed self," is part of this legacy, deeply embedded in the western novel, memoir, and autobiography (Fisher, 2009, p. 51). The recent presence of the autie-biography and the mother and father narratives are making deep dents into the notion of the autist as an un-self-reflecting body.

It could be argued that the autism conversion narrative is a result of internalizing the typical autism essay, which Phil Schwarz (2009) described as damaging to the psyche and self-esteem of the autist. Autists who read what neurotypicals write about the "disease" find their signifiers inaccurate at best. The mothers of the early narratives, in the wake of Bruno Bettelheim,[8] were held responsible for their children's condition and therefore felt they must use their mothering to cure them. John T. Fisher (2009) suggests that with the first autism diagnosis of Leo Kanner's eleven children, in a moment of bombastic self-promotion, Kanner and other psychologists such as Bettelheim theorized treatment and cures of this most intractable condition. Kanner was the first to use the term "refrigerator mother," which was accepted as authoritative for the next two decades, possibly in an aggressive move to invalidate family counter-narratives.

In the Introduction to Clara Claiborne Park's (1982, 2001) *Exiting Nirvana*, 34 years after her groundbreaking *The Siege*—the first non-clinical account of an autistic child—Park describes the moment she heard Kanner repudiate his implication of parents in their children's autism. "Herewith I especially acquit you people as parents," Kanner reported at the Autism Society of America, 25 years after identifying autism (as cited in Park, 2001, p. 11). Kanner and particularly Bettelheim's *Empty Fortress* did not disappear quietly, nor was there forthcoming alternative research (Park, 2001). Although Park was aware of fitting the profile of Kanner's/Bettelheim's professional mother, she did not submit to the temptation of the cure/recovery/triumph story, but rather presented a nuanced account of her daughter's gains and losses. In contrast is Catherine Maurice's (1993)[9] *Let Me Hear Your Voice: A Family's Triumph Over Autism*, in which ABA is the magic cure so totalizing that not a trace of autism is left. In the book's Forward, Bernard Rimland, founder of the Autism Research Institute, writes that the mother's aggressive search for treatment paid off:

> More recently, within the past five or six years, there has been a sudden upsurge in published reports of autistic persons who now function within the normal range. In virtually all of these cases, however, there still remain some residual traits of autism. I am happy to say, however, I have visited the Maurice home and seen the children, *delightful* children, on several occasions, and did not (thank heaven!) detect any such residual signs. (p. xivl)

A new literary genre has emerged, however, in the past several years in which the author is also the subject of his or her text. These autie-biographies/

memoirs/narratives challenge the conversion narratives, first by writing articulate, often lyrical prose by neurotypical standards and, second, by transforming the autism conversation from "no-self-there" assumptions to evidence of a highly sensitized self that can critique the conversion narrative. This literary movement is supported by the activist bloggers and web writers mentioned throughout this chapter. First, I will turn toward narratives written by mostly non-autistic parents who are also transforming the narrative from triumph to acceptance and advocacy, as discussed in Park's texts.

Mothering and Fathering Narratives

> *You can't be as special as he is and still fit comfortably in this world.*
> (Kephart, 1998, p. 167)

In "(M)Otheirng and Autism: Maternal Rhetorics of Self-Revision," Sheryl Stevenson (2009) points out that when women write family autobiographies about their autistic children, they reveal not only the coping experiences, but also "the pressures exerted by irreconcilable conceptions of a productive/unproductive, enabling/disabled motherhood" (p. 200). Sociological and psychological pressures of mothering extend far further into the past than Kanner's/Bettelheim's "refrigerator mother." She alludes to the American ethos of the mother as self-sacrificing, putting her child's needs before her own. Coupled with this historical undercurrent of central responsibility, evidence shows that more pressure is put on the mother than the father of an autistic child.

In *A Slant of Sun: One Child's Courage*, the lyrical writer Beth Kephart (1998) says the following about motherhood after the discovery of her son's autism:

> Pregnant, I supposed that mother's intuition was a hard, certain thing, a perpetually replenishing reservoir of basic instinct. If there were problems, the gut would howl it. If there were risks, the heart would rattle. If the jumbled trivia of daily existence pulled into and into itself like a knot, the mother's hands would separate the strands. . . . Every day since the first one with Jeremy has been a mystery. I am no wiser, or any less vulnerable, for having given birth to a son. (p. 53)

Kephart portrays in a poetic bricollage the story of her son, Jeremy. Her dedication reads, "For Jeremy, who leans over my shoulder even now, and shows me the way." The autobiography was not planned as such; she wrote the text as journals and read them to her son years later. Her story is an unfolding of a mutual learning between the mother and son, consciously sidestepping the inevitable tilted power relationship. Kephart's artistic soul perceives her son's hyper-activity as dancing, and his echolalia as singing. "At three months or four, Jeremy did not just bounce in that Jolly jumper; he danced, he danced resolutely. By ten months, he was uncanny and graceful" (p. 51). She was so tuned into difference that it was a surprise to find out that these displays would later be pathologized as autism. The reader, however, reads the signs: his obsession with a green hat, his fire trucks that he lines up with precision, his fear of house guests, and his unearthly ability to read at two years old. After several chapters of acquainting us with his uniqueness, Kephart says, "The hats, the cars, the fire engines were all signs I should have read, but I was thinking about predilections, not obsessions" (p. 52).

The reality of autism destablizes Kephart. She questions her instincts, that love might not be enough, that her husband is the better parent. Jeremy's solitude, rage, empty gazing, and indifference are "barometers not of an inherent disability but of my own inability to mother. . . . It is my fault, and I ask no one, save Jeremy, what to do" (p. 59). Far from the conversion narrative, Kephart's story is about her acceptance of herself as a mother, not her son's condition.

Both Kephart and her husband are appreciative parents who, possibly because they are both artists, see difference as an asset. Rather than warning signs, their son's obsessions were indicators that he too had an artist's sensibility. On a Halloween night, the family had their first official three-way interview with a hospital director of developmental medicine. Kephart's husband recounted to the doctor Jeremy's matchbox car play.

> "Jeremy is very smart. . . . We know he is. He has an extraordinary memory, and you should see the impressive patterns that he makes, the geometry he can fashion with cars."
>
> "Cars?" The doctor straightens the clipboard on her lap and pays attention.
>
> "Matchbox cars. He arranges them in spirals. Or pinwheels. And the colors are right."
>
> "The colors are right?"
>
> "Aesthetic. Well considered." (p. 68)

Kephart's rebellion on her son's behalf begins with the first testing "through the spectacles of science" (p. 71). How does one parse out personality, mood, and artistry, which are mutable, from biology, chemistry, and genetics, which are fixed? And how does one interpret behaviors to circumscribed tests? There is no way to fit Jeremy into one of the circles that Yergeau abhors. Even when the "symptoms" of the labels match his, they still do not describe Jeremy. At this point in the book the reader also gets to know Jeremy, and agrees: the label hasn't been made yet for Jeremy. Kephart hears only the language of deficit, "*but don't stop there*. Because my son's compelling. He's confoundingly bright. He's artistic. He's affectionate" (p. 84). Landmarks, such as bedtime punctuality, teeth brushing, shoe tying, and room cleaning were not priorities. What needed to happen first was communication and feeling safe in the world. She maintained communication through telling and reading stories. When Jeremy's words came they rhymed them, wrote them down, and turned them into stories.

Now *I*, the reader, am inside *her* head. Because she is a talented storyteller and poet, because her story is authentic, her voice has replaced my internal voice. I am reminded of Paul Broks's (2003) thoughts about the slippage of one's own story, living through another's as symptomatic of the storytelling device that is our consciousness. I experience her sorrow and struggle, not for the loss of a child to autism, but her struggle as a mother. Kephart tells a story within a story, her every nuanced feeling. She is not the hero/victim/martyr, but a mother who honors her son's way of being and thinking about the world, and what that means for a growing sense of self:

> I do not believe that my husband and I have healed our child. We do not even know what normal is, what finished looks like. . . . We don't know what could have been done that wasn't, what shouldn't have been done that was. The only truth we have in our house today is that we have given our son the room to heal himself. (p. 240)

In *Not Even Wrong*, writer Paul Collins (2004) writes an equally poetic report of his son Morgan, diagnosed on the autistic spectrum. His story is often parallel to Kephart's: the earth-shifting surprise of the diagnosis, the insistence that his son is "fine," that "he's just different from what they're [doctors] used to" (p. 9), and the incredulous, "how could I not have seen it?" (p. 58). Most important is the similarity between the two families' humanness, acceptance, and appreciation of their sons. Collins takes the reader on a journey to past autists, at a time too early for a diagnosis, such as the fascination elicited by Peter the Wild Boy of Hamelin[10] and his influence on Daniel Defoe and Jonathan Swift, particularly as immortalized in Swift's *Gulliver's Travels*. Before Morgan was diagnosed, Collins says, "I had been chasing a silent boy through the even greater silence of centuries, when my own boy was in front of me all along" (p. 58).

We are taken through the trials and errors of school placements, negotiating the balance between empowerment and conformity, maintaining the idiosyncratic nature that is his son's, and conceding to normality. Above all are the efforts toward Morgan's communication, the inventive, intuitive, spontaneous hunches that lead Morgan and his parents into mutual knowledge. Both Kephart and Collins, although submitting to worry and despair, resist the rescuer mentality, respecting the personness of their sons, which, if not encouraged to shine from the beginning, might be lost forever.

The meaning of Collins's obscure title, *Not Even Wrong*, is revealed during an instructive explanation of the famous Sally-Anne test devised by Uta Frith and the young Simon Baron-Cohen. The test is a traditional marker for theory of mind in which the psychologist places a box and a basket in front of two girls, Sally and Anne (who are actually dolls). Sally puts a marble in the basket and leaves the room, whereupon Anne removes the marble and puts it in the box. The young client is asked where he or she thinks Sally will look for the marble when she returns. Collins sums up the hegemonic neurotypical certainty of the testers and the assumptions inherent in theory of mind.

> Perhaps the most succinct expression of this dilemma comes quite inadvertently from a physicist. Wolfgang Pauli used to deride colleagues in theoretical physics who disagreed with him as "not even wrong." He meant this as a put-down—that the questions they were asking were so off-base that their answers were irrelevant. (pp. 85–86)

Frith and Baron-Cohen might applaud themselves with such a simple and accurate test for a complex and unstable diagnosis. However, Collins points out that "only a person working from the same shared set of expectations could give a truly wrong answer" (p. 86). Baron-Cohen concludes "that the core problem in autism is the inability to think about other people or one's own thoughts" (holah.co.uk). The questions Kephart asked while musing about the finality and judgment that underlies scientific testing for autism applies to this test as well: the displacement of prepositions, anxiety provoked by a test, and the literalness of autists. Specific to this test is the use of dolls as a representation of human beings, which increases confusion of pronouns and taxes literal thinkers. Given their worldview, they are not even wrong.

Collins's musings on the often used "Martian" and "alien" terminology by both insiders and outsiders of the spectrum produced the true-but-not-true conclusion. We define disability by lack, he writes, yet, they are us:

> But autism is *an ability and a disability*: it is as much about what is abundant as what is missing, an overexpression of the very traits that make our species unique. Other animals are social, but only humans are capable of abstract logic. The autistic outhuman the humans, and we can scarcely recognize the result. (p. 164)

"Human but more so" is an accurate phrase that captures Collins's observations (Belmonte, 2009, p.173). In these parents' reflective moments, the boundaries of autism become more permeable and open to expanded interpretations. For example, Issac Newton, notes Collins, was lucky to perseverate on something that was significant to everyone. We don't get the "Newton" without everyone else on the spectrum. The spectrum itself is important. "There is no way to know what an immense concentration and radically altered perspective will alight upon" (p. 214).

Drama, handwringing, and existential angst are not Collins's ways of communication. His live-and-let-live narrative, however, is disrupted by a man in a coffee shop he calls "the painted light bulb guy." The man at the coffee shop is asking no one in particular whether anyone has ever painted light bulbs. He does not wait for a response but continues to explain the nuance of color-mixing and its effect on light. Collins watches in horror as the University of Portland students sigh loudly and make scoffing sounds. "I just want to shake the bastard, snap his laptop in two, and—*Can't you at least be polite?*" (p. 211). Then it's Collins's turn to be talked *at*, "trapped in a conversation where I'm not even needed, because it's as though he's talking right through and past me" (p. 212). Later, four blocks from the coffee shop, Collins sits down on the steps of a church and cries with the unbearable thought that someday someone will pretend that his son is not even there.

Autie-Biographies and Narratives

> *I must send forward my bold appreciation for taking the soul of this topic . . . to be shared among the many and diverse hearts who will attempt a new understanding. It can be very lovely when curious old patterns of comprehension shift to a more connected and true demonstration of the improved focus. My deep thanks, then, for the spirit of change and challenge.*
>
> (Burke, as cited in Savarese, 2010, p. 1)

Wrested from the medical abstract object of inquiry, autie-biographies insert themselves in the discourse and disrupt the mainstream narrative with the notion of an "autistic integrity" (Barnbaum, 2008, p. 204). With these narratives, the autistic person becomes a member of a community, with her own agency and normality. Belmonte (2009) describes the output of autist narratives as "rendering such defenses explicit" (p. 173). The defenses he speaks of are the defenses against the onslaught of sensory experience, which causes perceptual disorder. The unusual effort it takes to write in the neurotypical idiom and, in the end, achieve a linear narrative produces the deepest of insights and perceptions of self and other.

> The narrator who is more conscious of the effort of narration can, almost paradoxically, in the end achieve a deeper understanding of the characters and events around him or her precisely because (s)he is so impaired at automatic social perception and must concentrate harder to construct a theory of reality, to piece it together from perceptual fragments. (p. 173)

Many autie-biographies are written after the author has learned speech, or sometimes has yet to learn and communicates solely by typing. The same issues of organizing perception into a story that all writers have, as mentioned earlier, is more evident in these authors. These deliberate narratives and the intensity with which they are composed make autists "human, but more so," in contradistinction with the sometimes unfortunate mainstream notion of "human, but less so" (p. 175).

Stories of Neurodiversity

In the *Disability Studies Quarterly*'s (*DSQ*) 2010 Special Issue, "Autism and the Concept of Neurodiversity: Prefatory Matter," co-edited by Ralph and Emily Savarese, half of the contributors are on the autism spectrum, several with the "severely autistic" label. The descriptions from these authors' narratives and cultural commentaries about living with autism follow below.

Ralph Savarese begins his "Introduction" to the special issues with a reference to *I Am Autism*, a video produced in 2009 by Autism Speaks. The video does more to externalize and demonize autism than any other form of propaganda yet produced.[11] The narrator, who is meant to be the collective anthropomorphized voice of autism, says Savarese, sounds like Satan himself. This voice concludes the video: "I derive great pleasure out of your loneliness. I will fight to take away your hope. I will plot to rob you of your children and your dreams" (p. 1).[12] **Ari Ne'eman**, one of the contributors to this special issue, effectively drove the video off the site within a few days with the help of his organization, the Autistic Self Advocacy Network (ASAN). ASAN has gone further by insisting "Nothing About Us Without Us!"[13] in order to divert funds from the search for a cure toward a quality of life focus.

In "The Future (and the Past) of Autism Advocacy, Or Why the ASA's Magazine *The Advocate*, Wouldn't Publish This Piece," Ne'eman traces the rise in autism self-advocacy to technologies that have alleviated the need for verbal communication and geographical proximity, as well as the increasing objections of autistic adults about decisions being made about their futures in their absence. With ASAN, policymaking, research, service-delivery, and media are under the watch of people on the spectrum. The organization also created a partnership with scholars (Academic Autistic Spectrum Partnership in Research Education [www.aaspireproject.org]), and the first article was published in 2014 about the computer program used to conduct the partnering study, an audio-computer assisted self-interview. This partnership, writes Ne'eman, is "laying the groundwork for a new kind of autism research paradigm, which includes autistic people as full partners in the creation and implementation of rigorous studies on issues relating to the quality of life of autistic people" (p. 2).

Ne'eman projects a future in which the world includes autistic people with the same "rights, opportunities and quality of life as any [of our] neurotypical peers" (p. 2). He objects to the proliferation of pseudoscientific treatments, such as those advertised in the magazine the *Autism Society of America*: "Vaccine recovery and Applied Behavioral Analysis, whose initial aversive-heavy experiments claimed to bring half of all children subjected to its methods to 'indistinguishability from peers'" (p. 2). "What do we want?" Ne'eman asks. It is *no*t never to have been born, as the catastrophe narrative would have the public think. "For many of us, the prospect of cure and normalization denies essential aspects of our identity . . . and to pursue normalization instead of quality of life forces us into a struggle against ourselves" (p. 3). He does not deny that autism is a disability, but rather argues that the best approach is not recovery and cure because it pulls out the supports that autistic people need, disavows the very real nature of developmental growth, and ignores the social and built environments that pose real problems. According to Ne'eman, the civil rights struggle lies in posing the question: does the problem lie within atypical behaviors or in the neurotypical community that does not accept them?

Amanda Baggs also writes about the social injustices in the autism community in "Up in the Clouds and Down in the Valley: My Richness and Yours." She writes, "My task here is to scale the cliffs of language and shout up to you the pattern of one or more injustices" (p. 1). As a typer and computerized-voice user, her essay is about the inherent exclusion of language. Like the obstacles made by the builders of environments that exclude wheelchair users, the world is designed to exclude non-speakers.

> The most important things about the way I perceive and interact with the world around me can only be expressed in terms that describe them as the absence of something important. The absence of speech. The absence of language. The absence of thought. The absence of movement. The absence of comprehension. The absence of feeling. The absence of perception. (p. 1)

Although her thoughts are personal, they apply to other autists who have expressed similar views. These disclaimers should be unnecessary, she says, "but I know that without them my readers' minds will likely be smothered by endless stereotypes" (p. 2). Without language she has been dismissed as having no thought, or even a lack of soul. Baggs quotes Jim Sinclair's (1987) thoughts about his asexuality as speaking closest to the degradation she experiences without language: "It is when someone who has not even bothered to look at my world dismisses it as a barren rock. . . . It is when my unique faculties are thrown back at me as hopeless inadequacies" (as cited in Baggs, para. 5). This paper is meant to describe her experiences, although she advises that words are mostly inadequate or inaccurate.

Baggs's first memories are of the complex sensations of colors, sounds, textures, flavors, smells, shapes, and tones. Whether or not she was consciously attentive to these sensory experiences, they were all absorbed by her:

> These sensory impressions were repeated long enough for me to become deeply familiar with them. This familiarity resolved into patterns that formed the basis for more patterns, and—to this day—all of this continues to form the basis for how I understand things. (p. 3)

These patterns are clues in how she processes sensory impressions and language. The patterns are not categories in the sense that groups of things are forced together, but rather things that fit together outside of herself. Because of this innate pattern-making, she was able to locate the correct responses before she understood the meaning of words. Not only did she not understand the meanings of words, but she also did not know that words had meanings.

> Conventional language, however, is based on categories rather than patterns, and it poses a great nuisance to me because of this. If I were merely a speaker of a foreign language, then I might be able to find ways to translate between my system of patterns and another's categories, but as far as language goes, I am something closer to a speaker with a foreign brain. (p. 3)

Even today, she is better at fitting together correct word patterns than understanding their meanings. She has made extensive and complex maps of long patterns of words and their appropriate situations prior to understanding language. This reverse order of acquiring language is typical of autism and hyperlexia.

Pattern-making is the way that she perceives the world, from her proprioceptive sense of her body in space to the olfactory sensations in the air, all are woven into similar kinds of patterns. These patterns and connections are what she refers to in the title of her well-known 2007 video, *In My Language*. Body language, interactions, rhythms, and arrangements of objects are the rich and varied vocabulary of communication.

Thought, which she describes as "the juggling of many layers of symbol and abstraction," takes place in her metaphorical sky (p. 4). Most people, says Baggs, don't consider the more direct relationships, connections, rhythms, and interactions with the world to be thought. "They expect thought to take place with a good deal of cognitive fanfare, so that they can hear or see themselves thinking" (p. 5). These she calls loud thoughts, and the quieter thoughts that neurotypicals *do* have are crowded out. Baggs's description of the loud cognitive fanfare of thought is reminiscent of Broks's (2006) explanation of internal dialog as reassurance that there is a thinking self:

> When I do scale the cliffs of language, people react to me strangely. They have lived on a mountain so long that they've forgotten the valley I come from even exists. They call that valley "not mountain" and proclaim it dry, barren, and colorless, because that's how it looks from a distance. (Baggs, 2006, p. 5)

Baggs develops this resourceful metaphor by describing the terrain as different (not lacking), with trees, creeks, rocks, and soil that are indigenous only to the valley. These are the kinds of beauty inherent in a different form of perception, and she shrewdly compares them to those of neurotypicals as "more filtered—perhaps in some ways more efficient—but irretrievably blocking out many things before they hit consciousness" (p. 5). Her richness, she says, is not a cheap copy of an idealized original, but people forget that richness can't be quantified.

Nick Pentzell was diagnosed as severely mentally impaired for the first thirteen years of life, and taught only need-based basic skills. He found facilitated communication (FC) when he was thirty, and at the time of writing he was a college student with an award-winning video *Outside/Inside*, produced by his stepmother, theater historian Gwen Waltz. He is still plagued by the "infant" stereotype of his past and, in frustration, often re-creates old behaviors and thinking patterns he calls "babyliss." In his paper, "Dissed Ability: Grappling with Stereotypes and Internalized Oppression of Babyliss," he describes how adult expectations also cause anxiety:

> Let me look back in time to the point where I crossed over to the talking world. It quickly became a fact of my life that the ante was upped: having to communicate causes your life to become much more difficult, even while it relieves frustration, dampens loneliness and gives you more control over your life. (p. 1)

Pentzell was also aware of the qualities he would have to compromise. He says with stinging truth, "I was becoming aware that I was losing a kind of purity by dealing in the hypocrisies and white lies accepted and required in social interaction. We all become complicit once we participate in society" (p. 2). With time his idealism was tempered by a little necessary cynicism in order to comply with the world.

But he is preoccupied with babyliss in his paper, which is also a consequence of trying to be equal to neurotypicals. It is his old way of coping with his (mis)label, defiance as the only semblance of power he could muster:

> I think it's very difficult for anyone who has been repeatedly stereotyped to escape fully society's pressure to conform to stereotypes, nor (when our resistance is fragile) can we hide from our self doubts that whisper that the negative things people have said to and about us are true or that somehow we deserve to be second-class citizens. I think Babyliss is my internalized oppressor. (p. 2)

At the same time, Pentzell remains committed as an autism activist, FC user, college student, and creative artist, to breaking down the barriers between typicality and atypicality. In contrast, **Dawn Prince-Hughes** was diagnosed with Asperger's syndrome when she was thirty-six. In "The Silence Between: An Autoethnographic Examination of the Language Prejudice and its Impact on the Assessment of Autistic and Animal Intelligence," she says that her gift of language is in the sensory synesthetic way she experiences the world. In her 2004 memoir, *Songs of the Gorilla*

Nation: My Journey Through Autism, she describes her love and comfort in sensory experiences as addictions, such as her memories of the sounds and scents of her grandmother baking biscuits, the heat of the oven as it permeated the house. "For me, language was blended inextricably to context and memory. . . . If a thing existed, it existed as a living part of language and had a deep understanding of its place in the vibrations of speech, in the vibrations of existence" (2010, pp. 1–2). Like Pentzell, Prince-Hughes learned that to use language in the social context meant leaving the safe house of non-human life. "It seemed that for most speaking humans, language could be considered a violent activity, in that it cut up the world, and in its use also cut groups of people from one another" (p. 2). Her use of language was centered in the concreteness of life, the *thisness* of objects rather than the abstractions that language made of them. Social language split things apart, created dichotomies and judgments.

> When I was young I talked in that language of silence. I knew what trees and streams were saying because they told me. I knew what sow bugs and snakes were saying because they molded me. I grew together with them because of the words of living together in a world where everything needed everything else. (p. 2)

In school she couldn't use the language of her teachers and her peers, and left high school before graduation. In her memoir she tells the story of finding gorillas at the zoo, and through them learning to connect to humans. She returned to school and eventually received her PhD in interdisciplinary anthropology, and is currently an adjunct professor of anthropology at Western Washington University. Her research was in the language of primates, somewhat of a taboo in the field. The academic position that primates did not have language, and so they were "stupid, and therefore, disposable," struck her as the same prejudice she encountered as an autist (p. 4). "All these creatures the normal world imagines silent. The autistic child, the ape in the zoo or in the laboratory, the homeless, the dogs in cages. Thinking their silence means they lack language, lack consciousness, is convenient" (p. 5).

Even with her accomplishments, Prince-Hughes is aware of her difference, of her "dis/order." She, like Pentzell and many other autists, feels the pressure to conform, cover-up, and compensate. This is an imperfect strategy, she says. "Like others who seek to be what they are not, we invariably end up with secondary problems engendered by chronic anxiety. As rage and frustration are pushed below our consciousness, we suffer depression" (2004, p. 32).

Ralph and Emily Savarese's adopted son **DJ**, who was neglected by his mother and physically abused in foster care, has spent his childhood and adolescence overcoming debilitating depression, anxiety, and rage. He was labeled "profoundly retarded" when he came to live with the Savareses at age six. He was twelve when he wrote the final chapter of Ralph Savarese's (2007) memoir, *Reasonable People: A Memoir of Autism and Adoption*, and a senior in High School when he wrote "Communicate with Me" for the 2010 *DSQ* special issue. After suffering through a special school, which he writes about in the chapter, he became an "A" student in a regular school shortly after arriving at the Savareses. In 2012 he entered Oberlin College as its first non-speaking student with autism.

DJ has been using FC for many years, and like Pentzell he needs a facilitator. In "Communicate with Me," DJ answers questions from his peers, such as why he needs someone to facilitate his typing. There are two reasons: first, the facilitator helps him to feel safe and regulate his nervous system. The facilitator is a buffer between him and his peers so that he does not become over-stimulated "and my feelings grow so strong that holding them inside is impossible. I desert reason, and my body repeatedly begins to flap" (p. 1). Second, the facilitator keeps him focused. Both in his chapter and in his paper for *DSQ*, DJ talks about breathing. Breathing easily means focus, relaxation, and centerdness. Once only able to *exhale* voluntarily, he has been practicing voluntary *inhaling* since childhood to regulate his sensory input.

> The Frees [speaking people without autism] who understand me know how to hear my dear self. They greet my dear self and free me to respond. Treating me as free, they tell me what to do until my breathing feels deep and slow, and my fingers and eyes can once again communicate with each other, so I can type my thoughts. (2010, p. 1)

He writes resolutely in *DSQ* that the facilitators do not control his hands. He learned to read before using FC in a regular classroom and was watched over by his teachers as he pointed to words independently. DJ knows about the controversy surrounding FC, and has responded to questions about it from Dr. Sanjay Gupta on CNN.[14] In the program, *Finding Amanda*, DJ types with Baggs and responds to Gupta's questions.

GUPTA: What is autism?
DJ: I don't treat myself as autistic. I treat myself as fresh thinking. Yes I look different. I hope fresh ideas get people to ignore my autism.
GUPTA: Is autism something that should be treated?
DJ: Yes, treated with respect.
GUPTA: What does it mean to be free?
DJ: To joyously get to live the dream.
BAGGS: Or to live things better than we dreamed.

The specialized school he attended remains a bitter memory, which he says was the result of inaccurate and harmful testing that did not reveal his intelligence. In a letter to his teachers at this school, he advocates for students in similar un-represented positions. The years of low expectations evidenced by the easy lessons were wasted, he says. "Why weren't you teaching me to talk, to read and to write?" (as cited in Savarese, 2007, p. 442). He asks his former teachers to re-estimate the children as smart. "I want you to know that easy effort estimates kids as retarded when they're smart; testing kids without encouraging them is wrong" (p. 442).

CONCLUSION: FROM NEURODIVERSITY TO NEUROCOSMOPOLITANISM

> *By "hope" I do not mean a cure, but, rather, a practice of full inclusion that might lead to enhanced participation and communication. I mean an ethic of humane discovery, not dire presumption and prognostication. I mean, finally, an appreciation for diversity in all of its forms.*
>
> (Savarese, 2007, p. xvi)

Ari Ne'eman, Nick Pentzell, Dawn Prince, Amanda Baggs, and DJ Savarese are only a few autists who write arresting memoirs and narratives. Many were once called "low functioning" with tics, flapping, and other behaviors that might appear "mentally retarded," as they were once labeled. A few are still without speech. The fact that they write with elegance and clarity is testimony to their diligence in reaching out to the neurotypical world. The fact that neurotypicals have not sought to apprentice themselves to autistic neurology is testimony to the failure of neurodiversity to do the work of including the full spectrum of sensory processing.

The goals of diversity are easily breachable; Savarese points out the misleading celebration of quantifiable statistics of increased diversity in the employment of teachers and the admission of students. Neurological difference easily falls through the cracks in these statistics, since they are the less visible and more silent of the disabilities, and more stigmatized and less supported by the disability rights movement (Osteen, 2009). Savarese borrows the postcolonial term *cosmopolitanism*, which designates "a transnational community, the feeling of being at home everywhere in the world" (p. 3). Given this metaphor, Savarese asks how neurotypicals might travel to both the nearer and outer reaches of autism, how we might create a public square in which we shed the notion of accommodation as a retrofit, add-on, or after-thought meant to make the "other" more comfortable. Rather, the notion of equal participation, or meeting "half way," is the meaning Savarese accords *neurocosmopolitanism*.

As reported in the majority of narratives in this chapter, autists tend to interact with the environment in a more sensory way, rather than as "a static interactive self" (Manning, 2009, p. 40). In this sense, Baggs and Prince-Hughes say that their interactions are fuller and livelier than the interactions neurotypicals have with their environment. What this perspective might imply is that the world—as neurotypicals interact with it—comes at a cost, as discussed earlier in this book. Given their unfiltered, un-unified consciousness, a less rigid and circumscribed perception is available to autists, one that would be richly rewarding for the neurotypical to participate in at an, as yet, unimaginable level. The arts might serve as a meeting ground in their discursive and metaphorical meanings. Many forms of art reveal for the producer and audience, open-endedness, infinite possible interpretations, and direct sensual experiences. DJ understood poetry for its embodiedness; poetry lured him into pragmatic language and might potentially serve as a conceptual and linguistic meeting place. The patterning rather than the categorizing of words of poetry recalls Baggs's exhortations about categories and her meaning-making through interconnecting patterns of light, sound, and rhythm. Like other autistic anthropologists and writers of autoethnography and autie-biography in this chapter, Baggs inhabits the culture of language in order to report to neurotypicals how her own subjective identity, un-mediated by language, is rich in its own ethnicity and culture.

NOTES

1. Autistic blogger Rachel Cohen-Rottenburg takes issue with several points that Simon Baron-Cohen makes about autism, particularly his characterization that autistic people are lacking in empathy. Baron-Cohen writes back with a ten-point response. See http://autistscorner.blogspot.com/2011/09/simon-baron-cohen-responds-to-criticism.html.
2. An MMR vaccine scandal in the UK was galvanized by the 1998 publication of *The Lancet* medical journal. Andrew Wakefield's data was falsely manipulated to suggest that MMR vaccines caused autism. Jenny McCarthy and others are attempting to revitalize the movement.
3. These writings can include formal scholarly writing and memoir, but also the more informal blogs and websites. As Murray notes, cyberspace has offered substantial freedom for autistic expression.
4. Elijah became a standup comedian appearing on MTV and traveling widely. But at the time of entry into community college, his interests took another direction.
5. The ASPIE school closed after the third year of operation when a new superintendent was appointed in the district and the program lost support and funding. It has served, however, as a model for other similar schools now operating in the New York region near Boiceville.
6. TEACCH stands for Treatment and Education of Autistic and Related Communication Handicapped Children. The autism program is based at the University of North Carolina in Chapel Hill.
7. James T. Fisher (2009) suggests that *Dibbs in Search of Self* by Virginia Mae Axeline (1964) is the most durable and classic American conversion narrative: "a youthful (extraordinarily youthful, in this case) subject, an estranged or 'divided self' . . . achieves wholeness and authentic selfhood following an arduous journey of self-discovery" (p. 53)
8. Bruno Bettelheim (1967), in *Empty Fortress: Infantile Autism and the Birth of the Self*, condemned mothers as the cause of their children's autism because of their coldness and reserve, famously calling them "refrigerator mothers."

In his experience, he found the majority of parents to be professionals who were not nurturing. Having been discovered to have no credentials, abusing his young clients, and falsifying data, he has since been discredited. But during the height of his influence he did considerable damage. After his death from suicide in 1990, news of mistreatment emerged from his former young patients.

9. Catherine Maurice is a pseudonym, used to protect the identities of her children.
10. Assumed to have autism, Peter has since been diagnosed with Pitt-Hopkins syndrome by professor of genetics, Dr. Phil Beale, based on his portrait in William Kent's mural at Kensington Palace. His webbed-finger and cupid's bow lips are typical of the syndrome. Christopher Mechling's (2013) *Peter: The Untold True Story*, links Peter the Wild Boy to James Barrie's *Peter Pan*. The theory is compelling, since Barrie was influenced by Defoe, who wrote a pamphlet about the Wild Boy. In *Peter Pan,* Peter lived at Kensington Gardens among the fairies before leaving for Neverland.
11. Savarese writes that *I Am Autism* is even more horrific than a previous Autism Speaks video, "Autism Every Day," in which a mother longs to drive off a bridge with her autistic daughter.
12. In 2011, DJ Savarese compiled a play in which he quoted the video as well as the voices of autists such as Jamie Burke and Tracy Thresher. It is read by the Grinnell High School Readers Theater and published on youtube (https://www.youtube.com/watch?v=HzTYKychygI)
13. For a complete explanation and history of the motto of the disability rights movement, "Nothing About Us Without Us!," see Chapter Two in Brenda Jo Brueggmann's (2012) *Arts and Humanities (The SAGE Reference Series on Disability: Key Issues and Future Directions).*
14. In the preface of "Communicate with Me," DJ explains that he is stunned that Sanjay Gupta would want to talk to him so much that he was flown to New York and stayed in a good hotel, "but ironically at my school, most kids choose not to talk to me at all. Why is that?" (p. 1).

REFERENCES

Asperger, H. (1944/1991). 'Autistic psycopathy' in childhood. In U. Frith (Ed.), *Autism and Asperger syndrome* (pp. 37–92). Cambridge, England: Cambridge University Press.

Autistics.org (n.d.). *In support of Michelle Dawson and her work*. Retrieved from: http://archive.autistics.org/library/dawson.html

Axeline, V.M. (1964). *Dibbs in search of self*. New York, NY: Ballantine.

Baggs, A. (2006). *Everything we have missed?* Retrieved from: https://ballastexistenz.wordpress.com/2006/05/17/

Baggs, A. (2007). *In my language*. Retrieved from: http://www.taaproject.com/in-my-language-by-amanda-baggs/

Baggs, A. (2010). Up in the clouds and down in the valley: My richness and yours. *Disability Studies Quarterly, 30*(1). Retrieved from http://dsq-sds.org/issue/view/43

Barnbaum, D.R. (2008). *The ethics of autism: Among them, but not of them*. Bloomington: Indiana University press.

Baron-Cohen, S., Leslie, A.M., Frith, U. (1985). Does the autistic child have a "theory of mind"? Cognition, 21. 37–46.

Barrie, J.M. (1911). *Peter and Wendy*. New York, NY: Charles Scribner Sons.

Belmonte, M.K. (2009). Human but more so: What the autistic brain tells us about the process of narrative. In M. Osteen (Ed.), *Autism and representation* (pp. 166–179). New York, NY: Routledge.

Bettelheim, B. (1967). *The empty fortress: Infantile autism and the birth of the self.* New York, NY: The Free Press.

Biklen, D. (2005). *Autism and the myth of the person alone.* New York: New York University Press.

Bizell, P. (1997). Cognition, convention, and certainty: What we need to know about writing. In V. Villanueva (Ed.), *Cross-talk in comp studies* (pp. 387–411). Urbana, IL: NCTE.

Blackman, L. (2001). *Lucy's story: Autism and other adventures.* London, England and Philadelphia, PA: Jessica Kingsley.

Broks, P. (2003). *Into the silent land.* London, England: Atlantic Books.

Broks, P. (2006, November 18). The big questions: What is consciousness? *New Scientist.* Retrieved from: http://www.mintinnovation.com/links/docs/Mind_and_consciousness/Big%20Questions%20-%20what%20is%20consciousness.pdf

Brueggmann, B. J. (2012). *Arts and humanities.* New York, NY: Sage.

CNN. (2007). *Finding Amanda.* Retrieved from: http://www.cnn.com/video/#/video/health/2007/11/21/gupta.amanda.inspires.others.cnn

Collins, P. (2004). *Not even wrong: A father's journey into the lost history of autism.* New York, NY: Bloomsbury.

Couser, T. (2000). The empire of the "normal." A forum on disability and self-representation: Introduction. *American Quarterly, 52*(2), 305–310.

Davis, L.J. (Ed.). (2013). *The disability studies reader.* London, England and New York, NY: Routledge.

Dawson, M. (n.d.). *The misbehaviour of behaviourists.* Retrieved from: http://www.sentex.net/~nexus23/naa_aba.html

Fisher, J. T. (2009). No search, no subject? Autism and the American conversion narrative. In M. Osteen (Ed.), *Autism and representation* (pp. 51–64). New York, NY: Routledge.

Grandin, T. (1995). *Thinking in pictures and other reports from my life with autism.* New York, NY: Vintage Books.

Grandin, T., & Scariano, M.M. (1986). *Emergence: Labeled autistic.* New York, NY: Warner Books.

Happe, F. (1991). The autobiographical writings of three Asperger syndrome adults: Problems of interpretation and implications for theory. In U. Frith (Ed.), *Autism and Asperger syndrome* (pp. 207–242). Cambridge, England: Cambridge University Press.

Harmon, A. (2004, December 20). How about not 'curing' us, some autistics are pleading. *The New York Times.* Retrieved from: http://www.nytimes.com/2004/12/20/health/20autism.html?_r=0

Kanner, L. (1943). Autistic disturbances of affective contact. *Nervous Child, 2,* 217–250. Retrieved from: http://neurodiversity.com/library_kanner_1943.pdf

Kephart, B. (1998). *A slant of the sun: One child's courage.* New York, NY: W.W. Norton & Company.

Lionnet, F. (1989). *Autobiographical voices: Race, gender, self-portraiture.* Ithaca, NY: Cornell University Press.

Manning, E. (2009). What if it didn't all begin and end with containment? Toward a leaky sense of self. *Body and Society, 15*(3), 33–45. Retrieved from: http://bod.sagepub.com

Maurice, C. (1993). *Let me hear your voice: A family's triumph over autism.* New York, NY: Random House.

Mechling, C. (2013). *Peter: The untold true story* [Kindle edition]. Retrieved from Amazon.com

Mitchell, D.T., & Snyder, S. L. (2000). *Narrative prosthesis: Disability and the dependencies of discourse*. Detroit: University of Michigan Press.

Mukhopadhyay, T.R. (2003). *The mind tree: A miraculous child breaks the silence of autism:* New York, NY: Arcade.

Murray, S. (2008). *Representing autism: Culture, narrative, fascination*. Liverpool, England: Liverpool, University Press.

Murray, S. (2012). Autism. New York, NY: Routledge.

Ne'eman, A. (2010). The future (and the past) of autism adovocacy, or why the ASA magazine, The Advocate, wouldn't publish this piece. *Disability Studies Quarterly, 30*(1), Retrieved from http://dsq-sds.org/issue/view/43

Oppenheim, R. (1974). *Effective teaching methods for autistic children*. Springfield, IL: Charles C. Thomas.

Osteen, M. (2009). *Autism and representation: A comprehensive introduction*. In M. Osteen (Ed.), *Autism and representation* (pp. 1–47). New York, NY: Routledge.

Paradiz, V. (2002). *Elijah's cup: A family's journey into the community and culture of high- functioning autism and Asperger's*. New York, NY: Free Press.

Paradiz, V. (2010). Leaving the ivory tower of Asperger syndrome. *Disability Studies Quarterly, 30*(1). Retrieved from http://dsq-sds.org/issue/view/43

Park, C. C. (1982). *The siege: The first eight years of an autistic child*. New York, NY: Little Brown.

Park, C. C. (2001). *Exiting nirvana: A daughter's life with autism*. New York, NY: Little Brown.

Pentzell, N. (2010). Dissed ability: Grappling with stereotypes and the internalized oppression of babyliss. *Disability Studies Quarterly, 30*(1). Retrieved from http://dsq-sds.org/issue/view/43

Prince-Hughes, D. (2004). *Songs of the gorilla nation: My journey through autism*. New York, NY: Three Rivers Press.

Prince-Huges, D. (2010).The silence between: An autoethnographic examination of the language prejudice and its impact on the assessment of autistic and animal intelligence. *Disability Studies Quarterly, 30*(1). Retrieved from http://dsq-sds.org/issue/view/43

Rimland, B. (1993) Introduction. In C. Maurice (Ed.), *Let me hear your voice: Triumph over Autism* (pp. xiii–xvii). New York, NY: Random House.

Savarese, D. J. (2010). Communicate with me. *Disability Studies Quarterly, 30*(1). Retrieved from: http://dsq-sds.org/issue/view/43

Savarese, R. J. (2007). *Reasonable people: A memoir of autism and adoption*. New York, NY: Other Press.

Savarese, R. J. (2013). From neurodiversity to neurocosmopolitanism: Beyond mere acceptance and inclusion. In C.D. Herrera & A. Perry (Eds.), *Ethics and neurodiversity* (pp. 191–205). Cambridge, MA: Cambridge Scholars Press. Retrieved from: https://www.academia.edu/5890492/From_Neurodiversity_To_Neurocos mopolitanismBeyond_Mere_Acceptance_and_Inclusion

Savarese, R. J., & Savarese, E. (2010). The superior half of speaking: *Disability Studies Quarterly, 30*(1). Retrieved from http://dsq-sds.org/issue/view/43

Savarese, R. J., & Savarese, E. (2012). Literate lungs: One autist's journey as a reader. *Research & Practice for Persons with Severe Disabilities, 37*(2), 100–110.

Schwarz, P. (2009). Film as a vehicle for raising consciousness among autistic peers. In M. Osteen (Ed.), *Autism and representation* (pp. 256–270). New York, NY: Routledge.

Sinclair, J. (1992). Bridging the gaps: An inside-out view of autism. In E. Schopler & G. B. Mesibov (Eds.), *High-functioning individuals with autism*. Retrieved from: http://pubpages.unh.edu/~jds/Autism.htm

Sinclair, J. (1993). Don't mourn for us. *Our Voice, 1*(3). Retrieved from: ww.autreat.com/dont_mourn.html

Stevenson, S. (2009). (M)othering and autism: Maternal rhetorics of self-revision. In M. Osteen (Ed.), *Autism and representation* (pp. 166–179). New York, NY: Routledge.

Swift, J. (1726). *Gulliver's travels*. Ireland: Benjamin Motte.

Waltz, G. (Producer), & Pentzell, N. (Director). (2002). *Outside/Inside* [Motion picture]. U.S.: Sprout Film Festival.

Weintraub, K. (n.d.). *A mother's perspective*. Retrieved from: http://www.asatonline.org/forum/archives/mother

Williams, D. (1992). *Nobody nowhere: The extraordinary autobiography of an autistic*. New York, NY: Times Books.

Williams, D. (1994). *Somebody somewhere: Breaking free from the world of autism*. New York, NY: Times Books.

Williams, D. (2003). *Exposure anxiety: The invisible cage*. London, England and New York, NY: Jessica Kingsley.

Wurzburg, G. (Director). (2012). *Wretches & jabberers* [Motion picture]. U.S.: Institute of Community and Inclusion, Syracuse University.

Yergeau, M. (2000). Clinically significant disturbance: On theorists who theorize theory of mind. *Disability Studies Quarterly*, *33*(4). Retrieved from: http://dsq-sds.org/article/view/3876/3405

Yergeau, M. (2009). *aut(hored)ism: Computers and compositions online*. Retrieved from: http://www2.bgsu.edu/departments/english/cconline/dmac/

Yergeau, M. (2010). Circle wars: Reshaping the typical autism essay. *Disability Studies Quarterly, 30*(1). Retrieved from http://dsq-sds.org/issue/view/43

Yergeau, M. (2013). Clinically significant disturbance: On theorists who theorize theory of mind. *Disability Studies Quarterly, 33*(4). Retrieved from: http://dsq-sds.org/article/view/3876/3405

Part II

The Artist's Identity

6 Emerging from Anonymity

Since the deinstitutionalization movement in the 1950s that restored to society the "mentally ill," and in the 1970s the intellectually and developmentally disabled, a variety of unconventional art centers have opened throughout the country and abroad for people with disabilities. The oldest in the United States, Creative Growth Art Center in Oakland, California, has become the model for art centers that reject medical methodologies in favor of non-traditional teaching methods. What has emerged are the artists' own narratives and self-representations, bringing art and education closer to eroding the boundaries between normality and disability as these terms are defined by western cultural standards.

The work that the artists do at Creative Growth is not considered by director Tom di Maria as strictly Outsider Art. And yet he is careful not to isolate the artists who are sought after by Outsider Art collectors and dealers. Rather, they are visibly part of the contemporary art world. The legacy of deinstitutionalized Outsider Art, which di Maria neither dismisses nor encourages, is only one among multiple cultural discourses. Creative Growth has arrived at an enviable and balanced position in a field that still inspires polemics and theoretical debates. Before revisiting Creative Growth toward the end of the chapter, I will begin with an abbreviated history of art made in institutions, initially used to recognize patients' mental conditions, but which evolved into an affinity for the artists' ideas, experiences, and aesthetics.

EFFECTS OF INSTITUTIONALIZATION

Michel Foucault (2009) describes institutionalization and removal from the community from the seventeenth to the nineteenth century as an encircling of the "insistent fearsome figure" (p. 5). Justifying the confinement of the "mad person," the catch-all for all that is menacing in the world, is dependent on the perceptions and causes of and reasons for mental illness, manifested with the metaphors and symbols of the time. Madness is perceived as deviant, lacking responsibility for the social good and, therefore, deserving of punishment. Reminiscent of Leslie Fiedler's (1996) secret self, Foucault (2009) writes that the Other's symbolic placement of madness is turned inward "if we admit that what was once the visible fortress of social order is now the castle of our own consciousness" (p. 11). The internalized "fearsome figure" conjured by madness within our consciousness is arguably mortality, death, forces darker than death, nothingness, or "the great solar *madness* of the world" (p. 28). If madness engulfs the world, then reasonableness (normality) cannot exist to oppose it; hence modernism's bifurcation. The notion of normal becomes the standard by which abnormal is identified, encircled, and removed from society. The abnormal then becomes the depository of the normal's own alienation. The scientific age of the nineteenth and twentieth centuries inherited the left-over morality and punishment, which "forms the bedrock of our 'scientific' knowledge of mental illness" (p. 106). All that was needed was the label "mental patient," and the proof of progress in the age of scientific positivism was sealed.

Also in the nineteenth century, the interconnection between the medical and judicial systems imposed a hybrid discourse in a power/knowledge structure of surveillance (Foucault, 2003). Foucault positions this discourse within the medicalized notions of abnormality and the suspicion that the mentally ill will commit violent crimes.

Institutional life continues to haunt us today, but with particular voracity for the poor, people of color, and the disabled. Whether we speak of prisons—which are operated much like mental hospitals—nursing homes, or "special" schools, the majority of the population within these institutions comprises some combination of the categories above (Ben-Moshe, 2013). Since the dismantlement of the United States' mental health complex and the lack of a sufficient community support system, many of the institutionalized mental patients have traded hospitals for prisons. *The New York Times* journalist Nicholas Kristoff (2014) reported that "more than three times as many mentally ill people are housed in prisons and jails as in hospitals" (p. 11). Liat Ben-Moshe (2013) states that "the American Psychiatric Association reports in 2000 that up to 5% of prisoners are actively psychotic and that as many as one in five of those prisoners were 'seriously mentally ill' " (p. 134). In addition, mental health deteriorates from confinement; particularly researched are the extreme forms of segregated and isolated incarceration. More important than the risk of incarceration, says Ben-Moshe, are the systemic effects of confinement in our culture, such as the dehumanizing disregard for human rights, citizenship, and personhood.

I turn now to the place that art has in this history and the changing cultural perspectives of mental and intellectual disabilities as modernist polarity gave way to postmodern pluralism. Colin Rhodes (2000b) describes this change as a shift from the isolation of the Other to the confirmation of individual subjectivity at the margins.

THE EMERGENCE OF OUTSIDER ARTISTS WITHIN INSTITUTIONS

> *From what psychic Elsewhere do such configurations emerge so assertively? Given the context of the artmaking, it is small wonder that our vocabulary falters, for this is no longer a readymade discourse which we can join (as when we step onto a moving escalator) but one in the process of being made, step by step (and so more like scrambling up a cliff).*
> (Cardinal, 2000, p. 54)

The wide spectrum of humanity subsumed under the term "outsiders," and their artistic practices known as Outsider Art, have captivated scholars in multiple disciplines since the early 1900s. The first examples, which tended to pathologize the artists, came from doctors in psychiatric institutions who wrote clinical studies about their patients' artwork. Jean Dubuffet, who looked for a raw, unadulterated approach to art that rejected the principles of modernism, repositioned the meaning of the inmates' work as an ideal art form. In recent decades, art historians (Cardinal, 1972, 2000, 2008; Foster, 2000; Rhodes, 2000a, 2000b), art educators (jagodzinski, 2005; Krug, 1992), and art therapists (Henley, 2012) have written compelling, intimate, and engaging responses to such marginalized artists, challenging traditional clinical discourses. They challenge Outsider Art discourses that stereotype people who exhibit atypical behaviors, which are often related to disabilities that affect communication, mental processes, and social interaction.

Morgenthaler and Prinzhorn

Historian of Outsider Art and editor of *Raw Vision* magazine, John Maizels (1996), begins his book *Raw Creation: Outsider Art and Beyond* as follows, "The gradual recognition of the art of the 'insane' is one of the most fascinating stories in the frequently astounding field of self-taught art" (pp. 12–13). Although stirrings of this growing recognition began in the late nineteenth and early twentieth century, I will fast-forward to 1921, during which the Swiss doctor Walter Morgenthaler published a study about the "psychotic" artist Adolf Wolfli in *A Mental Patient as an Artist*.

Wolfli is considered an archetypal master of a genre that would soon be called Art Brut. He lived at the Waldau clinic near Bern beginning in 1895, and after several years of isolation began to draw. Most of these early works were discarded, and it is likely that none would have survived if it were not for Morgenthaler's arrival at the clinic in 1906. These first pencil drawings are in his classic style of highly symmetrical, detailed motifs and lettering. Morgenthaler wrote in his book:

> Every Monday morning Wolfli is given a new pencil and two large sheets of unprinted newsprint. The pencil is used up in two days; then he has

> to make do with the stubs he has saved or with whatever he can beg off someone else. He often writes with pieces only five to seven millimeters long or even with the broken-off points of lead, which he handles deftly, holding them between his fingernails. . . . At Christmas the house gives him a box of coloured pencils, which lasts him two or three weeks at the most. (as cited in Maizels, 1999, p. 24)

Ans Van Berkum (2000) points out that Morgenthaler's careful descriptions of Wolfli appear repeatedly in the works of other Art Brut and outsider artists. Traits such as compulsion to make art as if from an inner force, the lack of conceptualization, commands from God, and immunity to external influences are familiar conditions of these "isolated" artists.

In 1908, Wolfli began his epic work of texts and illustrations. The first eight of the 45 volumes was called *From the Cradle to the Grave*, and the final 16 volumes, *The Funeral March*, comprised his fictionalized autobiography of exotic travels and experiences with friends and family. Upon his death after 35 years of internment, his massive body of work was preserved in the Waldau Museum in Bern, and in 1975 entrusted to the Adolf Wolfli Foundation.

The year after Walter Morgenthaler (1921, 1992) published *Madness and Art: The Life and Works of Adolf Wolfi*, German psychiatrist Hans Prinzhorn at Heidelberg University's psychiatric hospital published *Artistry of the Mentally Ill*, the first major initiative to systematically analyze the art of mentally disabled people in institutions. Although Prinzhorn's project began for diagnostic purposes, as an art historian his interest in the art of his patients appeared to be more subjective than clinical, more as "*artwork* than as *scientific document*" (Cardinal, 2008, para. 8). Heidelberg University hired the art historian-psychiatrist to expand its collection of over 5,000 artworks by about 500 patients of psychiatric institutions, now known as the Prinzhorn Collection, which is still housed in the Heidelberg clinic. The work of institutionalized people opened a window for Prinzhorn to attend to both the artists' clinical and artistic manifestations. His collection was the start of an interest in the mentally ill and disabled from less of a clinical perspective and more as a spectator of pioneers in a mysterious art form.

Of the 500 artists, Prinzhorn was careful to highlight ten he thought most outstanding, such as Karl Genzel. Genzel is known for his kopfflusslers, or head-footers, which are free-standing sculptures. They were at first made from chewed bread and later from more sturdy materials such as discarded pieces of wood furniture. After a leg amputation, his mental state declined, and these bodiless creatures with over-compensating legs must have been at least partially the result of his amputation.

By 1915, artists from the Prinzhorn pantheon, such as Karl Buhler, Johan Knupfer, and August Natterer, made deep impressions on the Dadaists who were their contemporaries, and later the French Surrealists and the German Expressionists. The artists' romance with madness was similar to their perceptions of other marginalized groups, who they valued for their simplicity and unsophisticated directness (Rhodes, 2000b). They borrowed the surfaces of the institutionalized artists' texts and imagery to promote their own anti-sense manifestos.

At the end of World War I, artist Max Ernst's introduction to the Prinzhorn collection, particularly the work of Genzel and Natterer, inspired a critical departure in his surrealist practices. Ernst introduced the collection to the Surrealist group, and many of their processes, such as automatic drawing and writing, bricolage, and trances "were generally regarded as equivalents for the creative process of schizophrenic artists" (p. 107). The romantic irony of these processes was that they appeared to be "liberating," especially from the dominant European tradition. It was not until the Surrealist writer Antonin Artaud was institutionalized that they felt the full weight of psychosis.

Dubuffet

Before the outsider movement, which drew directly from artist Jean Dubuffet, and before audiences acquired a taste for this peculiar artwork, Dubuffet made the case for a departure from the accepted codes of the art world, its conditioned responses, and its homogeneous frame of reference. When Dubuffet received Prinzhorn's *Artistry of the Menally Ill* in 1923, he saw in the artworks the manifestation of the surrealist ideals of automatism and delirium. Art unsullied by the stifling effects of culture was the pivot of his theories. By 1944, he began his quest for a "pure art" by visiting mental institutions, during which he saw Adolph Wolfli and Heinrich Anton Muller's[1] work at the Waldau clinic. He began his own commissioned book about the work he saw, and needing a title, he dignified the psychotic art with the official term *Art Brut*.[2] The term is a legacy of his days as a wine merchant in which "brut" meant raw, unadulterated, pure, "like the best champagnes" (Rhodes, 2000a, p. 24). Therefore, "brut" or "raw" is a metaphor for non-academic art, an art uncooked by culture.

Dubuffet found in the untraditional materials and artists on the fringes of society an escape from the culture of beauty and the undoing of centuries of indoctrination. "He thought the simple life of ordinary human beings contained more art and poetry than academic art" (di Maria, 2015). While "cultural art" maintained its dominance nothing original could endure, he thought, since the mainstream would make sure "to anesthetize its power and eventually asphyxiate genuine expression" (Maizels, 1996, p. 35). Dubuffet's Art Brut was meant to revise the western philosophical tradition from Plato to Kant that made claim to absolute or universal values. In connoisseurship and cultural hierarchies, beauty was by far the supreme value as the result of the search for an essence of aesthetic expression, which Duchamp rendered irrelevant with his Readymades, and Dubuffet rejected by preferring ugly but honest art.

Dubuffet also rejected the pathologizing of "Mad Art", and instead positioned the asylum inmate as a radical version of the romantic genius. He found in these inmates' spontaneous, socially and culturally unrestrained works a "truer" art. But his idealism was not sustainable, given that no one, as Cardinal writes (2000), is immune to culture, even those who might be psychologically resistant to it.

The first Paris exhibition of Art Brut in 1947 marked the beginning of Dubuffet's extensive permanent collection that he eventually housed in Lausanne, Switzerland. Intentionally avoiding the aura of the museum, he called the body of work the "Collection de L'Art Brut." In assembling his collection, he would need to make and re-make his borders as he debated whether or not to include artists with remote artistic backgrounds. By this time Dubuffet was a rich and well-known artist, and had amassed over 4,000 works by 133 artists (Maizels, 1996). About 1000 works that did not meet his exacting criteria for purity were set aside and ignored until he designated them as "Neuve Invention" in the 1980s. "Dubuffet eventually had to admit that even the craziest outsider grows up and lives in a cultural milieu whose traces can never be entirely eradicated" (Berge, 2000, p. 85). His obsession with cultural contamination would have a divisive effect on future Outsider Art historians who continue to police the borders.

The Collection de L'Art Brut opened in 1976. Dubuffet's purpose was not to promote a body of work or movement, but rather to present each artist with an individualistic style and vision. He appointed Michel Thevoz, the author of *Art Brut*—a rich text about the development and theory of Art Brut—to be the curator of the collection and eventually his successor as director.

Thevoz (1994) added to the contamination paranoia the notion that since the 1970s mass culture had dramatically changed the possibility of immunity. He asked if it is "possible that individuals could still exist who were so idiosyncratic and independent as to be capable of constructing a personal mythology and pictorial idiom?" (pp. 66–67). I suspect that the imagined threat of assimilation ignited Thevoz's paranoid fears that the collection would deteriorate into a mausoleum. He also pointed out that after the 1950s, the sudden introduction of psychotropic drugs in psychiatric institutions was an incursion of normalization that would be irreversibly damaging to the incarcerated artists. The ethical ramifications are rampant in his mourning of delirious artistic inspiration. Jos ten Berge (2000) also points out that Thevoz's over-romantizing of the "mad artist' was ill conceived, since artists rarely produce work during acute delirium. Yet, there is truth in the fact that the overwhelming sedating effect of early antipsychotic drugs did damage to inmates, as did the inhumane practices of lobotomy, sterilization, and shock treatment during this era.

The introduction of art therapy also appeared in the 1950s, and was mistrusted by Thevoz (1994). He believed that these projects stifled the spontaneity and passion of the artists. "The making of art as a hygienic practice dissuades the potential creator from tackling anything novel, for it preempts all initiatives and orients them in a preordained direction toward an orthopedic goal" (p. 68). Dubuffet's audacious intent, Thevoz reminds us, is not "to cure madness but rather to stimulate it" (p. 68). Dubuffet exempted the famous Gugging Artists' House from this category, and its director Navratil reassured him that interventions were minimal. Several of the Gugging artists, such as August Walla and Johann Hauser, were well represented in the Art Brut Collection.

Berge (2000) further questions the ethical stance of Art Brut artists in their vulnerable position in society and potential lack of voice in exhibition matters. This is particularly true when artists want to cross over into the mainstream, and "the alarm bells seem to start ringing for some *art brut* devotees" (p. 88). This contamination phobia limits the agency of the artist, whether or not the art world influences his or her work and its so-called quality.

Outsiderism and Legitimacy

> *Totally alien, the new art (an art that has always been) proliferates quietly round the outskirts of the cultural city. The present survey of what this art can offer, being only provisional and partial, thus ends not with the complacent humming emitted by art-books that fit snug next to what has gone before, but with the busy, uneven clattering made by the nameless creators presently engaged in erecting alternative realities, sounds which—such is the present state of our sensibility–are yet too disparate for us to apprehend as a single message. Whether or not the time will ever come when those untutored hands will fashion a Trojan Horse, the siege of the cultural city is underway.*
>
> (Cardinal, 1972, p. 180)

In 1972, Roger Cardinal coined the term *Outsider Art* for the title of his book, solving the need for an Anglophone version of *Art Brut* for his British readers. The term has stuck, albeit with changing meanings (Cardinal, 2008). Since Cardinal introduced it, the term has relaxed the boundaries of Art Brut, with an abandoned emphasis on the social position of the artist. Nevertheless, authenticity conflicts continue unabated, as the many letters by readers and advocates of Raw Vision attest[3] (Maizels, 1996). Cardinal (2008) retains the original usefulness of his outsider term as an equivalent for Art Brut while encompassing not only mental disabilities, but also artists who are socially independent yet work outside the standards and definitions of the art world.

"Outsider" is not the first signifier for the marginalized; the indigenous peoples of the colonial conquests still wrestle with the totalizing category of "primitive." When not disparaged, they are depicted as "noble savage[s] . . . better off than we civilized westerners in our over-cultivated, technology-obsessed society" (Berge, 2000, p. 77). In art, especially, primitivism is viewed as noble in light of the psychological costs that technology brings to bear on personal lives. Berge (2000) theorizes that because of a loss of intimacy—among other human behaviors—we have constructed an alternative reality: the romantic notion of the outsider as unspoiled and authentic. The majority of these Others, however, have rejected the primitive label, except for the most vulnerable among them, the mentally disabled. This unequal power relationship underscores the inherent bifurcation of the term "outsider," assigning a status to a group that remains fixed in place, of which the Italian artist Carlo Zinelli was an iconic figure. The attempt to relativize the outsider is continually met with counter attacks. I will revisit the polemics that inevitably arose from "outsiderism" after introducing Zinelli.

Disrupting Borders: Carlo Zinelli at the Venice Biennale

> *It's obvious that for this type of art-making, traditional academic training is irrelevant.*
>
> (Buzzati, 2013, as cited in *Il Palazzo di Everything*, p. 15)

The presence of the London-based The Museum of Everything (MoE) at the 2013 Venice Biennale, the barometer of the art world, disrupted the borders of the inside/outside binary. MoE's director James Brett shuns the term outsider as "the ghettoization" of the artists. His cause célèbre is to "reclaim the title of 'artist' as a basic human right" (Miller, 2013). The artistic director of the 2013 Biennale, Massimiliano Gioni, who is associate director of the New Museum in New York and an outsider aficionado, envisioned the broad scope of the biennale by installing "The Encyclopedic Palace," the symbol of 1950s Futurism. Leant by Manhattan's American Folk Art Museum, it was built by a self-taught Italian-American artist, Marino Auriti, who intended it to house "all the knowledge in the world" (Vogel, 2013).

One of Dubuffet's great artists, Carlo Zinelli, was featured at the MoE pavilion at the Biennale. The circumstances of Zinelli's life that led him to become a renowned and prolific artist are emblematic of the outsider mythic figure. He was born near Verona, Italy on a farm to a family of seven children. His mother died in childbirth when he was three, and rather than his father remarrying to secure the large family, as was traditionally done, their comfortable lifestyle crumbled as he spent the family fortune. The eldest son, and father of Allesandro Zinelli, who is currently the president of the Carlo Zinelli foundation in Verona, took over the family carpentry business when he was eleven. Ultimately the male siblings found other homes, while his sisters moved to a convent or were forced to work as housemaids for other families.

Zinelli was nine years old when he dropped out of school and moved in with a family in the remote Italian countryside to tend cattle. The loss of his mother and his removal from his family was a lonely and traumatic time. The symbols in his paintings, says his nephew Alessandro Zinelli, reflect his suffering during this period, such as the number four, which represents the number of his good friends. At 18 he reunited with his sisters in Verona. But it was at this time that he was called to the Spanish Civil War, ultimately to become a stretcher-bearer. The mutilated bodies and disembodied limbs that he witnessed are repeatedly depicted in his work. After only two months he returned to Verona psychologically devastated. His mental condition deteriorated after his removal to an asylum, where he was placed in isolation, his speech and communication faltering. "He spoke only in truncated, fragmented sentences of chopped up words, neologisms, and mutterings and repeated certain symbolically significant words and phrases such as 'the end of the world'" (Thevoz, 2001, p. 281). The doctors diagnosed him as schizophrenic and prescribed permanent hospitalization. His condition was considered irrecoverable and treated with the remedies of the day, "cold showers, strait-jackets, electro-shock therapy and insulin injections" (Zinelli, 2013, as cited in *Il Palazzo di Everything*, p. 16). Symbols of these daily regimes, such as the syringe, became ubiquitous in his work.

Zinelli's sudden urge to draw on the hospital walls with bricks, stones, and sticks motivated sculptor Michael Noble to demand that he be given

Figure 6.1 Michael Noble and Carlo Zinelli c. 1960 (© John Phillips, courtesy of The Museum of Everything and Fondazione Culturale Carlo Zinelli)

materials and a painting table. Noble entered the asylum to recover from alcohol addiction, and with the help of his wealthy and aristocratic wife, later funded the building of an atelier (studio) within the hospital to be used by Zinelli and twelve other patients. Until then a few patients had been working from observation and other traditional exercises. Now Noble "directed" the atelier to adhere strictly to the tenets of Art Brut by following the self-taught commandments, as Dino Buzzati called them in a 1957 exhibition catalogue, which was Dubuffet's rejection of all interference with the artists' work other than supplying materials. The artists also had the freedom to take walks, dance, and sing.

Zinelli completed his first painting on plywood in 1957, and Noble was struck by his genius. During the same year, an exhibition was held in a commercial gallery for the artists, which was of little interest for Zinelli. The conspicuously empty holes that appeared in his figures are as recognizable as his signature, and have been interpreted as windows, internal organs, bullet holes, or the daily pills he was administered between shock therapy. Artist Pino Castangna (2013), who worked with Noble in the Atelier, asked Zinelli the meaning of these white circles. He pointed to the nurse who showed Castangna a box of four white tablets of tranquilizers. "Pills are harder than bullets; and for Zinelli, as penetrating and transformative," says curator and film producer Pino Castangna (as cited in *I1 Palazzo di Everything*). These spaces inhabit both animate and inanimate figures, as if embedded in the landscape of his life from childhood to adulthood. The Museum of Everything describes his work as follows:

> Memories of the country-side, of wild animals and travelling circuses, were illustrated alongside bulbous figures, dying soldiers, congregations of priests and dancing women. Around them a swirling imaginary language echoed Zinelli's faltering speech patterns. It was as if the artist had found new life inside his own creations. (Always the Sun)

Zinelli's figures are in profile, in a procession going somewhere, shrinking in size toward the edges of the paper. They are silhouettes, maybe shadows, what is left of humanity after witnessing atrocities. Exposure and transparency act as metaphors for what he unavoidably saw. And, in addition to the feeling of inside, there is excess and chaos, the over-repetitive surfaces of his work: an excess of letters, figures, and design elements that mingle, inhabit space, but rarely touch. In the following paragraphs, I return to the present and the so-called outsider artist, whose work follows the trajectory of artists such as Zinelli, but who inhabits an art world(s) that questions the use and relevance of terms that delimit the "outsider."

Imagine Turning the Art World Inside Out

The BBC director Alan Yentob's documentary, *Imagine: Turning the Art World Inside Out*, begins with the question to outsider artists and experts

Figure 6.2 Carlo Zinelli (© Courtesy The Museum of Everything)

alike, "What is Outsider Art?" The outsider artists are in on the inside joke and answer with wit and sarcasm. Later the experts weigh in.

JOE COLEMAN: What is Outsider Art? Well you got me. I've been trying to figure that out. I've certainly been called worse things in my life than an outsider artist.

GEORGE WIDENER: Is that someone that's working outside, you know, that doesn't mind if it rains or something and they'll draw outside. In fact I was a bit of an outsider artist. I was over on a bench in Hyde Park laying low from the cops at night doing drawings.

PAUL LAFFOLEY: What do you mean?

YENTOB: Do you feel like an outsider?

LAFFOLEY: Well, I suppose so, but what does an insider feel like?

JOHN SALTZ, ART CRITIC, NEW YORK MAGAZINE: And by the way, excuse me, Caravaggio was homeless, incarcerated and insane. And 90 percent of the artists I've ever met are a little insane.

JOHN MAIZELS: One of the exciting things when seeing an artist you've never seen before is that you've never seen anything like it before, because each outsider artist is like an art movement of one, and they invent their own techniques, disciplines, ways of working, and their own visions. That's why they come up with something completely individual each time.

By way of introducing the first of several contemporary outsider artists featured in the film, Maizels shows Yentob a small self-portrait of Joe Coleman that he owns. Coleman's works are quite large and expensive, so he painted a small portrait of himself for Maizels, reminiscent of precious jewel-like medieval miniatures. The painting, in which Coleman is pictured in bloodied apron and gloves after performing an autopsy in a Hungarian hospital, is called *The Pathologist*. Yentob visits Coleman and other artists, such as Paul Laffoley, in their homes and galleries, as well as converses with curators at exhibitions.

Joe Coleman

> *It was a shitty hand, but I played the cards really well.*
>
> (Coleman, as cited in Lieb, 2008, p. 29)

Joe Coleman was expelled from the School of Visual Arts for making work his teachers called "fascist" and schizophrenic" (Strausbaugh, 2006). He was invited to be a student advisor many years later after establishing himself as a highly skilled and eccentric artist. He believes, however, that artists should live in the world rather than go to art school because they will not learn what they need to know inside a school. Coleman began making art as a child in Norwalk, Connecticut. In a home with a violent alcoholic father, he found relief in drawing. His obsession with religion and death germinated at this young age as a student in a school for "disturbed children" (Strausbaugh, 2006).

His fine artwork is made with a single haired brush and a magnifying jeweler's lens. He paints one square inch of the canvas at a time without forethought or planning. He was told to "loosen up" at art school, but he says he's at his loosest when he tightens up (Lieb, 2008).

> I'm looking for more and more information on the surface of the painting, even though it's coming out of somewhere, out there or in here, but it's appearing in here, and that's where I'm finding it, and the more minute that I look, the more that I find. I try to take care of the misfits and the losers. The losers never get to write their side of history, except in my work. (Coleman, as cited in Yentob, 2013)

Unlike his contemporaries, Coleman insists that there isn't an ounce of irony in his work because it comes from existential pain. "Nothing merits a knowing wink or nudge. This fact, more than any other, is why Coleman's paintings are so frequently compared to religious icons" (Lieb, 2008, p. 29). Artist and friend Tony Fitzpatrick calls him the only spiritual painter that America has produced.

Because of his success and the high prices he fetches for his work, he has been banned from the annual Outsider Art Fair in New York where he had been exhibiting for ten years. "What does this tell us?" asks Yentob.

Figure 6.3 Joe Coleman, *A Doorway to Joe*

"Perhaps we fetishize these artists. We prefer them to be poor and struggling." Coleman scorns the outsider artist label, "I didn't want to be burdened by a bunch of guys who nailed tin cans into a windmill" (Coleman, as cited in Lieb, 2008, p. 29).

Success such as Coleman's comes posthumously, if at all. Coleman's choice of subject matter would typically guarantee anonymity, but since 2008, when he mounted his retrospective at the Jack Tilton Gallery in New York, he has received the recognition reserved for so-called art stars. Prior to this large exhibition, writes Rebecca Lieb, it was not possible to view more than one of his work's at a time, since most of his work was owned by private collectors and a fairly substantial cult following. Rather than speeding up and working smaller, he's slowing down, going deeper, and working larger. One painting can take up to a year to complete, which keeps his buyers waiting.

Paul Laffoley

> *It's good to be unknown for a long time.*
>
> (Laffoley, as cited in Yentob, 2013)

Paul Laffoley passed away November 16, 2015. His several encounters with alien species re-directed his art and philosophy. Mark Pilkington (2013) calls his work complex systems of imagined technologies in which the viewer is vital to the work because it is made solely to communicate information and transform the viewer/operator. Laffoley studied art history and philosophy at Brown University and for a short time at the Harvard Graduate School of Design until he was kicked out for "conceptual deviance." "I was working against what they were teaching. . . . I had no interest in what they were doing. But I don't rebel against anything" (Laffoley, as cited in Rousseau, 2013, p. 71).

Laffoley worked with Minoru Yamasaki, the architect of the World Trade Center, until his life took a sharp turn in a different direction. In the 1980s, he designed what he called "physically alive architecture." His *das Urpflanze Haus* is based on the concept of a primal plant, or Urplanze, which generates infinite varieties of plant life. If, hypothetically, all forms of vegetation on earth were grafted together, he said, one would have a single plant. Cross grafting among different species is made possible by the gingko biloba. This plant would resolve many of the problems of poverty, such as providing low-cost housing. "You have a single plant with a multiple root system. . . . You can give a person a bag of seeds and have an entire world in two months" (Laffoley, as cited in Rousseau, 2013, p. 71).

At the exhibition *The Alternative Guide to the Universe* at the Hayward Gallery in London, Laffoley constructed a two-dimensional time machine entitled *The Thanaton III*, in which the viewer can project himself or herself mentally without physical travel. It was painted after Laffoley was visited for the third time by the alien he calls Quazgaa Klaatu. The encounter occurred while he was giving a talk in 1988 outside Boylston Street in Boston. The alien appeared as a body of light, and a photograph taken of Laffoley that day shows him covered in a nimbus-like cloud (Laffoley, 2013). Among the various information he received, he learned how to "link life to death in a continuous experience" (p. 48).

Laffoley (2013) called this work "a psychotronic—or mind-matter interactive—device" (p. 48). The painting enables the viewer to download intelligence from another dimension by placing one's hands on the surface and staring into the eye of the painting. Ralph Rugoff, director of the Hayward Gallery, says the exhibition harkens back to a time when science and art were not as divisible. The blurring of disciplinary boundaries fits Laffoley's experiments well, which Michael Bracewell (2013) describes as the "conversion of mysticism into mechanics" in the "tradition of esoteric scholarship connecting the experiments of medieval alchemy to philosopher-scientists of the eighteenth and nineteenth centuries" (p. 47). Bracewell describes Laffoley's work as a map that reveals social, scientific, and cultural codes directing humanity from the past into the future.

Pilkington (2013) researched the small print in Laffoley's 1989 painting, *The Eloptic-Nohmangraphon;* the text explains that "eloptic" was coined by Thomas Glaen Hieronymus as an electrical and optical hybrid. Three names were clues in deciphering the tautology of Laffoley's work: Albert Abrams, Ruth Drown, and Thomas Galen Hieronymus were early pioneers of radionic technology.[4] Hieronymus patented a device that worked as both an object and a two dimensional symbol of the device.[5] It relied "on the user's sensing changes in the 'eloptic' energy through the place on which the element sits" (Pilkington, 2013 p. 102). Even Hieronymus was not certain how the invention, which seemed to depend on the conviction of the subject, worked: "We can best understand them as technological adaptations of ancient, sympathetic magical practices, a magic that feeds on, and is fuelled by, the conviction of both the practitioner and the subject" (pp. 102–103).

As Rogoff takes Yentob through the exhibition, Yentob remarks how different the view of the world is from the artists' perspectives, a mutation of art, science, mathematics, and mysticism. Rogoff responds that contemporary artists have lost sight of this blended engagement in the pursuit of knowledge. These artists have their own concepts about how the world works, usually in opposition to scientists and other experts of their fields. In subsequent pages, I compare these artists—with their highly subjective and idiosyncratic perceptions of the world—with the organized system of the academy, which generates such experts.

Self-Taught Versus the Academy

I choose the term *self-taught* to make the distinction between the art school, or academy, and the binary positioning of artists who make their work outside these accredited institutions in America and Europe. The tradition that is enshrined in these schools—within a wide range of conservative and liberal practices—is founded on professional training regulated by a set of institutionalized standards and skills. These sets of practices result in diplomas that are purposed for future professionals in the official organization of the art world's network of museums, galleries, and foundations.

According to Matthew Higgs (2011a), who was an instructor at the Royal College of Art and Goldsmiths in London, the purpose of art school is to create consensus rather than encourage difference. The young artist exits the academy with identifiable mannerisms, processes, and structures, which makes contemporary art so homogeneous. While walking through Chelsea Galleries, Higgs automatically recognizes artistic references and relationships built from prior experience in the academy. On the other hand, his encounters with the work from art centers such as Creative Growth and Gugging are so different that he must recalibrate his responses to avoid defaulting into art historical knowledges.

In Steven Madoff's (2009) *Art School (Propositions for the 21st Century),* artist Ken Lun writes an ambivalent letter about being an educator in an art school. He left his tenured position at the University of British Columbia in Vancouver because of the ambiguity of his role. Questions that he thought needed to be asked seemed irrelevant within the institution, questions about "life knowledges," such as "What does it mean to be in someone else's place? How is it even possible to express something of the pain and suffering or happiness and joy of someone else?" (p. 331).

These knowledges, which Foucault (2003) spoke of in his lectures at the College of France, are subjugated, knowledges that have been "disqualified as nonconceptual knowledges, as insufficiently elaborated knowledges: naïve knowledges, hierarchically inferior knowledges, knowledges that are below the required level of erudition or scientificity" (as cited in Lun, 2009, p. 335). The irrelevance of these knowledges is produced from the increasingly high tuition that limits the population to privileged students who are well off, and thus have an insularity that distances them from other knowledges. Therefore, class and status do matter, imposing themselves on art production. Localized knowledges, as Foucault (2003) called them, are antipodal to institutions and their validated knowledges. Lun warned that art school knowledges that do not challenge the dominant ideologies of the capitalist art world do not serve art students who are, alas, too ready to accept its homogenized narratives and expectations, and the shiny surfaces of art objects they produce.

The self-taught curriculum, however, is neither written, formalized, nor shared (Cardinal, 2000). Nor are studios and equipment standardized, since resources are acquired ad hoc. "One of the basic lessons on the self-taught curriculum is how to assert oneself against the impediments of contingency—one's lack of finesse, one's obdurate materials, the interruptions and perhaps mockeries of one's neighbours" (p. 71). Cardinal exemplifies the artists in the landmark 1942 exhibition *They Taught Themselves* at the Sydney Janis

Gallery as changing the perception of folk tradition as timeless and conventional. Most likely this shift was produced by the outsider influence of favoring idiosyncrasy, individualism, and experimentation. The designation of "self-taught" appropriates the artist as both teacher and pupil, semi-independent of culture. Cardinal asks, "How can one really know nothing yet also be 'in the know?'" (p. 71).

Many self-taught artists practice inventive ways of accessing materials. For example, James Castle found discarded pencil stubs and used spit as an adhesive for "natural" pigments such as soot. In these highly idiosyncratic schools of self-taught art, Cardinal theorizes that the ultimate learning is in the consciousness of self, or selfhood, the memorializing of an identity. Rather than the mastering of the medium, the artist inscribes his or her presence in the material as a creative agent. This is the distinctive feature of the self-taught, an inevitable outcome of the process that Cardinal emphasizes—whatever the nature of the self might be—and therefore the release of its potential. The memorialization of an identity might be the secret of the personal style that makes the self-taught artist so distinctive from the professional academic.

In order to emphasize the thesis of this book, I suggest that the feelings of these artists may not be coherent, nor are their identities stable. Then, there is the contradictory character of self-taught art that has been described by Leo Navratil and others as selfless—a loss of self to an ecstatic and compulsive process. The artists foray into a space beyond the self, often romanticized as possessed by a spirit or guide. The ideal Art Brut artist, according to Dubuffet, created these other cosmologies, entire world systems that transcended the personal or single ego. They might also be reminders, or even evidence, of the several egos or identities that each of us inhabit, but of which we are not aware.

But whatever is at the interior of the "self," it is the inspiration for creation rather than what might be the current trend in the art world, and the reason that these artists' works have the character of a secret diary, as Cardinal suggests. The same self-reflexive nature of the self-taught artist, however, is criticized for artistic solipsism and psychological isolation. Yet there are always the cultural references in these artists' works that make them accessible, if not fully, at least in part.

The making of symbols indicates not only self-scrutiny, but also a need to make contact with the social order. This notion balances the self-reflexivity of self-taught art and endows it with practical meaning. Certainly the artists at Creative Growth Art Center are interested in audience reception and, as described in their biographies in the following chapters, the audience is often considered in the process. They are also aware, to a greater or lesser extent, of their own autobiographies, and the reductionist practices of curation, which Cardinal points out can be patronizing and further the "othering" of non-academic artists. Gallerists and curators know that collecting biographical information is usually the most important attraction of the outsider artist and, often, the more fraught the artist's life is, the more eccentric the biography, the more attractive it is to the audience.

Failing Categories

The diversity of artists and their biographies underlines the postmodern dilemma of divisive and bifurcated terminology, such as outsider, self-taught, vernacular, Art Brut, and any number of other categories that designate the Other. Randall Morris (2001) challenges this tendency to colonize or pathologize the Other in western-speak.

> We must look into this work for the first time on its own history and its own contexts and learn its languages. . . . The names chosen are not names coming from the nature or demands of the work being named, but rather from the "culture" of the hegemonic namer. (pp. 117–119)

Morris particularly dismisses the notion of an "alternative universe," a phrase too easily reached for when we are confronted with another's visual manifestations of interior reality, a way of safely keeping the Other in a defined place in the canon. An alternative universe is in fact the product of all artists, particularly those who are skilled at creating space; but here this terminology is used for the purpose of maintaining outsiderness. Morris uses the term "home-ground" as a common denominator with which to behold the "angst-laden stormscape by Henry Darger or a somnambulistic myth-ride by Francesco Clemente" (p. 118). Morris claims that the art that we have cast under the wide net of outsider culture is in fact *cultural art* with few exceptions. How many "wild children" have existed in history who have been brought up without knowledge of language or other forms of cultural communication? Morris compares the ahistorical curation that emphasizes formal affinities rather than contextualizing the artists within their intentional histories to the colonial approach toward tribal artifacts. He suggests that we restore the control of the narrative—sane or insane—to the artists, because whatever their perspective, the work itself is a narrative rooted in the world.

> Upon the home-ground thus created the artist thrusts the narrative. This further expands the possibilities. The traveler can be in a localized realistic scape, or be an unreal traveler in a real scape or a real traveler in an unreal scape. These reveal various choices and modes of control. (p. 126)

In an era of postmodern pluralism, the notion of outside/inside has been replaced by a more heterogeneous culture (Rhodes, 2000b). And yet the art world continues to operate as the mainstream. Whereas modernism produced internationally recognizable styles and practices, postmodernism has released artists from the conventional and arbitrary standards of art history. Thus, while the institutional power of the art world is maintained, its social and historical practices have been exposed, mainly by outsiders insinuating themselves into the mainstream.

High art, encoded in the theoretical language of art historians and shared by the initiated, exists in parallel with outsider artists who more or less are "discovered" by accident. Colin Rhodes (2000b) suggests that while the two zones—the art world versus outside the art world—have been historically and traditionally antipodal, the colonizing practices of the dominant art market are giving way to a more democratic landscape by developing more interconnections and fewer western categorizations. In the same way untasteful aspects of visual culture, such as funk and kitsch, have invited questions about aesthetic assumptions (Frudden, 2013). In the last section of this chapter, I suggest that two art centers—the Gugging House of Artists and Creative Growth Art Center—have found an "in-betweeness" by fostering highly individualized artists while maintaining a foothold in the art market. They signify the end of the fiction of the so-called authentic outsider.

DEINSTITUTIONALIZATION AND COMMUNITY ARTS PROGRAMS

Gugging

Cardinal's broad inclusion of non-institutionalized people under the outsider umbrella was undoubtedly influenced by the deinstitutionalization of mentally disabled people that occurred in the latter half of the twentieth century. In the course of deinstitutionalization, some institutions and institutional art programs that remained, evolved to reinvent the ways in which artists work and how they are defined. An early example is the House of Artists in Klosterneuburg, Austria, which Johann Feilacher restructured from Leo Navratil's 1954 Gugging program at the Sanatorium and Care Home that was founded on the principles of Prinzhorn (Gugging.org).

Gugging is a model unto itself that defies categorization, a residential institution that is more like a home than a hospital. It employs "art therapy," but without a formalized order, time-schedule, or process, nor does it make art obligatory. The House of Artists is separate from the general psychiatric ward, focusing not on the preparation for re-entry into society, but on the development of social identities (Navratil, 1994). The patients are treated first and foremost as artists; the merits of their artwork are emphasized, while their mental illnesses are regarded as private matters (Maclagan, 2009). The familial style of caretaking and personal freedom enables artists, such as internationally acclaimed Johann Hauser and August Walla, both deceased, to become successful and relatively autonomous given their conditions.

Navratil's interest in art began with a diagnostic drawing test of a human figure that he asked his new patients to perform over several years, and in which he found surprising mutations. He also found the drawings to be helpful in his therapeutic approach because they offered information beyond traditional conversational therapy. He came across the two texts by Morgenthaler (1921) and Prinzhorn (1922, reprinted in 1972 and 1995), and an article by the Swiss psychiatrist Alfred Bader.[6] It was Bader who became most influential in transforming his interest in art from a diagnostic tool to a creative experience (Navratil, 1994). But it was the contemporary Viennese painters, such as Georg Eisler, Ernst Fuchs, and Arnuf Rainer, who visited Gugging that inspired Navratil's ambitious project. By 1981, the reputation of the Gugging artists was such that an art center was built from an abandoned pavilion as a working and living space for artists.

Many thousands of miles away, Creative Growth Art Center in Oakland, California also established a radical model that situates the disability of their artists within a community, refraining from imposing the exacting standards of social and artistic norms.

Creative Growth Art Center

> *As I sit in my studio, usually alone and isolated, I sometimes think that maybe I'm the outsider. I struggle to get to the place that people here get to freely. This is a great creative hotbed that can be applied to other sites, not just for people with disabilities.*
>
> (M. Hall, personal communication, July 2012)

Creative Growth opened its doors in 1974 while psychiatric institutions across the country were closing. Many of the first generation of artists entered Creative Growth with the label "mental retardation," a catch-all label common in institutions. They chose instead to label themselves "artists," their personalities trumping their former institutionalized identities. Their artworks, once relics of anonymity and non-beingness, later revealed unexpected internal lives.

di Maria (2015) describes Creative Growth as forming at an intersection of two forces: the closing of institutions and a time of social and political upheaval. The founders, Elias and Florence Ludins-Katz, conceived a radical idea as ad-hoc micro-entrepreneurs by opening their garage to the ex-patients. To put this revolutionary act in context, di Maria described a 1972 book called *The Life of the Retarded Adult* found in a box of the Katzes' reading material, which provided detailed instructions regarding when to take a retarded adult into public places and when to leave him or her at home.

Also, by departing from the institutionalized version of Outsider Art, the Katzes eliminated the stereotypes that had preconditioned the art world to

Figure 6.4 Creative Growth Art Center, 2013 (photograph by Ben Blackwell)

this distinctive work. The Katzes looked upon their artists' works as meritorious and deserving of gallery presence. In addition to being the oldest arts center for individuals with disabilities in the world, Creative Growth's current gallery was the first in the country to focus on the art of the disabled, but with the vision of integrating their artists into the richly diverse culture of the community. The popular culture of Oakland and its surrounding artists played a large role since its beginnings. From the start, says Matthew Higgs (2011a), the Katzes envisioned the work of their artists in the public domain, not a privileged support network that perpetuated the isolation of the formerly institutionalized. They hired a professional curator to bind the two worlds together toward their future personal economies rather than relying on social services, even though California had the best services in the United States (Higgs, 2011a). Creative Growth remains vital, says Higgs, because of this forward thinking and its propitious location in the artistic community of the Bay Area.

> The work that comes out of the workshops is a hybrid; it's neither one, nor the other, not the clichéd *wild man* working in the woods with no external influences, nor the savvy MFA student reading *Art Forum* magazine. It's something else and it's that *something else-ness* that interested the Katzes in the first place. They certainly weren't interested in creating an outsider art factory. (p. 4)

Methods and Strategies

Creative Growth is located at the site of a former car showroom, and the large expanse of windows on the street level invites onlookers. The open floor plan, organized by medium, in the 10,000 square foot building makes room for 162 adults (speaking 13 languages) to participate each year. By 9:30 in the morning the first set of two hour classes are in motion. Typically, the artists take 15 minute breaks before the end of the morning and afternoon sessions. Lunch lasts for an hour between sessions in their dining room and then the afternoon classes begin. The schedule is fairly formalized and most artists will be found at the same tables each day. Some fluctuation occurs when a visiting artist takes up residence for several weeks, and all artists are invited to participate in the project. The volume level is fairly high with a healthy and continuous drone of conversation punctuated by exclamations, laughter, and the heavy power drilling in the wood shop.

Creative Growth is a "non-teaching institution" and studio staff act as facilitators, highlighting their equality with the artists. The staff say that their primary goal is to help achieve the goals of the artists. But while the program practices a hands-off approach, some media involve more intervention than others. For example, artists in the wood program would not have carte blanche because of potentially dangerous tools.

The intake process is a tour of the studio. If the artists are interested, they are accepted and stay even if they aren't productive. Making art is not always comfortable for most artists, disabled or not. The "sidelining" of the staff artists provides room for disturbing emotions and thoughts to be worked out through materials. But not all materials for all artists will translate their conflicts or demons into symbolic works. A range of media is useful in helping artists find their "voice." A well-known example is Judith Scott,[7] who was unproductive until she stumbled into the fiber arts "class," and went on to become an internationally recognized fiber artist. The studio staff looks for opportunities to introduce new ideas that different media might offer the artists, particularly if they are stagnating with the ones they are using. At the same time, di Maria's concern is not to introduce materials that seem foreign or arbitrary.

The studio staff are not trained or previously educated in theoretical knowledge or practical methods of teaching or working with people with disabilities, although di Maria began a lending library of relevant materials to study. Therefore, they instinctively privilege art over disability and work around the artists' limitations.[8] For example, Michael Hall comments:

> Carl Hendrickson[9] has severe cerebral palsy and can't do the physical work that he wants to. But he is *determined* to do as much of it as he can. And he can't communicate—he's non-verbal—so you just find a way to work with him. And he comes up with brilliant solutions all the time. So you're working with the person and then you run up against

part of his disability that is a challenge for a moment and then you find a way around it. (personal communication, July, 2012)

Probably because many of the artists at Creative Growth are not verbal, such as the well-known Dan Miller and Judith Scott, their work is often more intensely complex than that of mainstream artists. They are also not inhibited by "the stifling internal critic that is so lethal, nor weighed down by art history or academic training" (J. DeStaebler, personal communication, July, 2012). Matthew Higgs (2011a) suggests that each work speaks with its own dialect. "It's not about the literal manifestations of words or language, rather it's the idea that these objects or artworks are very heavily inflected, very specific and as such, profoundly subjective gestures" (p. 9).

Sometimes I stood in the doorway in the morning while the artists settled into their routines. The uninhibited energy and excitement of beginning another day of work was astonishing. Like Higgs, I was not prepared for such unrestrained artistic energy. He found Creative Growth accidently by taking a random route to his new job as curator at the Wattis Institute, and this spontaneous introduction changed his notions of Outsider Art. Higgs (2011b) says that "without exaggerating, Creative Growth is probably the most important cultural organization I've ever encountered" (p. 12). As a Bay area local, he was impressed by how, at the time of its founding, Creative Growth ran parallel to other radical movements. He calls it "extraordinary" and "unprecedented" because its founders were able to realize their ambitious and utopian vision of supporting the artwork of people with disabilities over their lifetimes. It was probably inconceivable to anyone but the Katzes that such voices could coexist. It should have been bedlam, Higgs says, but it wasn't because the artists' idiosyncrasies have been privileged, and the Katzes resisted the temptation to homogenize their voices into conventional forms.

An art institution where people with disabilities can go for life, if they choose, has never been available before Creative Growth (Higgs, 2011a). As mentioned earlier, Higgs compares his experience teaching in the prestigious art schools in London with Creative Growth; art is made at the latter for reasons that are out of reach, out of the realm of art schools:

> A really significant factor of what you encounter at Creative Growth is that you're looking at 162 idiosyncratic individuals. If you go to an MFA program most of the students have been taught the same art history, they've been given the same theoretical texts, they've been exposed to the same narrative about art and there's a shared language, a common base from which their individual works develop. (M. Higgs, personal communication, June 12, 2014)

What sharply distinguishes Creative Growth from the academy is that their 162 artists do not share the same educational history or social conventions.

Each artist brings to the conversation his or her own set of rules, thoughts, and observations.

The unknown reason for the Creative Growth artists' works—why they are made—is the basis for endless speculation. Because these objects remain unknowable, says Higgs, viewers as well as the objects are liberated. I think what is so attractive about these artworks is their rawness, realness, and unpretentiousness. What comes across so loudly is the need to make this artwork, and that power is translated by the artists in diverse ways, from the roughness of Carlo Zinelli to the obsessive neatness of Joe Coleman.

Although conveniently called outsiders by curators and gallerists, the Creative Growth artists do not fit the typical model of the lonely genius making art in isolation. Mostly all, however, are untrained, having no experience making art or knowledge of art history. Their gallery, as observed so richly by professional art handler and installer Joel Frudden (2013), who having an epiphany while hanging work, was astonished by the proximity of the gallery and the studio of artists. Visitors who enter the gallery must also enter the studio, separated only by an exhibition wall, and invariably hear the artists at work, "the greasy grind of power tools, the feathered texture of paper ripping, and the din of focused activity punctuated by occasional laughter, friendly pontification, and indecipherable exclamations" (p. 120).

The "white cubeness" of the gallery is a nod and compliance to art world aesthetics, offset by the "bruteness" of the artists' eccentric appearance, behaviors, and communications. But Frudden, recalling the comments of Michael Hall in the quote earlier, calls them the antithesis of the "tortured and isolated stereotypes" of the art genius (p. 123). Yet, prior to his introduction to Creative Growth, Frudden subscribed to the "intentionality" camp of aesthetics, by which art is distinguished not only because of its aesthetic value but also because the aesthetic intention of the artist is predicated on a dialogue with art history. Definitions of art pale with the daily confrontation of the work produced within a community that resists classification and art world commandments. di Maria's (2013) response to an interview question about success in the art world versus the meaning of success at Creative Growth is predictably about mystery and the unexplainable. Proof of artistic achievement to di Maria is the repeated production of beautiful and intriguing work in a voice that is unmistakable from any other. The artist who is "on a high wire without a safety net" is precisely what Dubuffet valued so passionately (di Maria, 2013, p. 126). "You just have to look without the benefit of a relationship to art history, for example, or academic bearing, or an artist's statement of intent; and trust that the work has that kind of meaning, or power" (p. 126). di Maria claims not to willfully choose the outsider label, but he also does not want to alienate the field that finds a kinship with the artists. For example, Lucienne Pierry, the director of the Collection de L'Art Brut, took an interest in Creative Growth and spent time in the studio observing how the artists work with the facilitators, which led to two exhibitions in Lausanne. She chose artists Judith Scott, Dan Miller, and Donald Mitchell to be part of the permanent collection because of their perceived imperviousness to outside influence.

Other than their participation in the Outsider Art Fair in New York, Creative Growth artists mostly exhibit in contemporary galleries, and it is within this context that di Maria would like them to be understood. Rather than biography, di Maria uses the term "culture" of the artists to present their disability appropriately within their work, a balance which he is effective in striking. Sometimes the disability might inform the artist's work, such as in Dan Miller's, whose autism raises questions about repetition, number and letter sequencing, and patterns (di Maria, 2013). Yet other formats of information in the gallery can be intrusive, particularly the use of the artist's photograph with his or her diagnosis.

In order to insure a non-biased eye, several people are responsible for curatorial decisions, including the artists' thoughts about their own and their colleagues' work. "That's a curatorial voice from a perspective that I'm never going to have. I'm not a maker in the studio. I'm not a person with a developmental disability, and I don't share table space, or studio space, with that person. We try to factor all of those things in" (di Maria, 2013, p. 130). Still di Maria worries that because of his or the staff's preconceived notions of art, someone or something might be missed.

Several artists, such as William Tyler and Dan Miller, have been at Creative Growth, sitting at the same tables, and working in the same medium for over 35 years. di Maria reckons that this is how their distinctive styles develop. Their increasing presence in the art world has not changed the artists' voices by catering to the art market or other external forces. And although working together for 20 or 30 years or more, rarely does di Maria see artists borrow from or imitate each other. Like the Gugging House of Artists, each artist is "an art movement of one."

CONCLUSIONS

The medicalized descriptions of disability in the past several decades continue to inform labels and practices that set up roadblocks for new discoveries made by activists and allies of disabled people, including families, caseworkers, non-professional acquaintances, and disabled people themselves. Experts in disability-related fields have a stake in protecting the worldview they created and, therefore, tend to ignore or fail to recognize evidence of the potential for disabled people to function more independently and contribute to society (Crossley, 1997). The progression of art from institution to art center demonstrates the importance of paying attention to how and what disabled people communicate.

Creative Growth constructs an environment that changes the staff's as well as its guests' perceptions of disability. These permanent changes in the perspectives of the non-disabled are usually motivated by friendship, which the carefully constructed relationships between studio staff and artists inevitably become. In the following chapters, I write short biographies of four Creative Growth artists on the autistic spectrum, Gerone Spruill, Dan Miller, William Scott, and R. B., whose work could only be produced in an egalitarian community. Their need to make art is the driving force for all institutional decisions, which possibly makes Creative Growth the purest existing form of support for art making with this population. Sometimes that need is obsessive, and sometimes it is derailed by the social or internal barriers of living with a disability.

NOTES

1. Most art historians agree that Dubuffet's most profound artistic influence came from the artwork of Heinrich Anton Muller.
2. "Art Brut translates literally into English as Raw Art—raw because it was 'uncooked' by culture, raw because it came directly from the psyche, art in its purest form, touched by a raw nerve" (Maizels, 1996, p. 33).
3. Jos ten Berge (2000) quotes several letters from Raw Vision, such as the following: "Dear Raw Vision, One thing bothers me. How long will it be before the mainstream art world, which is surely watching us closely, descends upon Outsider Art and takes it away from us? It troubles me to think that in a few years from now opinionated 'experts' and critics will have absorbed what they can of Outsider Art and will be spouting off their garbage to us all" (p. 90).
4. In *The Secret of Art: A Brief History of Radionic Technology for the Creative Individual*, Duncan Laurie (2009) writes that "ancient and traditional art forms worked with nature energies" (p. 5). Shamanistic artists of the past have used radionics, or moving invisible forces of energy, for "healing, changing weather, restoring harmony, divination, accessing and making the sacred comprehensible to culture" (p. 5).
5. Pilkington (2013) says, "It works like this: the item to be analyzed—which could be anything from a mineral to a blood sample—is placed next to a coil of wire, a pickup, which sends an electrical charge, via a rotating glass prism and an electrical amplifier, to another coil beneath a plate of glass or plastic. While stroking this plate the user rotates or 'tunes' the prism until they sense a change in the way the plate feels to the touch. They then compare the prism's turning to a chart of known frequencies and . . . voila, identify the sample. Modifications to the design allow users to diagnose illness in blood samples and, turning these eloptic energies around, to cure them" (p. 105).
6. I cannot find the title or date of Bader's influential article. Navratil and Bader became good friends, Navratil contributing to Bader's (1976), text, *Adolf Wolfli*.
7. Judith Scott had Down syndrome, and she was deaf and could not speak. She was institutionalized at age seven. Forty years later her twin sister removed her from the institution and brought her to Creative Growth.
8. di Maria said that "If the artist asks a teacher 'what should I draw,' we are trained to deflect, 'What are you thinking about?' 'Did you have a dream last night?' 'What color should I use?' 'What color do you like?' 'Do you think it's done?' 'Do *you* think it's done?' 'What happens if you work more?' 'You tell me.' To have that kind of patience for decades is difficult. We believe it allows the voice of the artist to come through."
9. Carl Hendrickson passed away in 2014.

REFERENCES

Always the Sun: Carlo Zinelli at the Venice Biennale. (2013. Retrieved from: http://smokinguns2011.blogspot.com/2013/06/always-sun-carlo-zinelli-at-la-biennale.html.

Bader, A., & Navratil, L. (1976). *Adolf Wolfli*. Lucerne, Switzerland: Bucher.

Ben-Moshe, L. (2013). "The institution yet to come": Analyzing incarceration through a disability lens. In L. J. Davis (Ed.), *The disability studies reader* (pp. 132–143). New York, NY: Routledge.

Berge, J.T. (2000). Beyond outsiderism. In J.T. Berge (Ed.), *Marginalia: Perspectives on outsider art* (pp. 77–101). The Netherlands: De Stadshof Museum for Naïve and Outsider Art.

Bracewell, M. (2013). Paul Laffoley. In R. Rugoff (Ed.), *The alternative guide to the universe* (p. 47). London, England: Hayward.

Cardinal, R. (1972). *Outsider art*. New York, NY: Praeger.

Cardinal, R. (2000). Marginalia. In J.T. Berge (Ed.), *Marginalia: Perspectives on outsider art* (pp. 51–75). The Netherlands: De Stadshof Museum for Naïve and Outsider Art.

Cardinal, R. (2001). The self in self-taught art. In C. Russell (Ed.), *Self-taught art: The culture and aesthetics of American vernacular art* (pp. 68–80). Jackson: University Press of Mississippi.

Cardinal, R. (2008, September). *Outsider art and the autistic creator*. Autism and Talent Conference: Royal Society.

Crossley, R. (1997). *Speechless: Facilitating communication for people without voices*. Victoria, Australia: Dutton.

Di Maria, T. (2013). Interview with Tom di Maria. In C. Daigle (Ed.), *Cultures of the maker: An anthology of subjectivities, dis/abilities, and desires* (pp. 119–123). San Francisco/Oakland, CA: San Francisco Art Institute.

Di Maria, T. (2015). *Proceedings from an Inclusive World: Bridging Communities*. Queens, NY: Queens Museum.

Fiedler, L. (1996). *Tyranny of the normal: Essays on bioethics, theology & myth*. Lincoln, MA: Godine.

Foucault, M. (2003). *"Society must be defended": Lectures at the College De France 1975–1976*. New York, NY: Picador.

Foucault, M. (2009). *History of madness*. New York, NY: Routledge.

Frudden, J. (2013). Hanging inside. In C. Daigle (Ed.), *Cutlures of the maker: An anthology of subjectivities, dis/abilities, and desires* (pp. 119–123). San Fancisco/Oakland, CA: San Francisco Art Institute.

Gugging.org (website). (n.d.). *History [of the House of Artists]*. Retrieved from http://www.gugging.org/index.php/en/haus-der-kuenstler/32/history

Henley, D. (2012). Working with the young outsider artist: Appropriation, elaboration, and building self-narrative. In A. Wexler (Ed.), *Art education beyond the classroom: Pondering the outsider and other sites of learning* (pp. 7–30). New York, NY: Palgrave Macmillan.

Higgs, M. (2011a). *Conversations with Matthew Higgs*. Retrieved from: http://www.museumofeverything.com/exhibition4/pdfs/MatthewHiggs.pdf

Higgs, M. (2011b). Conversations with Matthew Higgs and Tom di Maria. In *The Museum of Everything Exhibition #4.1*. England: The Museum of Everything.

I1 Palazzo di Everything (2013). *The museum of everything presents Carlo Zinelli*. London, England: The Museum of Everything.

jagodzinski, j. (2005). In the realm of the "Real": Outsider art and its paradoxes for art educators. *Journal of Social Theory in Art Education, 25*, 225–254.

jagodzinski, j. (2012). Outside the outside: In the realms of the real (Hogancamp, Johnston, and Darger). In A. Wexler (Ed.), *Art education beyond the classroom:*

Pondering the outsider and other sites of learning (pp. 159–186). New York, NY: Palgrave Macmillan.

Kristoff, N. (2014, February 9). Inside a mental hospital called jail. *The New York Times Sunday Review, 1,* 11.

Krug, D. (1992). Visual cultural practices and the politics of aesthetic discourse. *Working Papers in Art Education, 11*(1), 103–124.

Laffoley, P. (2013). The thanaton III. In R. Rugoff (Ed.), *The alternative guide to the universe* (p. 48). London, England: Hayward.

Laurie, D. (2009). *The secret art: A brief history of radionic technology for the creative individual.* San Antonio, TX: Anomalist Books.

Lieb, R. (2008, fall). From the sideshow to the big top. *Raw Vision. RV, 64,* 22–29.

Lun, K. (2009). Dear Steven. In S.H. Madoff (Ed.), *Art school: Propositions for the 21st century* (pp. 329–339). Cambridge, MA: MIT Press.

Maclagan, D. (2009). *Outsider art: From the margins to the marketplace.* London, England: Reaktion Books.

Maizels, J. (1996). *Raw creation: Outsider art and beyond.* London, England: Phaidon Press.

Miller, L. A. (2013). Museum of everything brings Carlo Zinelli to Venice. *Art in America.* Retrieved from: http://www.artinamericamagazine.com/news-features/news/the-museum-of-everything-brings-carlo-zinelli-to-venice-/

Morgenthaler, W. (1992). *Madness and art: The life and works of Adolf Wolfli* (A. H. Esman, Trans.). Nebraska: University of Nebraska Press. (Original work published 1921).

Morris, R. (2001). The one and the many: Manifest destiny and the internal landscape. In C. Russel (Ed.), *Self-taught art: The culture and aesthetics of American vernacular art* (pp. 117–128). Jackson, MS: University Press of Mississippi.

Navratil, L. (1994). The history and prehistory of the Artists' House in Gugging. In M.D. Hall & E.W. Metcalf, Jr. (Eds.), *The artist outsider: Creativity and the boundaries of culture* (pp. 199–211). Washington, DC: Smithsonian Institution Press.

Pilkington, M. (2013). Symbolic devices: Where art, magic and technology collide. In R. Rugoff (Ed.), *The alternative guide to the universe* (pp. 101–105). London, England: Hayward.

Prinzhorn, H. (1995). *Artistry of the mentally ill: A contribution to the psychology and psychopathology of configuration* (E. von Brockdorff, Trans.), New York, NY: Springer-Verlag Wien. (Original work published 1922).

Rhodes, C. (2000a). *Outsider art: Spontaneous alternatives.* London, England: Thames & Hudson.

Rhodes, C. (2000b). *Outsider art and the mainstream.* In J. T. Berge (Ed.), *Marginalia: Perspectives on outsider art* (pp. 102–117). The Netherlands: De Stadshof Museum.

Rousseau, V. (2013). Visionary architectures. In R. Rugoff (Ed.), *The alternative guide to the universe* (pp. 68–73). London, England: Hayward.

Strausbaugh, J. (2006, September 3). Joe Coleman gets a retrospective at the Tilton gallery in Manhattan. *New York Times.* Retrieved from: http://www.nytimes.com/2006/09/03/arts/design/03stra.html?pagewanted=all&_r=0

The Museum of Everything Presents Carlo Zinelli. Retrieved from: http://www.musevery.com/ilpalazzo/en/zinelli.php#zinelli.php

Thevoz, M. (1994). An anti-museum: The collection de l'art brut in Lausanne. In M.D. Hall & E.W. Metcalf, Jr. (Eds.), *The artist outsider: Creativity and the boundaries of culture* (pp. 62–74). Washington, DC: Smithsonian Institution Press.

Thevoz, M. (2001). *The art brut collection, Lausanne.* Zurich: Swiss Institute for Art Research.

Van Berkum, A. (2000). Outsiderkunst: From discovery to museum art. *Marginalia: Perspectives on outsider art* (pp. 12–50). The Netherlands: De Stadshof Museum.

Vogel, C. (2013, May 23). New guide in Venice. *The New York Times*. Retrieved from: http://www.nytimes.com/2013/05/26/arts/design/massimiliano-gioni-of-venice-biennale.html?pagewanted=all&_r=0

Yentob, A. (Director). (2013). *Imagine: Turning the art world inside out* [Motion picture]. United States: British Broadcasting Corporation. Retrieved from: https://vimeo.com/81888696

Figure 7.1 Photograph of Gerone Spruill (by Leon Borensztein)

7 Gerone Spruill

Chocolate City is inside of all of us, as long as we can have the funk and soul.

(Spruill, as cited in Bair, 2008, p. 2)

Gerone Spruill is a good-looking young Black man of medium height, appearing to be much younger than his 40-plus years. His gaze is disarmingly direct. Most days he wears a cap with his sunglasses perched above. He dresses in neat, sporty, casual clothes, sometimes wearing a vest over his T-shirt. Spruill mostly works with Prismacolor pencils and Sharpie markers on paper. His love for Funk and Soul music of the 70s and 80s drives his work and imagination to an ideal world of cool characters living a good life in his tri-Chocolate City region and home town of Oakland. The characters in Spruill's narratives are based on people he knew in high school when P-Funk (also called P-Funk All Stars, Funk Mob, etc.) was evolving. In his drawings, the conceptually developed characters perform the same kind of music as the original P-Funk artists. Spruill cites musicians such as Ms. Silvers, Brothers Johnson, the Commodores, and particularly the musical genius of George Clinton's Parliament/Funkadelic (P-Funk) as his inspiration. As a visual artist, Spruill is influenced by the album cover artists for Parliament/Funkadelic, Overton Loyd (Parliament), and Pedro Bell (Funkadelic). Loyd and Bell were also inspirations for a generation of African-Americans who found in them an alternate, sophisticated, and humorous view of living in America. Spruill's narratives are inspired by Clinton's wit as a writer, borrowing from Clinton his fictional "Chocolate City" surrounded by "vanilla suburbs" scenarios.

One day in September 2013 I interviewed Spruill as he worked on the back cover of a new album concept called *The Knights of the Chocolate Temple*. The songs read as follows. Side One: "Knights by Nights," "Freaky Dancin'," "I'll Always Stay," "I Like it." Side Two: "The Chocolate Table," "Don't be so Cool," and "I Never Knew." Nearby were the credits, which Spruill says explain who comprises the group Chocolate: Chocolate is Master Gee on Tenor, sax, electric, keyboards, lead and background vocals, words; MC Chuck on grand piano, electric keyboards and synthesizers, lead and background vocals; Ms. Gee plays drums; Ms.

Figure 7.2 Photograph of Gerone Spruill working (by Alice Wexler)

Chuck plays electric rhythm guitars; M. C. Gee plays electric lead guitars and background vocals; G. M. K. on bass guitars, alto sax, lead and background vocals; Milkjay plays trumpets, lead and background vocals; Ms. Jismo on congas and percussion; Ms. Milkjay on trombones. Spruill points to the bottom of the album, "Right here I was going to write, Recorded at Chocolate Studio of Oakland, Oakland California" (personal communication, September, 10, 2013).

Spruill shows me another album cover for the band *Chocolations* with Chocolate Girl. The members of the band include from left (see Figure 7.3), Sir Nose Senior with San Jose Funk, MC Chuk, GMX, and Sir Nose Junior. Mr. Shrimp, the fifth member of the band, Spruill tells me, is not in the drawing. But now he is lost in a fantasy narrative:

> But remember, you can say fried shrimp, but you cannot say, "Look at the shrimp, look at the shrimp," otherwise he'll get angry and start breaking things and you'll have to grab his arm and calm him down. He doesn't like it when people say "Look at the shrimp, look at the shrimp" it bothers him. Well, the reason why it bothers him is because he can't stand when people say "Look at the shrimp, look at the shrimp." I mean, he believes that some people would like to make fun of him. He

> hangs out with the others and they like to impress themselves as the Temptations, the Dells, and especially the Whispers. So that's the type of music that they got inspired, and they want to do the same thing as the Dells, the Whispers and the Temptations were doing back then. (personal communication, September 10, 2013)

In order to understand Spruill's adapted narratives, codes, and autistic iconography, in subsequent paragraphs I introduce a brief history of P-Funk cosmology[1] and compare Clinton's iconoclastic breakdown and recasting of white symbols and narratives to James Berger's (2005) commentary on the fall of the Tower of Babel as the prototype for the fragmentation of language—the genesis of the division between the word and thing that ushered in "ambiguity, irony, negation, artifice, the unconscious, ideology, the subject, the other" (p. 341). The breakdown of language and the counter-linguistic turn,[2] according to Berger, are post-apocalyptic symptomatic responses, the negation of conceptualization and representation following catastrophe. Spruill arrives at a multi-layered, wish-fulfilling narrative with an adaptation of P-Funk's iconography coupled with autistic fragmentation. I query how the linguistic alterity of autism is both a negation and symptom of symbolic, social order.

Figure 7.3 Gerone Spruill, *Chocolations*

P-FUNK COSMOLOGY

> *First we were straight. Straight suits and clean. Then, when the hippies came, we took it to exaggeration. We wore sheets, we wore the suit bags that our suits came in. And it was funny to us, 'cause we come from a barbershop, we knew how to make you look cool, so we never felt uncool.*
> (Clinton as cited in Mills et al., 1998, p. 29)

In *The Funk Era and Beyond: New Perspectives on Black Popular Culture,* Tony Bolden (2008) traces the word *Funk* to the Ki-Kongo word *lu-fuki,* which literally means the body odor of a hard-working man. Such negative associations linked funk to "the most degrading and dehumanizing racial stereotypes associated with blacks, including sexual profligacy, promiscuity, laxness, lewdness, and looseness," the qualities P-Funk celebrates as the antidote to the clean and white (p.15).

P-Funk arrived on the heels of the Civil Rights Movement of racial integration and ideological and political shifts in education, neighborhoods, and social relationships. Legislation[3] brought both gains and losses, writes Francesca Royster (2012), such as the assimilation and cultural possibility of the Black middle class, yet at the same time cemented the circumscribed Black urban areas. Legislation, and the changing living patterns it might produce, does not signify the end of underlying bias and racism (Royster, 2012). Unfortunate examples came at the close of 2013. At some of the most diverse universities, such as University of San Jose in California, racism reappeared in its most blatant and visual forms.[4]

The Vietnam War and the Civil Rights Movement were intricately connected, and the members of the P-Funk bands witnessed firsthand the trauma of the veterans' return. In the song, "March to the Witch's Castle" on the album *Cosmic Slop*, released toward the end of the war, a spare and passionate voice and guitar sings a hymn for returning veterans and condemns the United States government, "Oh lord, give us the strength to understand ourselves, for we are mysterious animals. And as the boys march home to the witch's castle, we will all need your help."

P-Funk is generally understood to refer to a cluster of bands under the guidance of producer and architect George Clinton. Parliament and Funkadelic, which are essentially the same band but with contractual differences, share from the same pool of musicians associated with James Brown's original back-up bands. According to the *Rolling Stone Encyclopedia of Rock and Roll* (2001), the bands were comprised of the most influential and adventurous musicians of the 70s, which left their impact on a broad range of subsequent musicians. In the Post-Soul era of emerging political and economic freedoms in the United States, Clinton imagined "an elsewhere, a space not yet invented" (Royster, 2012, p. 3). Musical performance became "the consummate form in which performers can negotiate the past as well as create new futures" (p. 3). Royster designates this time of shifting Black identity, gender, and sexuality as *Post-Soul eccentric* in which a space was created for non-normative Blackness. Clinton's genius was in fusing psychedelic with Funk and Soul, conceiving the surrealistic mythology and narratives that captured the African-American imagination, and possibly had, as Royster suggests, "a disquieting effect on notions of black nationhood" (p. 212).

Clinton, like other important players in Parliament/Funkadelic, has a mythological personal history evocative of the fictional characters that populate his music; one example is the rumor that he was born in an outhouse in North Carolina. Clinton grew up in Plainfield, New Jersey, forming a Doo Wop band called The Parliaments while working in a barber salon straightening hair. In the 1960s, Clinton moved to Detroit to work as a staff writer for Motown and in 1967, the band now called Parliament had its first major hit (Rolling Stone, 2001).

P-Funk was the platform on which archetypal characters and omnipotent demi-gods played out allegorical episodes of social and moral conflicts on stage, in the albums' cartoon series, and in the apocryphal song lyrics. Funk was the unifier, the cosmology, both deadly serious and riotously witty.

> The roots of this church lay deep in the African polyrhythmic pantheon; its disciples consisted of anyone who sought a quasi-cohesive view of a universe which included a god who danced, and who knew that having a loose booty to shake was as crucial to the keeping of the faith as the rosary was for the Catholic. (Hacker, 2011, para. 2)

If Funk was a religion, Clinton was the pope and messiah. Although the commandments were vague and few, Funk was the goal and the highest level of consciousness.

Clinton co-opted the white visual culture of the era, and "made it black, and made it intergalactic—in this case the mythos of (funky) contact" (para. 5). Kodwo Eshun (1998), in *More Brilliant than the Sun: Adventures in Sonic Fiction*, designates an erotic interpretation to Clinton's alien and mutant tropes. In *Clones of Dr. Funkenstein*, instead of resistance, the audience joyfully succumbs to mutation and de-humanization. Possibly, the most iconic image of Clinton's narratives was the Mothership, a flying saucer that alighted onstage, in Times Square, and in front of the United Nations at dawn, carrying Black space aliens. Mythological events such as this were couched in "real" events, such as the Apollo landing, which made deep impressions on Clinton[5] and the science fiction-Star Trek-Close Encounters-generation. What easily went unnoticed were that Stephen Spielberg's (1977) *Close Encounters of the Third Kind*, and Stanley Kubrick's and Arthur Clarke's (1968) *2001: A Space Odyssey* projected an all-white future. As science fiction writer Minister Faust (n.d.) says, the only Blacks in *Close Encounters* were literally animals. Clinton descended onto the stage as his alter-ego Starchild—evocative of the immortal space being in *2001:*

A Space Odyssey—amid backlit fog with the audience chanting ecstatically "The Mothership Connection is here." He confabulated religion with Black Power, Hindu, and Deaf symbols, such as the Mothership mudra of index and pinky finger extended upward, which Scott Hacker (2011) implies was an extrapolation of the Black-Power fist.

What was the Mothership's destination?[6] Scott Hacker (2011) suggests that the ship was an homage to the Pilgrims' landing on Plymouth Rock and a reminder that African-Americans did not arrive in America on these ships. This quasi-repatriation theme, writes Hacker, is "a semiotic breakdown of the dual meaning of 'funk' " (para 7). Both meanings are sensual and visceral: first the obvious musical meaning—the inexorable message of motion, the physical feel of funk, and second is the earthy, fertile smell of "conception and birth in dirt and secretions" (para. 8). But it was not to a location that African-Americans would go, but a return to roots, "The sense of undifferentiated cosmic unity inherent in Buddhism, the paradox, humor, and dance of Sufism, the ecological implications of quantum mechanics via the implicate[d] order of the universe's interconnectedness, and the surrealism of psychedelic awareness" (para. 12). Rickey Vincent (1996) writes that Funk has been part of the African cosmology; the universe is made of rhythm and harmony, its expression critical to spiritual and mental health.

Non-normative Sexuality

Clinton was confronted with media censorship, but the grassroots movement rebuked public constraints, transforming Funk into a linguistic symbol for all that was good in the world, or the defiance of western values (Gutkovich, n.d.). P-Funk was also misconstrued at times to be misogynist. Yet, the female, and particularly the Mother (or Earth Mother), was a persistent symbol in Funk cosmology. The bands were also reverent advocates of the struggles of Black women and pursued "them with open and ribald sexual aggression at the same time" (Vincent, 1996, p. 216). But P-Funk was the most direct in its overtly non-normative heterosexuality and Black masculinity, intentionally evoking white paternalized notions of erotic bodily encounters, and western anxiety of anomalous representations of desire. P-Funk provided a "new queer space for black heterosexual men" to experience ambiguous and vulnerable relationships with body, sex, and sensuality (Royster, 2012, p. 32).

Margrit Shildrick (2012) and Julia Kristeva (1982) point out the cultural anxiety that the body represents in encounters between self and other. The physically abject body as a threat of contamination underlines the need for body limits and control, and the distinctions and categories we make between ourselves and others. However, people with both visible and "invisible" disabilities are constrained by the same lack of social-culture capital and psychological limitations that are not self-imposed, but are internalized social expectations. Spruill, like other autists in this section, are affected by this internal/external reality. Because Spruill is cognitively astute about his position in the disabled world, he has been most psychologically affected. His psychic preoccupation with self-image most clearly plays out in the events and relationships of his fictional characters, and his admiration for the free-wheeling world of Funk. I will revisit the problem of living between the symbolic world and the "real" in Spruill's and other autists' narratives in this chapter.

SPRUILL'S INFLUENCES: ARTISTS PEDRO BELL AND OVERTON LOYD

In the early 70s fans did not have the internet, or even MTV and VCRs. Serious engagement with the P-Funk bands came through the over-the-top 3-D album covers designed by Pedro Bell and Overton Loyd, accompanied with inserts, posters, and T-shirts. As Clinton's website reminds its audience, fans were lucky to see their bands once a year on tour, and possibly a TV appearance. "Sitting with your big ol' headphones, you shut off the world and stared at every detail of the album art like they were paths to the other side, to the Escape" (Pedro Bell, para. 5). These visceral material things—T-shirts, posters, and LPs—were the stuff of the subculture's "badge of honor . . . your LP was a shield, your T-shirt was armor" (para. 6). Spruill was a teenager in high school, well tuned into his difference. To Spruill these bands were probably a way into a culture he understood, while "they scared the living hell" out of everyone else (para. 6). If you followed them, you were criminalized by polite society. As a Black autist, it must have been a revelation to find the anti-white culture of Funk and Soul visually manifested in Bell and Loyd's psychedelics and linguistic liberties.

Bell lived in the Chicago ghetto, where he learned to draw from his older brothers, and so he is essentially "untrained." He called his work "scartoons" because they were fun but they left a mark. Bell has been described as an urban Hieronymus Bosch and an erotic Black Salvador Dali, co-opting the psychadelia from the Beatles and other nice white bands. Bell first heard of Parliament and Funkadelic on an underground radio station, found the record company's address, and wrote a letter. His first album cover (the first he had ever made) was *Cosmic Slop*, which propelled Funkadelic in a new direction, crystallizing its identity. He populated Funkadelic's album covers under the name Sir Lleb (Bell spelled backwards), with surreal and florid pimps, gladiators, and other unsavory icons. In his liner notes he gave all the musicians nicknames, which is also one of Spruill's pastimes. Bell would draw 36 X 36 inch covers, but the record labels' reductions created tiny worlds of narratives that would often require the use of a magnifying glass. Most significantly, Spruill found a philosophy in this cosmology. His Chocolate City of Oakland, as he calls it, was most likely born in Bell's lexicon and visual world of "sci-fi superheroes fighting the ills of the heart, society and the cosmos" with their overt and covert political puns buried within a maddening visual cacophony (para. 7). Bell and Loyd's work made way for the counter-cultural street art and the bold graphics of graffiti artists of the 70s.

Writing came easily to Bell, while he says that drawing was hard work. He learned the power of words from his father's bible, specifically Genesis and Revelations. The innovative and wild use of hyperbolic grammar in his album cover essays introduced a new vernacular of Black language (Vincent, 1996). Bell writes on MySpace:

> My favorite books growing up were Genesis and Revelations, which somehow inspired me to become obsessed with science fiction. This led me to become fascinated with machinery, and subsequently, automotive technology. Though my teenage interest in sports cars may have been typical, my rabid studies of the infamous car customizer Ed "Big Daddy" Roth (who combined cartoon and horror imagery with automotive design) profoundly affected my outlook on life. (Bell, n.d.)

Loyd's cartoon illustrations, which have been called "Funk Aesthetic," are drawn in a loose pen and ink style. Spruill was particularly influenced by the characters in Parliament, which he brings back to life in his own (for now) fictional band, Chocolate. For example, Sir Nose D'voidoffunk, Starchild's arch nemesis, is featured in the tracks on Loyd's well-known album cover for *Motor Booty Affair*, with the rest of Parliament's cast of funky underwater city characters. Other Parliament characters reappear in Spruill's Chocolate band, such as Rumpofsteelskin, and he has given characters like Starchild and Sir Nose offspring and brothers, or for Master Gee, a twin brother named McGreed.

Loyd has also produced animations and a comic book that were included in Parliament's *Funkentelechy Vs. The Placebo Syndrome* album.[7] Spruill was working on his own comic book for a forthcoming exhibition at Creative Growth in September, 2013, which, like Loyd's, depicts the family of singers on his fictionalized albums. For *Funkentelechy Vs. The Placebo Syndrome*, Loyd illustrates the battle between "the extraterrestrial funk savior Starchild and Sir Nose D'Voidoffunk, who represents all that is unfunky and the suppression of free thought" (Funkatropolis blog spot, 2012, para. 4).

On his website, Loyd writes that he uses art to transcend social and cultural boundaries. His artist's statement reads, "I stand for the possibility that art can generate a breakthrough in communication that might allow us to shift our consciousness, embrace our humanity and access the eternal" (Loyd, para. 4). Loyd is currently the artistic director of Parliament-Funkadelic. Bell, however, has not prospered in later years. Since the death

Figure 7.4 Gerone Spruill, *untitled*

of his manager, Sharon Davis, Bell has been in poor health, living in a single residency occupancy in Chicago, and advertising his original art work for sale. In 2010, the Black Rock Coalition held a fundraiser for Bell to offset his medical costs. It is unclear what the results of the benefit were and what has happened to Bell since.[8]

FUNK AS A "METAPHOR" FOR TRAUMA AND SYMBOLIC DISORDER

Vincent (1996) writes that both orgasm and Funk "thrive in that gap in time when words fall away, leaving nothing but sensation" (p. 3). Funk can be described only by association, such as dirt, sweat, earth, low-down, hot, cool, sex. "Funk is whatever it needs to be, at the time that it is," says Clinton. It is "deliberate confusion" (as cited in Vincent, 1996, p. 4). When defining Funk, writers such as Vincent retreat to a poststructuralist counter-linguistic position because it invites the breakdown of language into pre-symbolic forms. James Berger (2005) defines the counter-linguistic turn as proceeding from transcendence after a traumatic breakdown of the social order. He conceptualizes the body as the default position, like Vincent's falling away of words, leaving only the sensation of the body as the locus of non-symbolic linguistic behavior. The transcendent, Berger writes, is deeply connected to trauma because it lies beyond conceptual categories and is found in the sublime as well as the abject as the progressive urge in the search for a new non-linguistic order.[9] In *The Curious Incident of the Dog in the Night-time*, discussed in Chapter Three (this volume), the wailing of Christopher's mother at the revelation of her husband's betrayal, and the simultaneous reunion with her son is an example of the breakage of the symbolic order followed by transcendence.

Under the influence of Saussure, nothing outside of language was real. Berger points out how poststructuralism of the latter half of the twentieth century reveled in the "post-Babel, Saussurean condition," liberated from the imaginary correspondence between life and language (p. 343). But the counter-linguistic turn, although motivated by poststructuralism, also emphasizes the language of local meanings and textual analysis, particularly with difference and alterity, and underscores the destabilizing effect of binaries, such as when a negative label is reclaimed by the population it categorizes, such as "crip" and "queer." Once owned, the signifiers take on political rather than pejorative meaning. Alterity, therefore, has had an important place in this conversation because of its position outside of, and defined in opposition to, the symbolic order. The cognitively and linguistically impaired, writes Berger, have helped neurotypicals understand how social trauma affects thinking and feeling in a symbolically mediated world. He points to the films *Billy Budd* and *Forrest Gump* as examples of normative self-scrutiny.

In this postmodern standoff between language and its representation of the traumatic and transcendent, the "wild children" of the Enlightenment emerge as Berger's postmodern (neurological) wild children. These are the non-linguistic children, who are not outside of social and cultural history as their eighteenth century predecessors were thought to be, but rather outside the social-symbolic order. By standing outside the order they are in the position to test the capacity of that order and present "traumatic-transcendent possibilities of human existence outside language" (p. 347). Berger asks how these children are the effects of modern social trauma in which language itself, as the transmitter of the social order, is also broken.

The African Diaspora, like the Holocaust, was a historical catastrophe, and as such an example of the breakdown of the social, symbolic order because, in its unimaginable horror, it defies representation and comprehension, consequently producing enduring effects on representation and communication. Clinton's neologisms, the hybridity of sacred signs and religious references, give form to the African-American Diaspora in the invented worlds of Funk, rendering the African-American experience as almost unrecognizable in the symbol systems of white visual culture. The P-Funk's Mothership, and its outlandish visual and musical performance, is an example of semiotic breakdown in Clinton's negation of the signifiers of white culture. Instead, he employs the open-endedness of extraterrestrial iconography and the reclamation of negative Black stereotypes and labels. Like the disability community's redemption of "crip" and "queer," Clinton reclaims all negative associations with the Black body.

In the following paragraphs, I question how the complexity of Spruil's response to the traumatic-transcendent iconography of P-Funk and his own linguistic disorientations are confabulated into narrative that sometimes overlaps, sometimes parallels, and sometimes diverges with his life.

THE LEGACY CONTINUED IN GERONE SPRUILL

Spruill is resurrecting Funk's sensational, sensual art form lost to the internet, hyper-media, MTV, and MP3s. Spruill's Sir Noses are not the anti-heroes of their predecessor. The two brothers—Sir Nose Senior and Sir Nose Junior—are hybrids, borrowed from Batman and Robin, living in the smooth White Chocolate City of San Jose. Like Batman and Robin, they have their female sidekick, Nosegirl. Spruill talks about the antics of his characters like a tolerant father who can't help being amused. He chuckles as he tells about another Nose character, Whitenose, who is "this crazy midget guy." The brothers "agreed that he should stay out of the way, let them do their business their way. And although he does have a crush on Nosegirl . . . I tell ya," he laughs, "and I'd say they're doing just good to protect and defend the smooth White Chocolate City of San Jose." Spruill shakes his head again and laughs:

> It's going to be really cool when I get those in check. Yeah, and of course the Sir Noses, they also have girlfriends as well. Well, Sir Nose senior has a girlfriend named Percia Baxtin, because he loves dark-skinned women. And Sir Nose Junior, he dates Percia's sister, Rhonda Baxtin. (personal communication, September, 12, 2013)

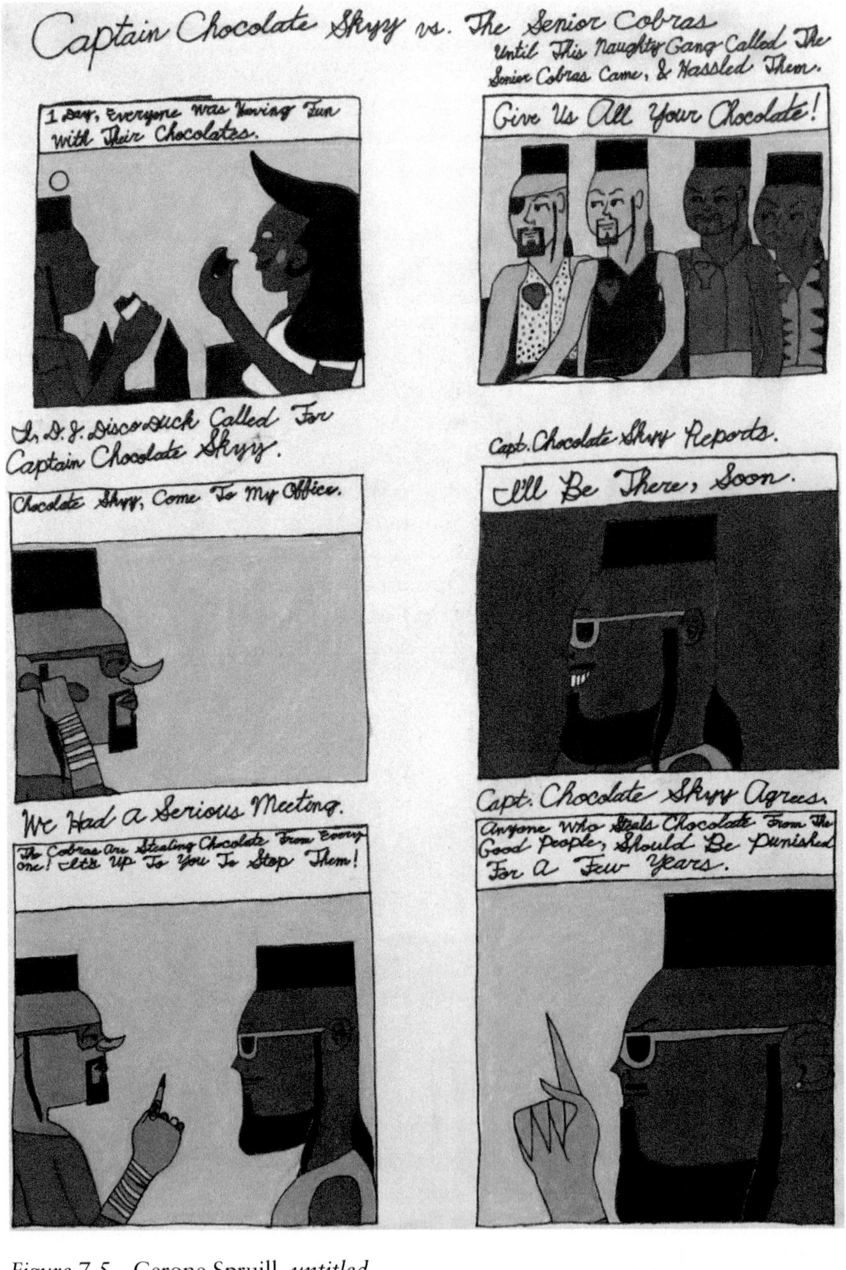

Figure 7.5 Gerone Spruill, *untitled*

The next exhibition at Creative Growth, *Recto Verso*, opening September 19, 2013, was a week away, which would feature several of the artists' work in visual and textual images. I asked Spruill about the characters in his comic book *The Chocolate All-Stars*, included in the exhibition. The main characters are Captain Chocolate Sky and his tall women Fudgie and Brownie. The Captain's mission is to defend the Sweet Dark Chocolate City of Oakland, a recurring theme of Spruill's. "And he has a cool weapon called *Shotgun*, that's spelled *Chokgun*," he says with a sly smile. He uses the gun to capture criminals, which shoots chocolate liquid that hardens into a dark chocolate coating, "like you see on the dip cones. And then the second heroes, these are beautiful, they're called Women in Black," who are meant to be similar to *Men in Black*:

> They wear black casual shirts with their black coats. And yes these ladies, and yes these women in black do wear black penny loafers as well. So the first one, Mimi, the intelligent one, and her side kick Zayna, are really cool as well. And a lot of people say, "How do you spell Zayna?" And I say you spell Zayna (writing in the air) Z-A-Y-N-A. And then the number three, the third superhero, is Hong Fong Chewy. He's half black and half Chinese because his father is Chinese and his Mom is Black, and he also likes to defend and protect the Sweet Dark Chocolate City of Oakland. And so he gets along with Captain Chocolate Sky, and he also gets along with Women in Black. And so the fourth superheroes, they're really cool, the fourth ones are Lady Stretch and Micro Man. [He visibly delights in his puns]. So Lady Stretch, she's similar to either Plastic Man from VC comics or she's like Mr. Fantastic from Fantastic Four. While her hubby Micro Man can shrink into miniature size, and you can use the microscope to see how short he gets. So they're all working with me to help protect the Sweet Dark Chocolate City of Oakland. (personal communication, September 12, 2013)

Parliament's 1975 album *Chocolate City* probably had the most influence on Spruill, who makes it relevant again to life in Oakland. The record was an unequivocal statement about the Civil Rights Movement and the "Blackification" of Washington, D.C. as the "Chocolate City." On the cover the Washington monuments drip with melting chocolate, the inspiration for Spruill's chocolate ammunition. The lyrics of the title song prophetically sing out, "We're gainin' on ya."

"When I Was a Baby I Did Good"

Spruill described himself as a healthy baby until age two. But in November, a month after his second birthday, he had an asthma attack. His mother took him to the general hospital, where he was diagnosed with autism. His mother, he says, did not understand what autism was, not surprisingly since it was only in the 1960s that autism was a diagnosis independent of schizophrenia. Spruill, however, is acutely aware of the diagnostic medical language, quoting from memory the classic "Terrible Triad" of impairments of communication, imagination, and social interaction, which he says can be found in combination with other disabilities. "It is also abnormal subjectivity, accepting fantasies rather than reality" (personal communication, September 12, 2013). Ironically, his description reminded me of the infinite variation of the label and the distortion of its clinical representations. His affected objectivity masked the burden of his intellectual understanding of the label. "But then sometimes I just wish that my life would have been cool if I had never been diagnosed with autism. Then I would have been able to communicate, reason, and interact around age two and three, age four, and age five" (personal communication, September 12, 2013). His yearning for normality and feelings of loss were a constant theme in his life and caused severe depression.

Because his mother "didn't understand what autism was," she sent him to Birch Children's Center in San Francisco. Spruill became agitated while talking about being a four-year-old away from home:

> And I was so young. I wasn't ready yet, 'cause I got homesick. I just didn't like the idea of not being with my mom and stuff. But she said, "Well, you have to do this in order to communicate, you got autism." So I stayed at the Birch Children's Center from Friday June 23 of 1978. But the good news is that my mom came to visit me. My birthday was here and all sorts of stuff. And the best part was I got to spend a few weeks with her. But I was glad when they helped me to communicate, to reason and interact with others more around ages five, six, and seven. (personal communication, September 12, 2013)

Spruill graduated from Birch Children's Center on December 4, 1980, and, he says presciently, the 70s were gone. He was learning to talk when introduced by his mother and three cousins to Parliament/Funkadelic. "When I was in a residential school I was going to tell everyone that I liked Parliament/Funkadelic, and they also understood that I liked classic disco as well" (personal communication, September 12, 2013). But they knew he didn't like rock music, he says, smiling. After graduating he returned home and entered East Bay Activity Center in Oakland, a private school for children with disabilities.

Spruill received special education services on entering the Oakland public schools. Toward graduation he was mainstreaming in several classes and receiving high grades. After graduating Oakland Technical High School in 1992, Spruill wanted to go to California College of the Arts (CCA), "but it turned out that no one had a check of 50,000 for me to pay tuition"

Figure 7.6 Gerone Spruill, *Lady Stretch and Micro Man*

(personal communication, September 12, 2013). He went to a community college instead, which didn't work out for him. His reason was simply that it wasn't the right college. I suspect that a two-year college signaled failure, having anticipated going to a four-year art college.

Spruill's voice during his disclosure about dropping out of college and his hopes of going to CCA further revealed his mourning for a life that might have been, a life of "normalcy." This notion is substantiated by the beliefs of others at Creative Growth that he would rather not be presented under the banner of a disabled or outsider artist. Gallery director Jennifer Strate O'Neal has known Spruill for twelve years, and has seen his growing awareness of difference and its social limitations devolve into a deep level of sadness. She sometimes accompanies Spruill to art openings and "for 15 or 20 minutes people don't know that he has a disability. And it's maybe a little more heartbreaking that way because all of a sudden people realize it, and then he realizes it" (personal communication, September 16, 2013) O'Neal says that Spruill does not take advantage of the Creative Growth community, unlike most of the artists who are immersed in the social and professional environment that the center offers. On outings to galleries, museums, and picnics, he alienates himself from the group or doesn't go at all.

Spruill looks forward to starting a business he calls *Chocolate City of Oakland Records and Film-Works*. He said during one interview that being at Creative Growth was a sort of holding space until "things get real cool," and his business gets started. Several of the staff are frustrated and concerned by his distractedness, restlessness, and impatience, the self-imposed quasi-isolation in which he waits for a music career like George Clinton's, and for his life to imitate the elaborate relationships he gives to his cast of characters. Spruill lives with his mother and works as a DJ at night. He longs to find his own apartment, which has become a source of anxiety and depression. But of the greatest importance for him is to find a partner.

His erotic preoccupation with feet, however, has narrowed the field. The fetish began, he says, at age three while watching what he called a "classic" Popeye cartoon episode. Popeye's future girlfriend, Olive Oil, wore black steel-toed boots. He liked them not only because they were black, but also because the soles were dark grey. "And I just imagined her touching Popeye with them . . . like her boots touching his face, and I said sssshh, man, I wish one lady could do that to me one of these days." As Spruill grew into a teenager he watched comedy shows and saw girls wearing dark brown penny loafers with black socks. "That also encouraged me to appreciate a woman's pretty feet more." Later, a high school junior touched him with her "glamorous feet. That's when she tapped on one of my white tennis shoes nice and slow." Spruill likes penny loafers by Bass, black steel-toed shoes made by Dr. Martens or Golden Fox, and black RTC dress shoes from the Navy, as well as working shoes made by San Antonio Shoes (SAS). Spruill showed me Take Time shoes made by SAS on his cell phone. "And I also find these attractive on a woman, no matter what they say and what they think. And it's perfect for walking tours and sight-seeing. And they'll make a woman's pretty feet feel comfortable no matter what." He adds, as long as they are worn with black socks, black tights, or deep black nylons. "And I hope that one day one special single lady will come to my rescue. That's only if she likes a man who appreciates feet" (personal communication, September 12, 2013).

Spruill is aware of censorship and negative responses to his obsession, and he is forthright in claiming his right to his sexuality. In a collection of written works compiled by Creative Growth writing workshop director Matt Dostal in 2009, he writes in "My Manifesto:"

> What is wrong with you? What are you so afraid of? Are you afraid of me? Well, guess what, I'm one of those cool freaks. Yes, I have a foot-fetish. Not the kind that you think I have. And I for one would rather be with people who can love and accept me for what I am and who I am, than people who thrive on hate. Yes, I have a foot-fetish, a different type. The same man who does cartooning and deejaying for you. Do you hate me now? Do you? Do not hate me, hate yourselves. I used to be afraid like you back then. The good news is I'm not afraid anymore. I'm proud of who I am and I'm also proud of other people that care for me so much that they're willing to stand up and fight to be what they wanna [sic] be. Guess what, I'm proud to be a footplayer. I don't care what you think is wrong. I'm tired of hearing what's appropriate and what's not appropriate.

The sexual pleasure of disabled people is usually fetishized, denied, or ignored as inappropriate behavior by heteronormative standards. While all responses are damaging, the negative meaning that silence conveys is harder to challenge (Shildrick, 2012). Devaluation of the sexuality of disabled people occurs in myriad ways beginning in childhood, in which negativity is internalized because of the intentional omission from sex education, the close adult surveillance of social events, and the inaccessibility of sexual healthcare. But the pervasive, sometimes subtle, infantilization is probably the most humiliating for young adults, such as Spruill (Shildrick, 2012). Shildrick examines these unquestioned conventional responses to non-normative sexuality and the tenuousness of the social sexual order in general; tenuous because most covert and overt sexual rules are driven by unconscious fears. Thus, the potential of a breakdown of order is persistent. Because Spruill exists with other disabled people in a community controlled by normate[10] standards, his displays of eroticism outside the parameters of a white heteronormative society is problematic for the Creative Growth staff responsible for any discomfort or transgression within the community. In such cases, Creative Growth assumes institutional governance in maintaining social order.[11]

In *The History of Sexuality*, Michel Foucault (1979) notes that although sexuality might be constructed and controlled by hegemonic, heteronormative

Figure 7.7 Gerone Spruill, *untitled*

power, it is too volatile to restrain. And, as Shildrick theorizes, it is this fear of sexual volatility that threatens normative categories, self-control, and self-definition. So, while supposedly a private matter, sexuality has always been under watchful government scrutiny, particularly impacting people with disabilities whose self-control is suspect and therefore threatening to normative stability. "This discourse on modern sexual repression holds up well, owning no doubt to how easy it is to uphold," writes Foucault (1979, p. 5). It becomes a "natural" part of the political, capitalist, and middle class order. To speak of sex outright, then, is in itself a subversive act. "We are conscious of defying established power" (p. 6). The boldness with which Spruill discusses his fetish can be interpreted as either autistic or courageous. It is probably both. The artists in the subsequent chapters each manage their sexuality in ways that are not optimal, and reflect the impoverished sexuality and disability discourse. But as a Black man, Spruill also found in the Funk cosmology the deep roots of African philosophy of spiritual and sexual comfort, and all aspects of the body. I imagine that Funk is for Spruill the refutation of western culture's censorship and repression. In Spruill's manifesto, he repudiates appropriateness for the covert message of control it sends Black sexuality, exposing "the unpackaged self for all to see" (Vincent, 1996, p. 5)

NOTES

1. Scott Hacker offers a florid and comprehensive summary of P-Funk cosmology:

> Dig: The secret of funk was placed inside the pyramids 5,000 years ago. If we had stayed tuned (To pyramid power? Connect this to the Chariots of the Gods melieu of the same era, and the visiting spacemen theme of P-Funk) to The One, we wouldn't be in the mess we're in. "Mother earth is pregnant for the third time. We all have knocked her up." It took the arrival of Dr. Funkenstein to unearth the funk and usher its viral spread over the de-funkatized surface of the planet. The problem with earth is that it is devoid of funk—earth is the "Unfunky UFO"—due to the unfunky operations of the white house, the pentagon, Nixon, businessmen and greed in general, and an overall lack of supergroovalisticprosifunkstica-tion. The symbol for the collective greed/war mentality is embodied by Sir Nose, D'Void of Funk ("I have always been D'Void of Funk, I shall continue to be D'Void of Funk . . ."), who relentlessly pimpifies the people "By sucking their brains until their ability to think was amputated . . . pimpifying their instincts until they were fat, horny, and strung out" in pursuit of "financial security or an eternal supply of TRIM," the result being that "the very source of life energies on earth have become the castrated target of anile bamboozelry from homo sapiens' rabid attempts to manipulate the omnipotent forces of nature."
>
> The ruthless whoring of Funkentelechy has brought mother nature to her knees, and we're pinned beneath them. "The frenzied incipience of pimpification hath risen to the point of cosmicide." In other words, we all have a bad case of the Placebo Syndrome, having traded in "the real thing" for a civilization comprised of cheap imitations, which is now crumbling around us. The Placebo Syndrome has given the body politic weak knees, which

are doomed to give out from under us at any moment. We no longer feel the pulse, or smell the deep draughts of the Cosmic Slop which generates the funk. "When the signal is too weak, you're in the syndrome." (http://stuckbetweenstations.org/2011/01/11/cosmology-of-pfunk/)

2. Berger's (2005) terminology for the "counter-linguistic turn" is derived from the variations of the linguistic turn, which has "provided the theoretical bases for the humanities and some of the social sciences for much of the twentieth century. Concurrently, however, and with increasing influence over the past fifteen or twenty years, we can see in the academic humanities, in some literary fiction, and in areas of popular culture varieties of what we might call a counter-linguistic turn" (p. 344). It is not meant to be, Berger says, a direct repudiation of the linguistic turn, but rather that there *is* an other of language, whether or not this other can be conceptualized, and the language does not go 'all the way down' " (p. 344).
3. Royster cites the important legislation of the Civil Rights Act of 1964 and the Voting Rights Act of 1965, ushering in greater representation and access.
4. See *New York Times*: http://www.nytimes.com/2013/11/23/us/racial-abuse-is-alleged-at-san-jose-state-university.html?_r=0
5. In Ricky Vincent's review of *George Clinton and P-funk: An Oral History*, he quotes Clinton as saying about Apollo, "I doubted logic . . . 'cause the minute you say what goes up don't have to come down . . . it was no longer true. So to me, everything else was suspect" (http://www.amazon.com/exec/obidos/ASIN/0380793784/gemotrack1–20/ref=nosim).
6. The final destination of the Mothership was actually the Smithsonian Institution, where it still remains. But Minister Faust believes that Clinton's message is that the Mothership is in your mind (http://io9.com/minister-faust-explains-the-meaning-of-george-clintons-487712241).
7. Funkentelechy, or Funk, intellect, and technology, evokes the Nation of Islam's term "Tricknology." Clinton often parodied the nation's invented terminology. However, Minister Faust writes, "Clinton's Mothership mission wasn't NOI radioactive vengeance, but radio-active dance" (para. 25, retrieved from: http://io9.com/minister-faust-explains-the-meaning-of-george-clintons-487712241). According to Brian Benson, Clinton might have been referring to the transcendentalist term *entelechy*, which is a realization rather than a potentiality, or a vital agent or force directing growth (para. 7, retrieved from: http://archive.birdhouse.org/words/benson/transcefunkadentalism.html).
8. At the time of the benefit concert, Bell was suffering from a foot infection, on dialysis three days a week, and losing his sight to macular degeneration.
9. The after-effect of trauma, however, can be either conservative or progressive, terrorism or transcendence. "Terrorism holds that the original, primal, pre-Babel language must be restored, and that the restoration can be achieved only through violence. The move toward transcendence finds revealed in the catastrophe the idea that language in any form is inadequate" (Berger, 2005, p. 343). The Tower of Babel serves as Berger's metaphor for the symbolic order. But it is also a trope for the Twin Towers and describes the post-apocalyptic years after the fall as a return to the old symbolic order, led by President Bush.
10. *Normate* is a term coined by Rosemary Garland-Thomson (1997) in *Extraordinary Bodies*. Normate is a general term designating the imagined and unexamined "everyman" who is the self-determined, independent, and rational narrator of neurotypical texts: "This neologism names the veiled subject position of cultural self, the figure outlined by the array of deviant others whose marked bodies shore up the normate's boundaries. The tern *normate* usefully designates the social figure through which people can represent themselves as definitive human beings" (p. 8)

11. According to Foucault, underneath the appearance of democratic decision-making, government is at the center of the social order through the network of institutional regulation.

REFERENCES

Bair, M. (2008, Spring). The Cocoa-flavored world of Gerone Spruill. *Oakbook, 3.*

Bell, P. (n.d.) *georgeclinton.com.* Retreived from: http://georgeclinton.com/family/pedro-bell/

Bell, P. (n.d.). *Myspace.* Retrieved from: https://myspace.com/pedrodelic

Berger, J. (2005). Falling towers and postmodern wild children: Oliver Sacks, Don DeLilo, and turns against language. *PMLA, 120,* 341–361.

Bolden, T. (Ed.). (2008). *The funk era and beyond: New perspectives on black popular culture.* NewYork, NY: Palgrave Macmillan.

Dostal, M. (2009). (Ed.). *When in the world did I think of?* Oakland, CA: Creative Growth Art Center.

Editors, Rolling Stone. (2001). *The Rolling Stone encyclopedia of rock & roll.* New York, NY: Touchstone.

Eshun, K. (1998). *More brilliant that the sun: Adventures in sonic fiction.* London, England: Quartet.

Faust, M. (n.d.). *Minister Faust explains the meaning of George Clinton's mothership.* Retrieved from: http://io9.com/minister-faust-explains-the-meaning-of-george-clintons-487712241

Foucault, M. (1979). *History of sexuality. Vol. I.* (R. Hurley, Trans.). London, England: Allen Lane.

Funkatropolis blog spot. (2012, April 22). *Overton Loyd makes the p-funk universe just a little bit funkier with his cool artwork.* Retrieved from: http://funkatropolis.blogspot.com/2012/04/overton-loyd-makes-p-funk-universe-just.html#.UqtQiPRDuSo

Garland-Thomas, R. (1996). *Extraordinary bodies: Figuring physical disability in American culture and literature.* New York, NY: Columbia University Press.

Gutkovich, V. (n.d.). *Funk is its own reward: The moving power of Parliament Funkadelic.* Masters Thesis. Wesleyan University. Retrieved from: http://wesscholar.wesleyan.edu/cgi/viewcontent.cgi?article=1023&context=etd_hon_theses

Hacker, S. (2011). *Can you get that? The cosmology of p-funk.* Retrieved from: http://stuckbetweenstations.org/2011/01/11/cosmology-of-pfunk/

Kristeva, J. (1982). *Powers of horror: An essay on abjection.* New York, NY: Columbia University Press.

Kubrick, S. (Producer and director), & Clarke, A. (Writer). (1968). *2001: A space odyssey* [Motion picture]. United States: Metro-Goldwyn-Mayer.

Loyd, O. (n. d.). Retrieved from: http://www.overtonloyd.com/exhibits6.htm

Mills, D., Alexander, L., Stanley, T., & Wilson, A. (Eds.). (1998). *George Clinton and p-funk: An oral history.* New York, NY: Avon.

Royster, F. (2012). *Sounding like a no-no: Queer sounds and eccentric acts in the post-soul era.* Ann Arbor: University of Michigan Press.

Shildrick, M. (2012). *Dangerous discourses of disability, subjectivity and sexuality.* London, England: Palgrave Macmillan.

Spielberg, S. (Director). (1977). *Close encounters of the third kind* [Motion picture]. United States: Columbia Pictures.

Vincent, R. (1996). *Funk: The music, the people, and the rhythm of the one.* New York, NY: St. Martin's Griffin.

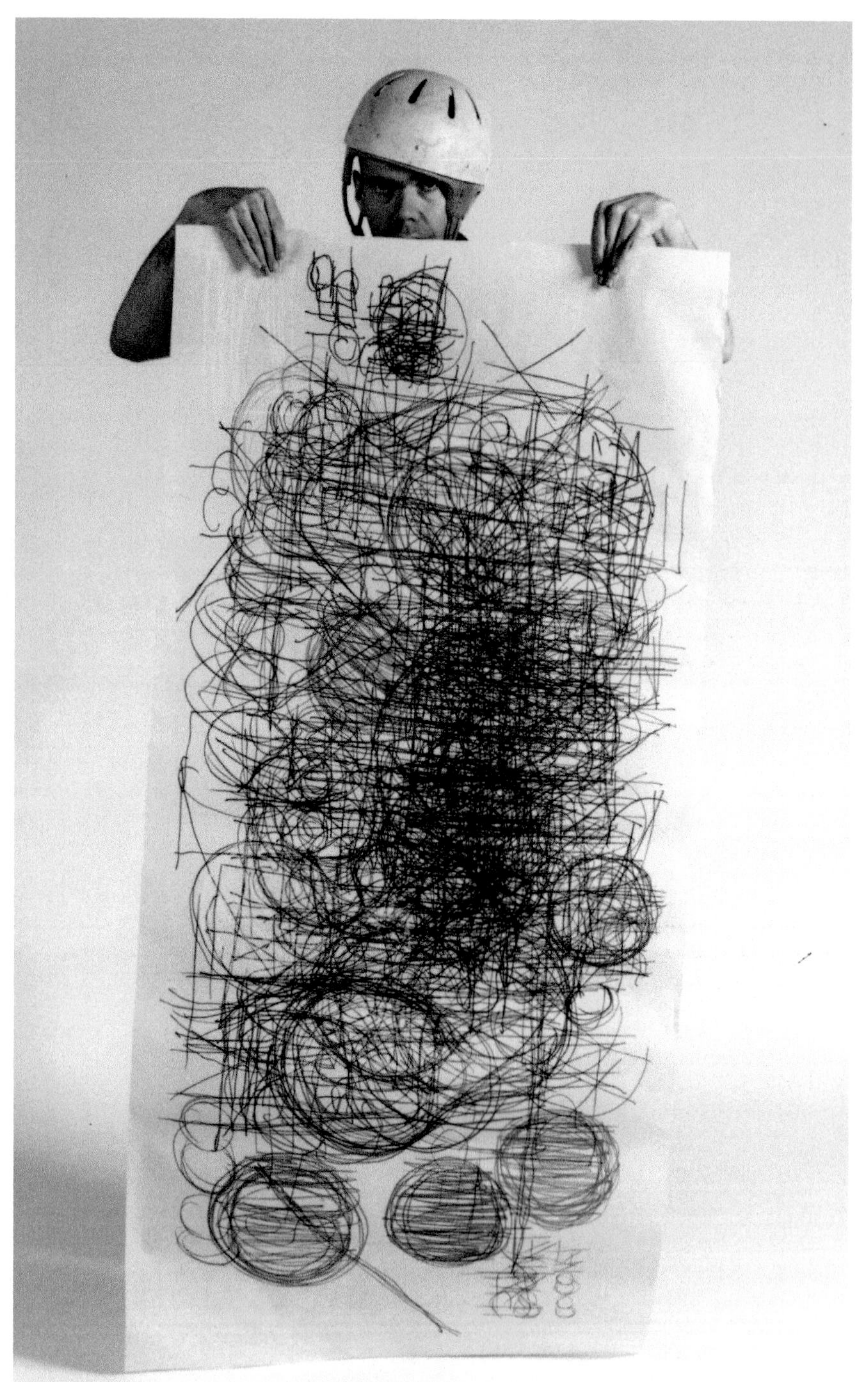

Figure 8.1 Photograph of Dan Miller (by Leon Borensztein)

8 Dan Miller

Dan Miller is a 53-year-old man on the autism spectrum diagnosed with a seizure disorder. His seizures have caused him to fall on several occasions, which is the reason that he wears a bicycle helmet at Creative Growth. His helmet has become an endearing accessory and as identifiable as his textual paintings and drawings. Director Tom di Maria calls Miller's introduction to art accidental. He spent school hours in special education classes and weekends in his uncle's hardware store. As an adult, he attended a day center in Castor Valley in which the staff noted his drawing skills and contacted Creative Growth. Miller lives as a legal adult at his caretaker's private home with two other clients, and uses assisted transportation to commute to Creative Growth. His mother passed away in 2002, but his sister Cara lives nearby and he visits her often. The Regional Center of the East Bay (RCEB) acts as a representative payee for Miller's social security benefits and makes sure that funds are handled appropriately. The RCEB funds a case manager who visits the facility at least four times a year to monitor services. According to their 2010–2012 annual review, Miller requires staff assistance when visiting the local community—which he enjoys fully—because he lacks safety awareness. Also, according to the RCEB, he has a history of aggression when upset, but these outbursts no longer occur.

Cara is seven years younger than Dan and therefore her memory of his nascent years is vague. Their parents were divorced early in Cara's life, their mother remarried when she was six, and their biological father died when she was 18. Their grandmother, Helen Chase, lived next door and took care of them when their parents were at work. Dan's love of language is traced back to his grandmother, an elementary school teacher for over 30 years, who taught him how to read, write, and talk. Chase appears in his work often, says his studio assistant Veronica Rojas. When Cara was past the age of learning to read and write, Chase and Dan continued to study these childhood textbooks. She used basic spelling drills, and Dan committed the words to memory. His excellent spelling is attributable to these nightly drills, and his visual texts, Cara says, are also directly related to them.

In hindsight, Cara admits to sibling rivalry, jealous that her older brother with a disability needed extra attention from their busy and strict parents. Although they attended to her needs, she thought her life was limited by the restrictions of Dan's more compelling needs. Her childhood was a process of learning and understanding that her older brother could not provide her with the conventional relationship she wanted. Cara is still learning and understanding what autism means for her brother. As an adult she reflects on her childhood feelings and impressions of his disability, and she might have wondered in her own limited way, she says, "How much was in there?" With his artistic success and subsequent social awakening in the past ten years, she speculates that "he can be himself, more. I think he has learned that, as well as the rest of us. I think it makes him happy, too" (personal communication, July, 15, 2014).

Because Miller has worked in a community of artists at Creative Growth for twenty years, he has become a better communicator. Cara says that he still cannot understand nuanced questions or abstract concepts that take him out of the context of the moment. She is not sure "what he gets and doesn't get," but she thinks it unlikely that he would respond appropriately to a critical injury, such as calling an ambulance, or any spontaneous event that disrupts his fairly regulated world.

But Miller can take a clock radio apart and make it work, "he can understand patterns and machines, he can figure those things out" (C. Miller, personal communication, June 13, 2014). His uncle owned a shop that did custom building work for bakeries and aircraft. The shop used the hardware and parts that attract Miller, and although she believes his obsession with utilitarian objects is innate, it was a likely place for it to germinate. Outings with Dan are typically to hardware stores, where he buys light bulbs and tools. "He's always loved them, he will go to the lighting section and turn on and off the lights, switches, or anything with a mechanical value" (personal communication, June 13, 2014). He has made three-dimensional toilets, drills and staple guns in clay and wood, all of which can be found in his drawings and paintings. It was also at his uncle's shop that he discovered the Granger catalogue, a favorite amongst his magazines. Since childhood he confiscated the catalogues and drew on their pages in black pen, which is still his favorite drawing tool, "even though we had big boxes of crayons." In these earlier times, Dan could draw through a ream of paper in a day. But Creative Growth has slowed him down, encouraging him to develop his drawings more fully, which includes an increased use of color.

STUDIO RELATIONSHIPS

Miller enjoys summer camp every year, from which he had just returned during my visit in early September, 2013. Miller and Rojas were working on multiple prints that he painted in quick succession. The edition of 40 prints was left to Creative Growth from a commission with the New York Hilton Hotel. The large painting with its many color tones and layers that the Hilton chose to reproduce in silkscreen did not transfer well into the new medium. They subsequently chose another painting and donated the first edition to Creative Growth. At our first introduction he held out his hand, made direct eye contact, and asked if I was Judy, which he calls many female guests. Cara says that Judy was one of his first counselors as an adolescent who made an impact on him, and she speculates that he is looking for her:

> She was an older counselor/helper to him and probably one of the first people he remembers who was kind to and supportive of him. . . . I also think it was when he started to have feelings for girls at that age; a first love type of person, if you will. I think he really liked her. (C. Miller, personal communication, July, 15, 2014)

According to the RCEB, Miller can write up to 100 words. While I observed him painting he said, "Click, click, click, right. The light goes click, click, gently. Fire, right, fire. Aunt Jean had a fire. Aunt Jean, right? Light bulb goes click, click, click. Gently." Miller asks Rojas to spell "gently." Then he asks her to spell "get down," and she spells it. "Right, light, goes click, click. BEHAVE, right?" Rojas adds "gently" after each sentence. She tells me that when Miller is agitated he says click, click loudly. The same content of dialogue communicates his changing moods by the tone and volume of his voice. Today his agitation is escalating, but he can also be very playful with his "clicks." It is a hot day and Rojas reminds him to add "gently."

Figure 8.2 Photograph of Dan Miller working (by Alice Wexler)

The clicks and light bulbs are detectable in his thickly layered work. Miller began his work on a table but now Rojas moves it to an easel, and he asks for dark brown paint (see Figure 8.2). He stops and waits restlessly as Rojas finds the paint. He will usually choose one color scheme if he decides to use paint. Depending on his mood, he might choose to work in ink, graphite, markers, or pencils. He works so quickly that Rojas must be ready with new paper before he over-works his drawing, which seems to be a concern of the Creative Growth staff and part of her job as an assistant. Rojas has been Miller's assistant since the "Large Works" exhibition at the Ricco/Maresca Gallery in New York in 2010. Large paintings were commissioned by the gallery, and an assistant was needed to accommodate Miller with the large-format paper and change of workspace. She cut the paper, set up a studio space with materials, and made sure he had the environment he needed to produce large works. The relationship was so beneficial to Miller that di Maria asked her to continue working with him, which she has done until now.

Miller leaves the easel and begins a new work on the table. He writes MARIA in rows (see Figure 8.3). Maria Hartikainen is a personal ceramics instructor he works with on Tuesdays. He chooses light blue and later picks up a black pen. Miller says "Maria, right? Maria, right?" This is an unusual painting, says Rojas, he doesn't often repeat one word. "This is a love letter to Maria" (personal communication, September 5, 2013). Miller asks for red, a big departure from the blue that is fading to white. He adds red to the perimeter of the painting, sometimes intruding onto the blue until he veers off into the middle.

Figure 8.3 Letter to Maria (photograph by Alice Wexler)

TUESDAY WITH MARIA

The following Tuesday in September, Miller rolls out clay for his slab boxes. His work with Hartikainen is fairly minimalist in form, but his glazes and sgraffito mirror the complex calligraphy of his two dimensional work (see Figure 8.3). Miller announces, "Richard isn't here. Richard went to Berkeley." Miller's spontaneous thoughts lead to light bantering between them. Maria answers, "Richard's not here, right, Danny." "No, No, Maria, No, No."

As Hartikainen helps Danny choose the size of the cardboard that will become the sides of his boxes, he says, "Pick up the empty cans, no, pick up the empty cans, no. Leave it in the ground."[1] They return to rolling clay and Danny says, "Dark brown, right." He moves closer to Maria and smiles, "Maria, Maria, Maria, right." Miller gives me a sidelong glance as if looking upon an interloper, the eavesdropper that I have become.

Maria pats down the clay, and Danny watches and says, "No, no, no." Maria says, "No, Danny." As he is about to put the clay through the roller he says, "It's not a toy, it's not a toy." And Maria leaves him to roll the clay. He turns toward her and repeats, "It's not a toy." He stops one more time, looking back, perhaps wanting to know where Maria went. He gets an exacto knife to take off the extraneous clay from the roller and looks for Maria.

Danny finds Maria and brings her back. They roll the clay together. Danny says "Around." Maria says, "The other way," and Danny says, "The other way, right . . . with sausage? The Pepsi can will cut you awful bad."

Danny cuts out the clay with an exacto knife. Maria walks away and comes back with another piece of cardboard. Danny says, "Light bulbs are round." Maria repeats, "They're round, right?" Danny changes the subject, "Pancake and bacon and eggs for dinner, right? Light bulbs are round." Maria says they are round. Danny says, "Jennifer, right?" Maria looks at Danny and says, "Jennifer, right, where is Jennifer?"[2]

"Down here, light bulbs are round. Dark brown."

Maria points to another piece of clay for Miller to pound, he says, "Light bulbs are round." Maria asks if the clay is sticky, Danny says, "Yeah," and Maria pulls out some dryer clay and says, "This is better." Maria walks away. Danny pulls clay out of the bag and pounds it.

DANNY: "Wait wait, right right."
MARIA: "What did you say?"
DANNY: "Get more clay."
MARIA: "More clay? You have clay here, this is good. You see here?" Maria points to the seam of the slabs meeting to form the box and gives him instructions.
DANNY: "Don't break it, no, don't break it no, right. Dark brown, no white. Light bulbs are round."

MARIA: "Do you see this is coming off, you need to push it in more." Maria rolls her chair next to Danny and Danny pushes the clay in with the heel of his hand.

DANNY: "Right right, light bulbs, don't break it, no, light bulbs break easy. Brown and yellow and red go together, right?"

MARIA: "Right, they do. Light bulbs break easy." "Is it hard enough?" Maria asks looking at Danny's work. "It looks great," she says looking at Danny meaningfully. "What happened to the tree?"

DANNY: "It died."

MARIA: "It died?"

DANNY: "It died, it died, it died."

MARIA: "The only kind of tree you should cut down is a Christmas tree, right?"

DANNY: "Pine tree died, the pine tree died."

MARIA: points to another seam, "This side too, Danny."

DANNY: "Died, the pine tree died."

MARIA: "We don't want that do we?" Maria walks away. Danny works for a second or two and then looks around, I suspect looking for Maria. She comes back with a tool.

MARIA: "Do you see this tool here? You can use this, and do this." Maria removes the extra clay from the seam. "And with the left-over you can put it there" (on the side).

DANNY: uses the tool and says, "Tree no, Tree dies, right. Light bulbs break easy, pick up the can, no, leave it in the ground." Maria repeats each word. Danny taps on the side of the clay wall with a hammer and Maria directs him to tap in another area.

DANNY: "Cans no, throw them away, throw them in the garbage." (Maria repeats). "Pick them up."

MARIA: "So what do you think?"

DANNY: "Good, pick up the can no, leave it in the ground."

MARIA: "So you want to start with this one now?" She moves another slab toward Danny. "Start with this tool?"

DANNY: "Yeah, yeah."

MARIA: "I'm going to see if I can get them a little more even than they are." Danny uses the tool to roughen the surface of the seam before attaching it to the floor of the box. He mistakenly works on the side of the slab and Maria explains what to do by holding up the side to the base.

MARIA: "This side you have to do," pointing to the seam of the side wall, and asks Danny where he'll put it when he's done.

DANNY: "Not Oakland, Reno, right."

MARIA: "Who lives in Reno?"

DANNY: "I do" (smiling and Maria looks up questioning).

MARIA: "Do you? (Smiling). Do you live in Reno?"

DANNY: "Yeah."

MARIA: "No you don't." (They both smile and enjoy each other). "What do you do in Reno, gambling?"

DANNY: "Gambling, yeah."

MARIA: "I think this is good. Now you have to place it on this side, there you go." She helps Danny pick up the side and place it on the base.

DANNY: "Reno, right."

Hartikainen explained that Miller uses cardboard as a blueprint for the boxes (see Figure 8.4); he draws the size he wants and then cuts it. With this method Miller can visualize the size he will work with. Hartikainen's objective was to make an easy transition from Miller's two-dimensional drawings to clay. "His work is very busy and I try to keep it to simple forms. We also talk about building houses, so we talk about building walls." She showed me work that he had done with other ceramic instructors, such as cars and light bulbs (see Figure 8.5). "So I think different teachers work differently with him which I think is very good because he gets the broad spectrum how to do his art work" (personal communication, September 10, 2013). I asked her why or how she thought that Miller's other teachers inspire him to produce a different kind of work. She thought that chemistry had a role,

Figure 8.4 Ceramic Boxes (photograph by Alice Wexler)

and I suggested that the subtle expectations of the instructor might also influence his work.

> It's funny with Danny because he's like that with many things. He talks different ways to different people. So I don't think he would do this with me. It's a snack thing with Danny too. He asks me to get him chips or crackers. With another teacher he just gets pizza, and another he just asks for soda. He would never get ice cream with me because I'm the chips person. So I think this goes along with how he works. (M. Hartikainen, personal communication, September 10, 2013)

Hartikainen was hesitant to consider the possibility of aesthetically influencing Miller. Her own work is abstract, elegant, and minimal. This issue is a constant question that arises within art communities. The Creative Growth artists are unyielding in their own purposes for art making and the idiosyncratic iconography that arises from these purposes. Yet it would be difficult to live without unconsciously interiorizing the constant information and stimulation of the community. Hartikainen says that she does not direct Miller toward these products, and that her role as an instructor is purely technical. They began work together six months earlier and she has seen much progress in Miller's technical skill and independence.

Figure 8.5 Ceramic Cars (photograph by Alice Wexler)

The verbal repeating back to Miller's dialogue that Rojas and Hartikainen employ works well and probably achieves several social objectives.

As discussed in previous chapters, Creative Growth's model does not subscribe to the romantic notion of the isolated outsider unscathed by culture, whose worth is in his or her singlehanded reinvention of art. It was a radical position, says Matthew Higgs, which the founders took in imagining what the relationships would look like between artists with disabilities and the professional counterparts who assist them in fulfilling their artistic visions. The Katzes visualized "an ambitious and wildly utopian" organization where nothing would be taught and nothing would be analyzed in any conventional pedagogical and therapeutic way (personal communication, June 12, 2014). Higgs points out that Creative Growth's practice is also a disavowal of the vocational purpose for "disabled art" that greatly underestimates the aesthetic authority and autonomy of these artists. The Katzes have found a "miraculous balance" of support, says Higgs, in a community of peers in which influence inevitably plays a part in the art making process. The fact that work is being made in public generates a "communal osmosis," although each artist remains distinctly apart. Higgs also points out that having assistants is commonplace in the contemporary art world for such artists as Jeff Koons and Richard Serra. In the context of Creative Growth, this practice is probably more complex and nuanced, and more difficult to grasp with artists, like Miller, whose intentions and ambitions are not communicated.

THE ISSUE OF "DIFFERENCE"

Like other assistants, mentors, and facilitators, Miller's "difference" is invisible to Rojas, except, she says, when he is perseverating or obsessing on a topic. She uses his perseverations, such as light bulbs and other household appliances, to guide their conversations. The artistic vision of Miller's artwork, and that of many other artists at Creative Growth, is so impressive that they have achieved a valorized status. While he is not skilled in language, he can communicate what he wants and needs. Because of their long relationship, his communication with Rojas has become a "normal" and efficient way of interacting. I conjecture that this achievement of "normalcy" in his communication, in which there is understanding, is one of the causes of his nascent social skills. His sister Cara says that while he was never completely withdrawn at family gatherings, he has now become proactively engaged. He will say, "I love you," or "I'm happy," which he never had before; she attributes the change to the comfort he found at Creative Growth.

When Miller first came to Creative Growth about 30 years ago, he walked compulsively up and down the stairs. As time passed his comfort level and orientation "stabilized" sufficiently for him to focus on the opportunities that drawing materials afforded. "We've seen him come from not lifting his head from the table to very engaged in his work," says Project Director Jennifer Slate O'Neal (personal communication, September 16, 2013). She attributes his social development to his success in the art world. He was the first artist at Creative Growth to have his work in the permanent collection at the Museum of Modern Art in New York, followed by William Scott and Judith Scott; he is represented at the Berkeley Art Museum in California, and in the homes of New York art collectors. As di Maria looks back at his early figurative work, he remembers that it was not the complex, abstract, and sophisticated (in the eyes of the art world) work that he is so prolific at today (see Figure 8.6). Yet, it is not intentionally abstract, sophisticated, minimal, and contemporary, as it has been described. Miller's trajectory is on a different track. And although he is inevitably involved with the aesthetic of his work, it is removed from the formal concerns of the academy and the art world. Rather, his work is the outcome of an intense investigation into the graphic form and visual representation of language. The imagery, such as his abstractions of light bulbs, mingle in the spaces between his memories of places and people, and the significant objects that conjure his past and shape his identity. As a young boy Miller broke a light bulb in his uncle's store, which frightened him. The breakage is still a significant event that continues to appear in his work. di Maria (2015) commented that the words in his drawings, such as router, paper, click, and switch "suggest communication,

Figure 8.6 Dan Miller, 1998, Creative Growth Art Center

connectivity, process, and articulation of his thoughts and their inability to become verbal." Jennifer Borum (2015) writes about the impossibility of categorizing such work: "Layered elements appear to be in a constant flux emerging into view while being scratched out of existence. Simultaneously poetic and artistic, expressive and conceptual, his work renders distinctions between such categories meaningless."

Miller's Indexical Language

As mentioned in Chapter Three (this volume), Terence Deacon (1998) speculated that indexical thinking exists in our neural impulses, but it is most fully manifested in atypical thinkers, particularly in the non-symbolic speech of autists. Miller's layered visual symbols become the equivalent of the word, which then dissolves into the increasingly illegible field. New semantic meanings emerge from the "ruins of the literal sense" (Ricouer, as cited in Berger, 2014, p. 216). This insistence on pairing the word with the thing is probably an indication of Miller's perception of the world, the concreteness of places and things existing before the organization of coded associations swept away their individuality.

According to Charles S. Peirce's distinctions between sign and symbol, the indexical sign is inevitably linked to its referent, while the symbol is more unstable and may shift according to other associated symbols or through semantic triangulation. James Berger (2014) observed that Plato also made the distinction between the word that has only one meaning and the word whose meaning is conventional or arbitrary. The language speaker's fascination with humans and non-humans outside of the social sphere structured by language has existed since *The Epic of Gilgamesh* and the Hebrew Bible (Berger, 2014). The Adamic language, the biblical language of Adam, the language of bestowing each object with its proper name without multiple signifiers is therefore without ambiguity. The final fall of Babel symbolizes the disruption of this unambiguous, "perfect" language "into ambiguity, duplicity, multiplicity, jokes, puns, lies, translations, fictions, and truths in the plural" (p. 16). Berger's claim is that language speakers are both fascinated and terrified by Adamic, indexical language—or the total absence of language. This ambivalent relationship, beginning with the child's introduction to language, is never lost. The presence of the non-linguistic other is a reminder of both one's difference and affinity—the purity and truth that once existed prior to symbolic language and, simultaneously, the fear of chaos and alterity. In other words, our profound ambivalence toward disability.

Historically, the breakdown of speech is also associated with the sacred, the oracle, the vision or revelation outside of language (Berger, 2014). Confronted with divinity, according to several scholars (Benjamin, 1978; Marks, 1987), one's auditory faculty is impaired, and *the word* is transmitted in a more immediate gestural and visual way. Hearing invites multiple interpretations, points of views, and relative truths. But seeing, according to this biblical interpretation of the divine, can leave no deception or uncertainty. Vision implies immediacy, while language and hearing imply mediation and distance. But the significant point that Berger draws from these theories is that humans are neither divine nor animal, nor self-sufficient and complete without the embodiment of the other. If language was sufficient in defining oneself, then human beings would be self-sufficient, a perfect form of being. The ethics of imperfect beings should include recognizing their own and others' incomprehensibility. Emmanual Levinas questions all representation of the Other: how we enframe others in language. Without the inclusion of the Other within oneself, we would have a compassionless form of ethics. According to Berger and Levinas (1969), only an ethics that concerns otherness as existing both inside and outside oneself can avoid the colonization of the Other.

Without the complex association among symbols, Miller communicates directly by visually representing both the object and its referent simultaneously. This pairing might be an example of the Platonic and Adamic perfect correspondence between the word and the worldly thing. Miller employs the sign without the ambiguity of the symbol, or the full range of its potential interpretations. As such, Miller's representations of light bulbs are indices rather than symbols, the intrinsic association between the word and thing. The contiguity of Miller's letters and numerals are a visualization of indexical thought.

Miller's associative and indexical thinking was recorded at the 2012 Cutlog Art Fair in Paris, where Creative Growth worked with the Seymour+ Space[3] to produce an interactive installation with Miller's work. In addition to telling the story about how viewers interacted with his work, a video of Miller working in real time is also available.[4] Miller stands behind a translucent screen, with only his arm and brush visible. He begins the drawing by writing the word "HOUSE." Directly on top of and touching the word he writes another word that looks like "ROOF." Below "HOUSE" he writes, "CARPENTER," and then below it, "ELECTRICAN." Miller draws two oblique lines through these words that become an iconic representation of a roof, followed by two perpendicular lines on the opposite ends, forming the walls of the house. (See Figure 8.7). Words as verbal representation also serve as visual representation, revealing the way that Miller imagines the world.

THE INFLUENCE OF CULTURE

Unlike Gerone Spruill and William Scott, Miller hasn't had the stimulation of living with his family in adult life. Even so, says Higgs, his work is distinctly autobiographical, an accumulative self-portrait, a visual narrative of

Figure 8.7 Dan Miller, Film Capture, 2012 Cutlog Art Fair, Paris

his development from adolescence to adulthood and the influences of family and objects of importance. A few years ago Miller found an old typewriter at Creative Growth and typed the same words he had been writing for the previous 25 years. di Maria observed in the typed pages the same decisions about space, form, and structure as he makes in his paintings and drawings. But new memories surfaced, possibly because of the change of process material. The repetition of the words "brown sweater," "car," and "diner," appeared. Cara told di Maria (2015) a story about her sweater:

> When I was 11 we went to this diner and I left my brown sweater there, and we drove an hour when I realized I lost it. And I was crying. Dan was in the back seat, and I had no idea that he was even aware of what was happening. And 30 years later he's typing about it.

Although Miller did not live in an institution as a young person, O'Neal thinks that he stands amidst these artists in his disinterest in, and possibly oblivion, to popular culture. The staff at Creative Growth recognize a difference among the artists who have been institutionalized and artists who have grown up in the public school system. The latter are influenced by popular culture and so have the same footing as any contemporary artist with or without a disability. Miller, she says, operates more like an artist who was institutionalized, having lived in his caretaker's home for most of his life. He has missed an era of technological change, the shifting of our visual world. "But he has this private thing going on. And although there are these touchstone words that come up and get repeated . . . we just can't know" (J. S. O'Neal, personal communication, September 13, 2013). Cara theorizes that it is not an oblivion to computer technology, but his disinterest in it. He was indifferent to the Ipad that she bought that had programs designed for autistic people. Television doesn't occupy him; he would rather look at magazines and books. "Why would a magazine be more interesting than a moving picture?," she wonders:

> It may be in part due to his preference of mechanical things—that he can get something more real, more tangible from something that is somewhat real in front of him. I find myself to be a bit of the same way. I use computers because they are a powerful tool but I prefer to write on paper, and read real books. I think and learn through writing things down and looking at them. So I can find Danny's preference of that to make sense. I also think that perhaps some concepts are past his ability to understand, or at least the concepts of what the ipad app or the computer program may offer. He knows what books and paper and tools do. He sees that and understands it. He likes it. He prefers it. (C. Miller, personal communication, July, 15, 2014)

Miller experiments with a variety of materials, goes back and forth freely from typing, painting, and drawing, and likes to integrate them. di Maria (2015) says that he liberates the myth that artists with disabilities are one-trick ponies, "they learn to do one thing and they'll do it again and again. They do not evolve and therefore they are not serious artists like academic artists. There isn't the interactive discussion, intellectualization, the evolution." Since we cannot read an artist statement, we can only conjecture what Miller is saying. His work is most clearly understood when we look back and see his development. For di Maria, Miller is an artist who is continually evolving, his work is complex and invigorating. "The form and the content are inseparable: the form is the word, the content is the word. You can't have one without the other" (di Maria, 2015).

While di Maria has never seen an artist copy another, their proximity, Higgs believes, makes it impossible not to be influenced by the radical diversity of individuals who inhabit the space, such as Gerone Spruill's obsessions with popular music and visual culture, if only by osmosis:

> Even if it's not consciously or self-consciously understood, I think there's an intimate relationship between different artists and their work. So there's a kind of slippage where this sort of atmosphere or energy remains and shared amongst the artists in the room. So where the facilitators are all practicing artists and even some of the administrative staff are practicing artists, it seems to me it's a culture around making and

> it's a culture around artists regardless of who they are and their circumstances. (M. Higgs, personal communication, June 12, 2014)

Creative Growth's location in downtown Oakland, in the midst of a thriving and political art community so reflective of contemporary life in America, must also be part of the daily reality for Miller, says Higgs. The Oakland popular culture holds a strong presence in the artists' work, which is most apparent in William Scott's and Gerone Spruill's. "It's there if you walk around the streets, if you go two blocks south and two blocks north, you're confronted with this extraordinary mix of cultures, and it reflects in the artists" (M. Higgs, personal communication, June, 12, 2014). Higgs observed that the building's former car showroom glass walls were intentionally left standing as both a literal and symbolic, thin and flexible, threshold between the outside and inside. It would have been more practical to make more working space with walls, but transparency between the street and the life inside is perhaps more important.

Yet, there is, an inconsistency between the art world's appreciation of Miller's work and how I observed his process. There is a sameness in the critical analysis of his work, implying a consensus by the initiated about the seductive aesthetics, the pleasing layers, and what appears to be a sophisticated use of text; curators and critics speak of his "intensive body of work," "descriptive texts," "an idiosyncratic hybrid form," all of which rings with the normative standards of artistic achievement (White Columns, 2007). His work is compared to the great modernist masters, such as "Jean Tinguely's rattletrap sculptures," or how his work marries "Cy Twombly's graffiti-like scratching with Jackson Pollock's skeins of dripped paint," or his conceptual kinship with "Yayoi Kusama's hallucinatory 'Infinity Nets,' or the 'Involuntary Sculptures'—rolled-up bus tickets and slivers of soap shaped by repeated unconscious gestures—documented by Brassa and Salvador Dali in the Surrealist magazine *Minotaure*" (Doran, 2010, para. 1). Effusive flatteries have a hollowed sound when one meets the ingenuous Dan Miller. He inexplicably has made iconic surfaces, and makes them almost in assembly-line fashion, that seduce the art world with their unfailing grace and tastefulness.

O'Neal suggests this paradox while resisting an analysis of Miller. She describes what she observes: his ritualization and repetition of words, images, and gestures, both graphically and verbally. But she prefers to tell an anecdote that she says reveals an obscured intelligence that reveals itself when no one is paying attention:

> I had this run in with Dan that really got me looking at him differently. . . . I was trying to clean something up that I spilled in the gallery one day and I went back by the sinks in the studio where all the mops are. And I picked up the mops and they were all tangled together, and I was struggling trying to get them apart, and he came up behind me and

> pushed me out of the way and he grabbed the mops and went (gestures with her hands) and completely untangled them and handed them to me. And I went, OK, you just don't know what's going on with Dan Miller. He is a really bright guy, and I think that he's good at a lot of things. He can't really tell us, other than these repeated words, which seem to be key things that happened in his life that he's reliving, and that might be comforting or it might be something difficult he's recounting, but I think there's a lot more going on there, you know. (personal communication, September 16, 2013)

Roger Ricco, co-owner of the Ricco/Maresca gallery, is convinced that Miller's artistic decisions are intentional. As an artist himself, Ricco is fascinated by Miller's artwork and how Miller informs him about his own work as a painter. Ricco compares the astonishment he feels on viewing Miller's work to the song of a new species of bird "that's never been heard before" (personal communication, March 22, 2015). Ricco also invokes sound when he describes Miller's layers as not only visual and cerebral, but also as happening in time. It's not the detailed subject matter he says that is astonishing, but the intentionally detailed way that Miller uses paint and responds to the materials. Ricco conjectures that the materials provide Miller with a kinetic satisfaction and a rhythmic feedback that envelops him in a sensual world. Ricco also recognizes a similarity between Miller and Judith Scott in their focused and obsessive layering of materials. The work of these two artists, he thinks, suggests an intensely different form of consciousness.

NOTES

1. Miller is referring here to an incident that happened at summer camp.
2. Miller is referring here to project manager Jennifer Strate O'Neal.
3. The Seymour+ Space describes their mission as follows: "The SEYMOUR+ space is a haven for the mind, a place devoid of technology and all external distractions. It provides an opportunity to disconnect in order to reconnect with yourself. No computers, cell phones, books or magazines. Just you, and a pencil and paper" (http://seymourprojects.com/sspace/).
4. See: seymourprojects.com/project-results-of-our-interactive-installation-at-the-cutlog-art-fair/

REFERENCES

Benjamin, W. (1978). *Reflections: Essays, aphorisms, autobiographical writings.* (P. Demetz, Ed., E. Jephcott, Trans.). New York, NY: Schoken.

Borum J. P. (2015). *Dan Miller.* Retrieved from: http://outsiderartfair.com/artist/949

Di Maria, T. (2015). *Proceedings from an Inclusive World: Bridging Communities.* Queens, NY: Queens Museum.

Doran, A. (2010). "Dan Miller: Large works:" This self-taught autistic artist creates works of astonishing complexity. *Time Out New York:* Retrieved from: http://www.timeout.com/newyork/art/dan-miller-large-works

Levinas, E. (1969). *Totality and infinity: An essay on exteriority* (A. Lingis, Trans.). Pittsburgh, PA: Duquense University Press.

Marks, H. (1987). On prophetic stammering. *Yale Journal of Criticism, 1,* 1–20.

Ricco/Maresca. (n.d.). *Dan Miller: Large paintings.* Retrieved from http://www.riccomaresca.com/dan-miller-large-paintings/

White Columns. (2007). Retrieved from: whitecolumns.org/sections/exhibition.php?id=1117

Figure 9.1 Photograph of William Scott (by Leon Borensztein)

9 William Scott

Once upon a time in a rough part of San Francisco, there was a boy named William. He was different from the other kids and they would tease him at school. He would walk home and try to ignore the drunk men shouting in his street. Sometimes he heard gun shots outside his window. He wished they would go away. And then one day he came here and began to draw. He drew the people who had been shot, back to life. He drew his city, but the way he wanted it to be. And he drew beautiful and strong women he'd never met.

(Yentob, *BBC: Imagine: Turning the Art World Inside Out*, 2013)

William Scott is a 52-year-old African-American man. While growing up his family didn't make accommodations for his disability, so he was placed in a regular classroom in public school, functioning at the lowest level of performance. But he liked to draw in the library and the librarian noticed his talent. The librarian knew about Creative Growth and gave him a train ticket to Oakland. "He showed up at our door when he was 17 and we took him in" (di Maria, 2015).

Scott sits in the kitchen area of Creative Growth and paints on an easel. Like Dan Miller, Scott has recently been assigned a mentor, Kathleen Henderson. The two artists sell their work for high prices, and each has a mentor for specific reasons. Henderson is usually present, looking out for Scott's personal and aesthetic needs. Sometimes he will call her at home if he needs to talk about a new idea. One of her primary purposes is to keep him on track.

As a sought-after artist, Scott's output is important to Creative Growth; Henderson says "it's a matter of him finishing pieces, getting them to the places that is needed," which sets up an interesting dynamic for her (personal communication, September 11, 2013). His process of creating alternative realities is of primary importance to him and requires a certain amount of dreaming time, which Henderson wants to support. But like other artists at Creative Growth, money also has an important place, and he uses it for both necessities and pleasures. Matthew Higgs holds a long view of the artists' work in the larger context of their disabilities. It would be unrealistic to expect a consistency in production from many of the artists given the complexity of both their internal and external lives. Also, the artists are not on a production schedule driven by the art world, and therefore they work at a different tempo. Higgs credits the Katzes' model of Creative Growth for providing the infrastructure necessary to support such irregular shifts in their work. He can't imagine any other therapeutic or institutional situation that could make these commitments to artists. Creative Growth, he says, allows us to see the totality of the artists' work over decades and bear witness to their maturity.

Scott has recently been persuaded to work on canvas. His works until now have mainly been on paper. He has an identifiable and audacious style; his subjects are primarily portraits of healthy, wholesome church women, his home town of Bay View/Hunters Point, San Francisco, and his family, which he paints in bold colors with equally bold renderings and informational text. Scott's family features prominently in his life and paintings, and they also become the subject of current events. The day of my interview, he was approaching the completion of a portrait of himself as a young adolescent with his stepfather, mother, and Jesus. He used an image of Jesus he found on the internet and photographs of his family as reference (see Figure 9.2). Scott shared his thoughts about the portrait as follows:

> This is me and my mother and stepfather, to reinvent them, to reinvent my family, to reinvent them. So they can put them into another life, put them in another life, that's what Jesus is about, because they need Jesus. I made a drawing of my family to reinvent, like in the 70s again; to return to the 1970s again, to return to another life. So I would be a kid again, with an afro. I'll be a basketball kid with an afro in the 1970s. When another life comes, I'll be a basketball player when another life comes; to be in another life, to be born again in another life. To be a basketball kid with an afro with the Lakers as, to be a Los Angeles Lakers, Los Angeles Lakers. Then I'll be a professional kid, a professional kid in another life, another life. I will be born again as a new baby, as a new baby. I'll be grown up to be a basketball kid in the 70s, 80s, and 90s, I'll be a kid again, to be young again, will be in the 1970s again. (personal communication, September 11, 2013)

REINVENTING THE PAST

> *You want to change your life, you want to change your neighborhood, you want to make it safe, you want your disability to go away, you want a new reality, you want to build new cities, you want to make everything positive, you're going to find a girl and settle down and you make that happen through art. That's the challenge that William has posed for himself, and you can't fault him for that.*
>
> (di Maria, 2015)

Scott has a complex relationship with the past, which has its roots in his Baptist religion. He filters all his memories through his sense of justice and

Figure 9.2 William Scott, *Family with Jesus*, Creative Growth Art Center

morality. He will often repeat, "I will obey the past," or "obeying the past," by which he means that he will erase his mistakes, and in some cases sins, and replace them with cautious and willful acts. One of his paintings is a re-envisioning of trouble he got into in 1982. "When I will be a teenager again, because I'll be out of trouble in 1982, when another life comes." He alludes to an incident that happened on Halloween night, about which he says "never again." When 1982 comes around again on Halloween night he will not go out again, "to start over again in 1982, to not get myself in trouble again, I will stay in the house" (personal communication, September 11, 2013).

Scott's content of troubling memories is often painted in a series of redemptive works, which adds to the power of his style. After completing his family portrait with Jesus, Scott began a tentative portrait the following morning of his step-sister Charlesetta, who died as a one-year-old. He fell asleep after lunch, and Henderson saw that he was struggling with the memory. It was meant to be a reconstruction of the past, bringing his sister back to life as she would look in the present. Scott was working from a photograph of his mother, but it was not adequate; he needed a photograph of the one-year-old, which was unavailable. The painting was put on hold, and Scott turned toward making a self-portrait as a young child on the beach in Santa Cruz (see Figure 9.3). He printed several computer images of beaches as reference. It seemed to Henderson that he was painting himself at the age he would have been when his sister died, "on the beach, alone on the beach" (personal communication, September 11, 2013). He had just been to Santa Cruz with his family for his forty-ninth birthday, so Santa Cruz was on his mind.

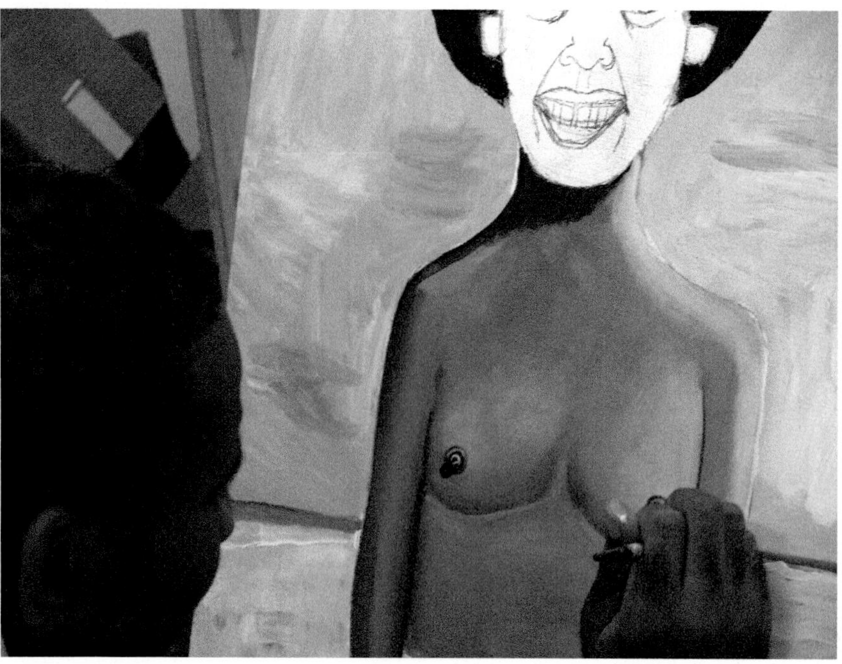

Figure 9.3 Photograph of William Scott working (by Alice Wexler)

KATHLEEN HENDERSON'S ROLE

Several of the staff at Creative Growth noticed Scott laboriously re-painting the eyes of his portraits. Henderson thinks that perfectionism plays a small role compared to his fascination with the gaze: "He studies the gaze, the way one looks at another, and he is making an intellectual connection about its importance" (personal communication, September 11, 2013). This is particularly true of his self-portraits as a youngster, in which he uses the canvas to rehearse what he has trouble doing in life. His youthful portraits might return him to an early stage of his life to learn these communicative skills. Henderson found that sitting in silence can be the most productive way to support these expository works: "I think if I sit long enough next to William he'll start talking about his fears and concerns. That's when he tells me he's worried about his mom getting older; that's when I feel that I know what he's thinking about." Scott has also been worried for the last two years about his approaching 50th birthday and making art works about it for several years. His "Friendship Party" T-shirts describe who he would like at his party. "Those considerations are in all his work" (K. Henderson, personal communication, September 11, 2013).

Scott shifted to canvas under Henderson's influence, completing over a dozen paintings within the year. She found him bent over a table working on paper. She thought his back must be hurting and found an easel and canvas. Those subtle changes redirected Scott's focus, leading him toward a fuller completion of his ideas. Canvas offers a longer-lasting relationship than paper, which had been his primary surface material, and demands fuller and more deliberate artistic decisions. The flat file cabinets overflow with his drawings and paintings, many of them unfinished, and others have been lost or given away. "A canvas is harder to carry home under your arm, and I think he's compelled to finish them because they're more object-like. So he's become increasingly more prolific, and I think part of it was having material support" (K. Henderson, personal communication, September 11, 2013).

September was not too early for Scott to think about Halloween, and he alternated between painting and working on a Darth Vader mask. I learned from Henderson that without an agreement about his schedule, Scott might work only on masks and costumes. But an agreement was made and an allotted time was designated to Darth Vader. As a 6'2" man, says Henderson, Scott moves silently and gracefully through the world, often unnoticed. He enjoys putting on the Darth Vader costume, even on hot days, and walking through the neighborhood. "So I don't know if he's a performative artist or wants to hide, or both" (K. Henderson, personal communication, September 11, 2013). Scott made a video as his Darth Vader persona with teaching artist Michael Hall titled *Beautiful Peace on Earth* that I will return to at the end of the chapter. He also officially welcomes the viewers of several documentaries to Creative Growth as Darth Vader. In the 2013 BBC documentary, *Imagine: Turning the Art World Inside Out*, Scott stands at the door of Creative Growth, faces the camera and says, "Welcome to Creative Growth Art Center. It's a good place. Let's do it."

SCOTT'S COSMOLOGY

Praise Frisco

Scott grew up in Bay View/Hunters Point, the roughest area of San Francisco, and he has expressed fear to former studio manager Jordan Destabler about taking the bus in dangerous situations. These encounters might have been one of the motivations for his lengthy *Praise Frisco* urban project of re-imagining his neighborhood. In this imagined topography, the current San Francisco is "cancelled" and the new San Francisco, which he christened *Praise Frisco*, will replace it (see Figures 9.4 and 9.5). The re-constructions are at once joyful and disquieting, joyful because he is fully engaged in his belief and optimism about a utopian future, and disquieting because utopianism is generally considered improbable. Scott's abiding belief in the Baptist Church is probably the origin of his unflagging commitment to seeing his architectural plans and theories come into being. In a ten-inch long panel now housed in the Museum of London, Scott painted San Francisco from memory, whited out the buildings and painted in new ones. He stops short of a finished painting because, di Maria (2015) explains, if reality won't change according to his specifications, it will be because he's not a good enough artist. By not finishing the work he can avoid future contradictions.

Figure 9.4 William Scott, *Praise Frisco*, Creative Growth Art Center

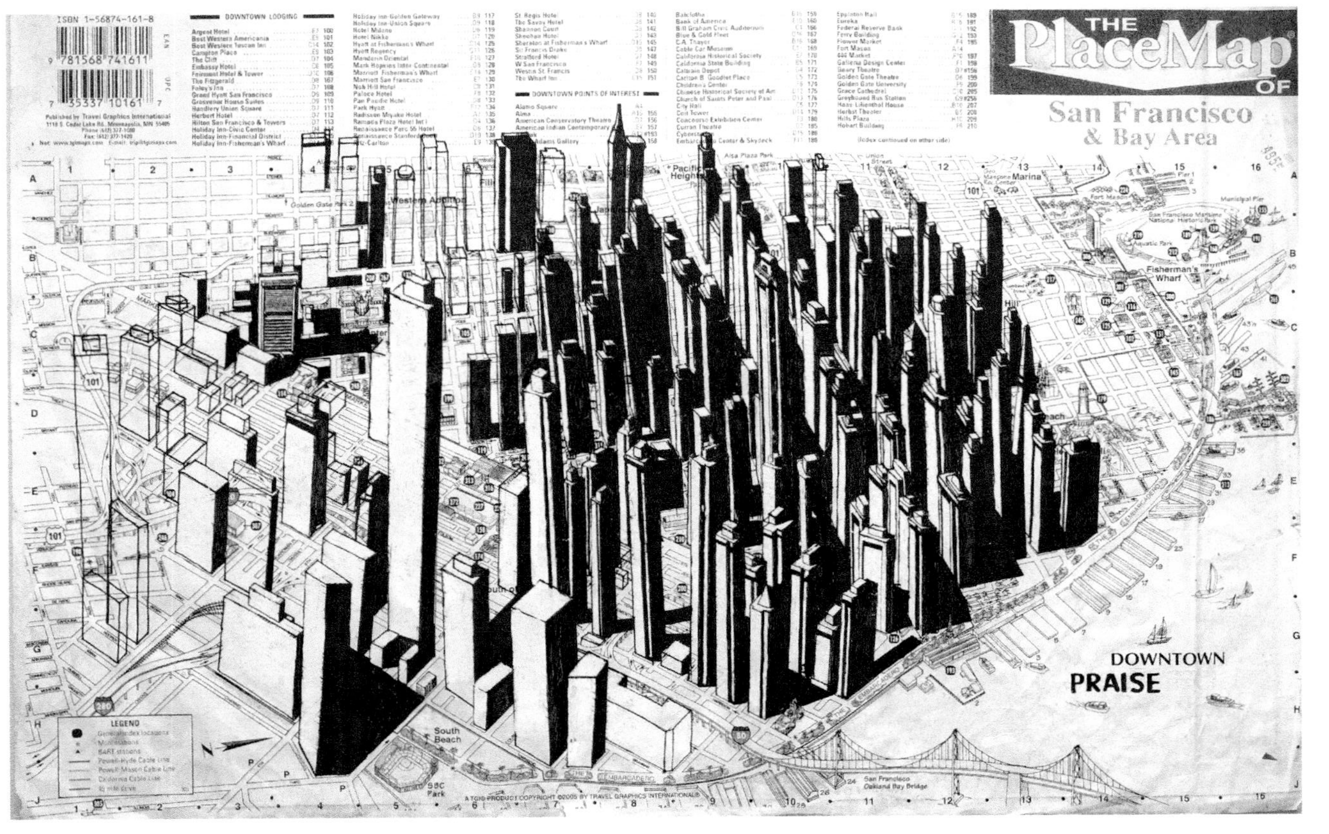

Figure 9.5 William Scott, Architectural Drawing, Creative Growth Art Center

Scott participated in the San Francisco World's Fair of 2007, an event organized by the California College of Arts' graduate curatorial students, led by their instructor Will Bradley. The event included art, film, poetry, and hip hop by the artists of the community. The organizers proposed the re-envisioning of Third Street along Hunters Point and Bay View, beginning with the question, "What would today's World's Fair look like if it didn't privilege a singular ideology, and how would it define itself?," (http://curatorial-practice.blogs.cca.edu/?page_id=735, para.1) which was meant to invite a dialogue about the relationship between nature and progress. The occasion was linked to the Third Street Light Rail, a project launched by the San Francisco County Transportation Authority and Muni, connecting residents of several communities to San Francisco's urban network. Hunters Point would be most affected, having long been abandoned by city and county officials since its Naval Shipyard closed. The students considered Hunters Point and Bay View San Francisco's "final frontier." The Light Rail would connect this area with an artistic community, "one of the harbingers of gentrification" (para. 2).

The Third Street Light Rail was emblematic of economic possibility, but also "tied to the identity politics of isolation, colonization and mobility" (para. 3), a perfect venue for Scott's re-envisioning of a just, healthy, and peaceful San Francisco. The World's Fair mission statement echoed Scott's processes and imaginings about time:

> The predictable future of Third Street shows that it is possible to conflate time; to see the past, present, and future existing simultaneously in one social field where power is unevenly distributed. In light of this, we invited artists, activists, and other practitioners as both individuals and community members to reflect on current and future needs and desires within this complex reality. How do we adapt to our surroundings, how do they adapt to us, and who conducts this exchange? (para. 5)

Scott exhibited a large architectural mural, a large canvas, and several drawings in the Third Street Opera House, an important institution for the neighborhood. It not only offers neighborhood events but also free meals on Wednesdays. The architectural mural was titled *50 Towers on Third Street*, which Scott said were for "good people and the healthy people of the gospel superstars."

In a series of architectural drawings, Scott showed with precise and microscopic detail his vision of *Peacetown*, in which the liquor stores disappear to make room for "a gospel town for building people's lives. They're going to build people's lives down there, to make the people come back as a new people" (*CCA SF World's Fair*, Part 4). In one of the segments of the six-part documentary about the San Francisco World's Fair, Scott turned to a drawing with a re-invented Denny's Diner logo, and answered a visitor's question about it. "Denny's Diner will be a healthy foods restaurant, fast foods for making people healthy and strong" (*CCA SF World's Fair*, Part 4). The blueprint for *The Union Heights Villa* was an embellished drawing of a re-envisioned project, probably like the one he grew up in, but now with pools, gardens, stores, sidewalks, and a football stadium for the 49ers. He told the visitor while pointing, "The parks are where the greens are with a sunny pool. Kids will play right there by the swimming pool and the good dancing people swim right there; the cultural people swim right there" (*CCA SF World's Fair*, Part 4).

One of his works was titled *United Peace Union States*, a cityscape with delirious gospel super stars dancing in the foreground dressed in colorful Sunday suits and brimmed hats. Scott called it the "Peace Cityscape to the building of peace in the city. Take down the original skyscrapers, with no penthouses . . . will be taking it down to re-build the new city into peaceful . . . make it peaceful" (*CCA SF World's Fair*, Part 5) (see Figure 9.6).[1]

Scott's participation was described on the World's Fair website as the rebuilding of San Francisco, "in search of the elusive 'normal' life, one of Baptist-sermon ideas and gleaming, safe, artistically franchised city centers" (http://outsiderartfair.com/artist/1084, para. 1). The "last day" of San Francisco, and the start of *Praise Frisco*, is a critical moment that changes as the final dates come and go. Scott began the series of paintings in the early 1990s, and the most recent final date is in the 2030s. Scott's

Figure 9.6 William Scott, *Balcony Resorts*, Creative Growth Art Center

prophecy of demise and re-birth is tied to the Baptist notion of the resurrection of Jesus and the returning dead, says Project Manager Jennifer Strate O'Neal, and the sudden appearance of a Black Jesus series marked the beginning of the project (see Figure 9.7). Scott says in the documentary *Peace Worlds* that the world has been bad for years: "I am making it for the re-planet."

Figure 9.7 William Scott, *Black Jesus*, White Columns Gallery

An Alternative Guide to the Universe

In June through August, 2013, Scott exhibited his paintings and architectural drawings at the Hayward Gallery in London. The exhibition, titled *Alternative Guide to the Universe* (see Chapter Six, this volume), included self-taught visionary artists who, like Scott, were motivated by concerns beyond the aesthetic, imagining prophetic landscapes that reinvented the world. The unguarded and unmediated works were described as science fiction, with the exception that the artists believed in the validity of their inventions. In the exhibition press release, gallery Director Ralph Rugoff wrote:

> These brilliant mavericks expand the spaces in which our own imaginative thinking about the world may venture. However farfetched or outlandish it may seem, their work possesses an intensity and bracing originality that gives it a compelling reality all its own. It invites us to think outside of our conventional categories and ultimately to question our definitions of "normal" art and science. (Hayward, para. 5)

Scott's compulsion to contribute to a just and peaceful society in his lifetime is infectious among the staff at Creative Growth. They support his project but also temper his preoccupations. Higgs calls Scott's self-reflexivity about his own life, the life of his immediate community, and global social concerns a collision of real desires and imagined solutions. He is not satisfied to fix himself and his family, which his series of "reinventions" are meant to do; his sense of social justice is equally dominant, indicating a deeply felt link to the world. The pragmatic use of his art form is impressive to Higgs, given the lack of voice of the developmentally disabled community. The space ship *Inner Limits* (see color plate) began to appear in his paintings, which di Maria (2015) interprets as the transformation of the dead to life. People in his neighborhood who have died from drugs or violence come back to earth, transformed to wholesome citizens. Without differentiating the past and the future, 1950s street-cars can co-exist with new buildings. "He changes the past and the future to affect the now, to craft a new reality in the moment of time, now" (di Maria, 2015).

Higgs is also impressed with the open and generous way that he applies his beliefs. What might elsewhere seem contradictory, Scott's visual texts are "completely reasonable, legible, and makes absolute sense" (personal communication, June 24, 2014). He holds his work in check, explains Higgs, so that the tension between his Baptist faith and his sexualized church women reads as a perfectly controlled and believable narrative (see Figure 9.8). The history of the church women began after several paintings of Diana Ross and Queen Latifah, whom di Maria explained were women Scott wanted to meet. Since he would probably not meet them, his mother suggested that he should meet a nice church woman. His citizen girlfriends were his solution. If he paints them, he will meet them.

Figure 9.8 William Scott, *Lavonn and William*, White Columns Gallery

Higgs curated two solo exhibitions of Scott's work at White Columns Gallery. The *White Room* exhibition in 2006 focused on his visionary plan for San Francisco to be torn down and rebuilt following more humane civic impulses. Scott presented two models of his neighborhood projects, one intact and the other in ruins, which Higgs interprets as the city's inevitable collapse in the future. He interprets Scott's role in the show as *citizen*, a term that Scott uses often: a citizen who is using his art work as a platform. With his bold black pen and signature print, Scott wrote to local architects introducing his work, and to Higgs, beseeching him to invite city developers to the gallery opening (see Figure 9.9). Higgs compiled into a zine the dozens of letters he sent by fax. Mayor Gavin has Scott's drawings in his office, so the fact that his work is reaching this audience must make an indirect impact whether or not it affects public policy.

The second exhibition at White Columns in 2009, titled *Good Person*, centered on portraiture of self, family, community, and church life. Included was the series that Higgs calls "In Another Life," in which he becomes someone else under a different set of more normalizing circumstances. Like the more deliberate costumes he constructs and wears of heroes and anti-heroes such as Darth Vader, Frankenstein, and Spider Man, Higgs interprets the portraits of himself as policeman, basketball player, prom escort, and married man serving as costumes and masks[2] for "another life" he might have had (see Figure 9.10).

Church Women, Science Fiction and Religion

Scott populates his idealized San Francisco with women who attend his Bay View-neighborhood church. Scott's church publishes an annual directory with photographs and information of the members, which he uses as reference for his series of wholesome church women. O'Neal refers to the series, painted in the early 2000s, as posters or advertisements seeking a wholesome, tolerant, and spiritual woman. Like Spruill, Scott has been looking for the right woman and, like Spruill, he is looking for a specific kind. But he has shied away from exploring friendships with women at Creative Growth because he wants to have a "normal" girlfriend, says DeStabler. "He wants to be normal, whatever that is. He's brought us letters when I was a client service coordinator and to my colleagues since, letters asking for help to find a girlfriend and things of that nature" (personal communication, September 12, 2013).

In *Imagine: Turning the Art World Inside Out*, Director Alan Yentob reads aloud an undated letter that Scott wrote to a caseworker, Christina Hernendez:

> I have been single for a long time I am tired of being, it bothers me too much. I wanted a wife real bad. I have never had any kids. I want to be a father for good. I would like you to be putting me on Praise Team in this month of spring. Christina, I wanted you to be putting me in to friendship and social skills.

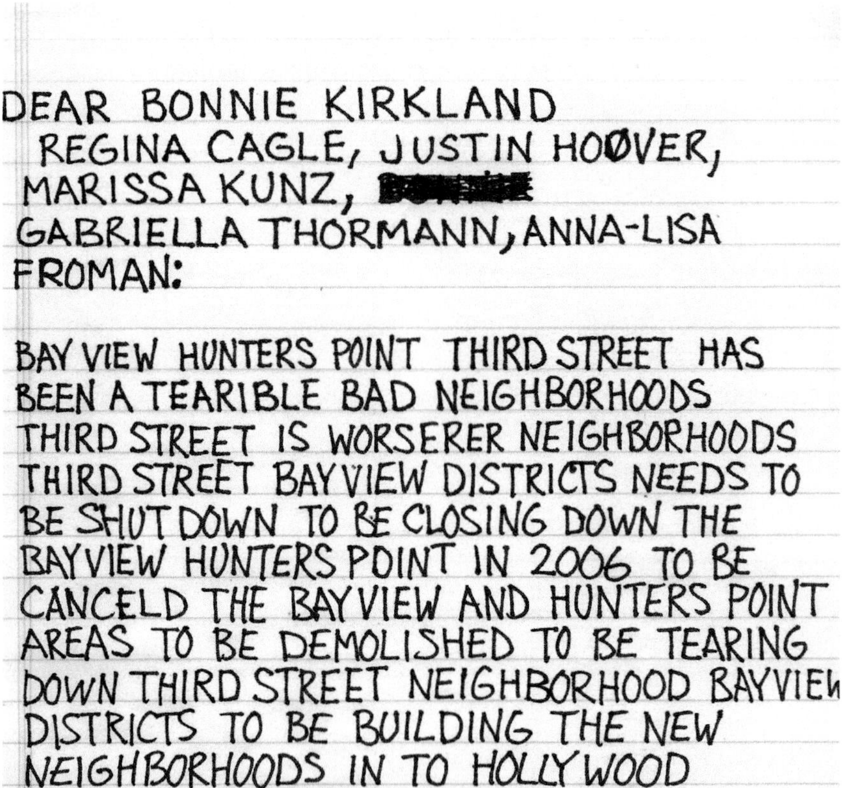

DEAR BONNIE KIRKLAND
REGINA CAGLE, JUSTIN HOØVER,
MARISSA KUNZ, [illegible]
GABRIELLA THORMANN, ANNA-LISA
FROMAN:

BAY VIEW HUNTERS POINT THIRD STREET HAS
BEEN A TEARIBLE BAD NEIGHBORHOODS
THIRD STREET IS WORSERER NEIGHBORHOODS
THIRD STREET BAYVIEW DISTRICTS NEEDS TO
BE SHUT DOWN TO BE CLOSING DOWN THE
BAYVIEW HUNTERS POINT IN 2006 TO BE
CANCELD THE BAYVIEW AND HUNTERS POINT
AREAS TO BE DEMOLISHED TO BE TEARING
DOWN THIRD STREET NEIGHBORHOOD BAYVIEW
DISTRICTS TO BE BUILDING THE NEW
NEIGHBORHOODS IN TO HOLLYWOOD
DISNEYARENA GOSPEL TOWN. APOLLO
TOWNS AND PEACE NEIGHBORHOOD
NEW NAME IS ROYALNIECE DISTRICTS
SAN FRANCISCO WILL BE CLOSED DOWN
TO BE SHUTTING DOWN THE CITIES
TO BE CLOSED FOR PEACE CELEBRATING
THE NEW CITIES IN TO PRAISE FRISCO CA
THE GOSPEL CITY' PROMISE LAND AND
PRAISE PARADISES AND NEW HUNTERSVIE
IN TO DISNEYWOOD [illegible] HALLELUGAH POINT
PUBLIC [illegible] HOUSING COMPLEXES AND
CONDOMINIUS NEW HOUSING AREAS

Figure 9.9 William Scott, *Dear Bonnie Kirkland*, Creative Growth Art Center

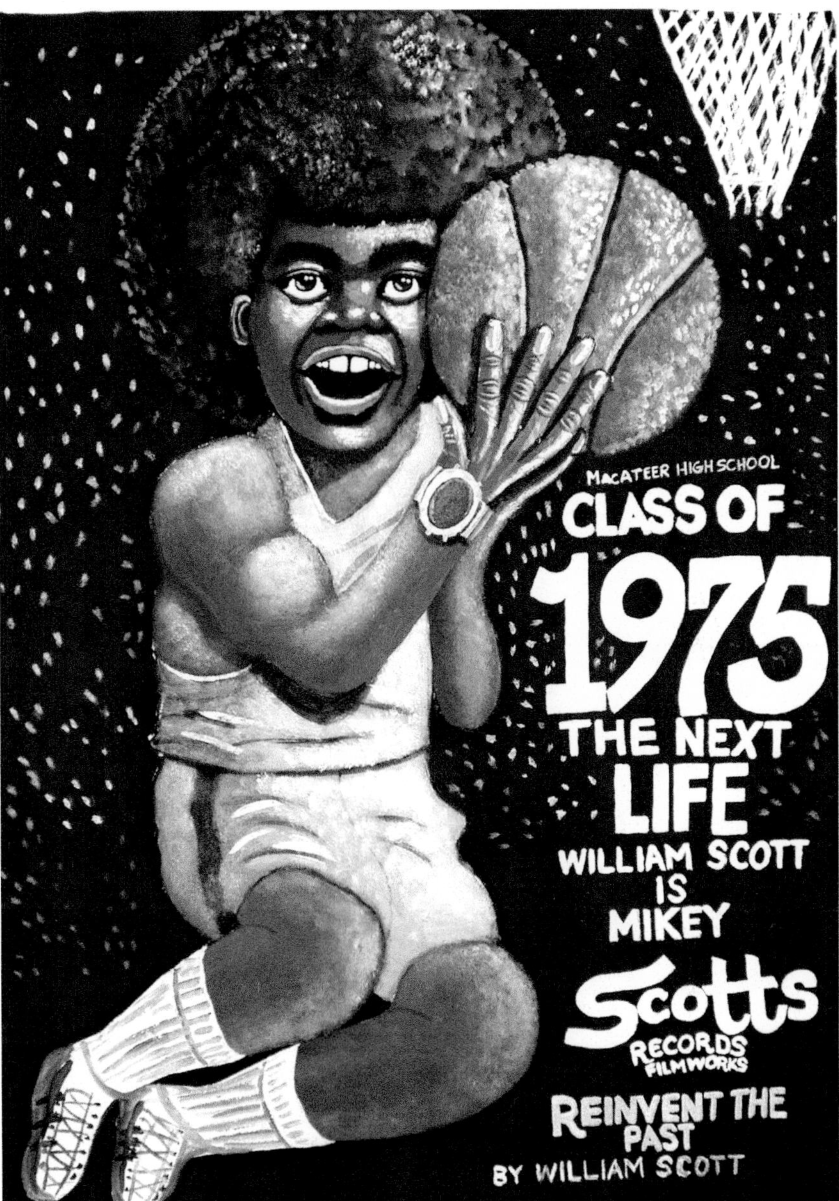

Figure 9.10 William Scott, *William Scott is Mikey*, Creative Growth Art Center

In another letter, addressed "Dear Scientologist," Scott writes that "religions will become all new animated as new encounters of wholesome fictions. . . . Inner skyline will replace the outer space in to inner skyline as a new planet earth of wholesome and humorous people." Evils are replaced with wholesome encounters, tough-love gods put the misguided back to wholesome work, and war turns into peace. Scott incants a new reality, an inner skyline infiltrated by Darth Vader and science fiction. Gallery assistant Catherine Nguyen interprets the Scientologist he addresses as not in the form that is currently known, but most likely as an entity of another universe. And while science fiction will be cancelled, he uses it as a way of accessing a new reality where it can bring good. His concept of aliens,

Figure 9.11 William Scott, *Wholesome Woman*, Creative Growth Art Center

she says, is not the traditional meaning of alternative beings, but rather "extremely positive, happy people that somehow live outside of this reality. He is constantly oscillating between creating this reality, and then dealing with what he knows within the church, his relationship with his family, and what he craves for in terms of companionship and reinventing that past" (personal communication, September 11, 2013).

The theme of religion is the undercurrent that links Scott's other desires. Religion in art is most often found among so-called outliers and other artists who defy categories. Few existing discourses about religion can be found in mainstream contemporary art history, art journals, and art schools, unless they are transgressive, deconstructivist, or a curiosity of popular culture. James Elkins (2004) notes that contemporary western art is further from organized religion than it has ever been. When religious art does exist, the religious iconography usually goes unnoted and subsumed under the formal properties of the work. In this sense Scott sets up a further division between the mainstream and the un-trained disabled artist. But paradoxically, in its postmodern form, art has never been so varied and unpredictable. Almost anything, in the Duchampian sense, can be filed under art. Yet it appears that the art world has arrived at an unstated consensus about religious iconography. That Scott has exhibited in highly regarded galleries and museums is a testament to the position of Creative Growth as a respected, yet-to-be-classified entity in the art world. "We'll never fully understand why they're being made, whereas with a more conventional trained artist we're usually in full awareness of why the work exists," says Higgs in a 2011 interview with The Museum of Everything. "There is a kind of *here* narrative" where art making is not bound to the contemporary art world and its history, where ideas are materialized in a community and in partnership, such as the partnership between Scott and Henderson (Higgs, 2011, para. 7). The remaking of what art is here, at Creative Growth, challenges the viewer to release presumed notions about the finality of aesthetic definitions.

THE POWER OF MYTH: DARTH VADER

Scott chooses as his alter egos Frankenstein and Darth Vader of *Star Wars*, the archetypal (sometimes misunderstood) outcasts legendary in the United States via the movies, the most popular mass mode of storytelling. Both personas are symbolic of Scott's ethos of redemption. In his cosmology, all forms of human life, particularly the most negative and destructive, must "obey the past" and return to the new life as wholesome and peaceful members of the utopian community. I will focus on Darth Vader because this persona appears to capture Scott's attention so fully.

Myth, according to Alan Watts (1968), is defined as a collection of factual and fanciful stories that have "universal" inner meaning about life.[3] Myth, which includes symbolism, images, narratives, and rituals, appeal to Scott's sweeping message of reform. Myth has also been used to establish social and moral codes. For Scott, having an authoritative persona, albeit one connotative of darkness, might help to make his call for renewal more dramatic and visible. Characters in myths are generally edifying and embody archetypal characteristics or primal reasons for being, such as the prodigal son, the divine messenger, or the selfless hero. Archetypical mythic characters often have prominent physical characteristics. Scott is a tall man, although he does not compare to Darth Vader's height played by the 6'7" actor in *Star Wars*.

Watts is concerned with the Christian myth in *Myth and Ritual in Christianity*, the divine revelations that are the preoccupations of Scott. The Christian mythic events organize Scott's complex cosmology in which he feels free to borrow from popular culture, such as movies, caricatures, and aliens, without seeing an internal contradiction. Watts also finds that the most powerful myth, the Christ myth, does not exist in isolation, but conflates similar myths of other civilizations, for example, the Egyptian god Osiris. Scott's compulsion to don the Darth Vader mask might not then seem that far afield from religious re-enactment and ritualization.

The purpose of myth, theorizes Watts, is not to explain phenomena, as anthropologists sometimes want to believe. Rather, Watts takes the Jungian view in which myth arises from dreams and fantasy. Carl Jung (1981) arrived at the theory of the Collective Unconscious[4] from his patients' fantasies, all of which comprised similar motifs, patterns, and iconography that resembled ancient mythology.

Scott, as a limited linguistic speaker, might be prone to the numinosity of symbol, myth, and story, and in touch with their significance far more than the linguistic speaker in which non-verbal information is less compelling. "Indeed, there are ways in which the symbols express their truth more adequately than the more formal and exact language of doctrine, for the truth in question is not an idea but a reality-of-experience" (Watts, 1968, p. 18).[5] Watts's premise is that Christianity, at its height in the thirteenth century, was not so much about fact and history as it was about the power of a symbolic Christian story. For example, the Feasts of the Church were not as important as historical commemorations as they were about the participation in the divine life. I am suggesting that Scott is not concerned with the potential contradictions of his curvaceous dancing church women and flying space ships within a Christian narrative because they are important symbols in the story of rebirth in which all aspects of life become wholesome. The following paragraphs that highlight the mythology of the *Star Wars* movies illustrates how Scott's appropriations of popular culture are woven into his artistic and world view.

THE *STAR WARS* TRILOGY MYTHOLOGY

The Father

According to Joseph Campbell (1991), the son's search for the Father is one of the most powerful quests because it encompasses the son's initiation into adulthood and the revelation of his identity and destiny. Darth Vader symbolizes the "Dark Father," and the threat to the son who must either defeat him or come to terms with him.

Scott has performed the ultimate reconciliation with the Dark Father by taking on his persona and transforming it into the selfless hero, what Darth Vader might have become had he not betrayed his own destiny as a Jedi. On the Jungian journey, the hero must first overcome his own limitations and flaws. Scott follows this trajectory, meticulously re-living by re-painting the past and learning the lessons, as he says. At the same time, Scott creates new myths by his conflation of religion and film. In order to put Darth Vader in perspective, I will follow with a brief synopsis of the *Star Wars* movie trilogy.

Star Wars begins before the audience was witness, in a time in a galaxy when gods, demons, and heroes battled to establish the social order. Darth Vader represents the evil Galactic Empire. The blond and blue-eyed Skywalker and Princess Leia are played by archetypical white actors, both of whom dress in white; Vader wears black. Although underneath his disguise, Vader is played by a white actor, his voice—all that is available for us to perceive—is the voice of the Black actor, James Earl Jones.

The Jedi Knights, a secret order, once the guardians of peace and justice, were defeated by the evil Galactic Empire, the Sith, and its leader Darth Vader. The Jedi are instructed to use the power of "The Force" in positive and constructive ways in the service of others. The Sith are eager to maintain power for their own benefit, and live in anger, aggression, and the desire for domination, while the Jedi live in balanced benevolence. Vader, having been seduced by the desire for power, left the Jedi knights. The fact that Darth Vader is Luke Skywalker's father is not revealed until the second movie of the trilogy, *The Empire Strikes Back*. In the third movie of the trilogy, *Return of the Jedi*, the father-son conflict is consummated by Darth Vader sacrificing his own life for his son, and therefore saving himself in his last selfless act.

Darth Vader was originally Anakin Skywalker, born into slavery. He has no known father and a strong bond with his mother. Injustice and suffering affected his perspective of life, and his emotions eventually betray him. His inability to perform the first task of self-reflection and transformation renders him unfit for the Jedi Order. He later forsakes it, and allows the dark side, the Jungian shadow, to take control. The identity of Anakin is literally swallowed by the persona of Darth Vader,[6] and he is transformed into a figure that is more machine than man (Hirschman, 2000). Luke Skywalker tries unsuccessfully to restore his father to his former goodness before the tragic yet redemptive end of his life. Luke Skywalker's inner victory is in sparing his father's life in a saber-battle, and therefore he enables his father to make the final choice that will redeem his life. James Iaccino (1998) describes the scene as follows:

> The spacefather's last request before he dies is to see his offspring without the mask. Luke obeys and is greeted by the kindest of faces, which

> emits nothing but unconditional love and affection for the boy. Apparently, all the hate and evil left Vader's form when he accomplished his self-sacrificing deed, leaving in its place the man Anakin once was. (p. 12)

Is Scott's resurrection of the archetypal "fallen angel" a cautionary tale for the populous—that we might all succumb, like Vader? Perhaps Scott views San Francisco in a losing battle with the dark forces, but by obeying the past like Vader, the city will ultimately be redeemed. Scott takes on Vader's identity, assumes spiritual power, and is therefore assured to complete the mission. We can never fully understand Scott's intent, as Higgs observes, but we glimpse his interior world in a short film, *Beautiful Peace on Earth*. The subsequent paragraphs describe this film in which Scott performs a daily ritual of feeding seagulls within the persona of Darth Vader.

Beautiful Peace on Earth

The camera follows behind Scott/Vader walking on the streets of Oakland toward a park as he repeats along the way, "It's a beautiful day outside." Once Scott/Vader reaches the park, he sits on a low branch of a tree among a fleet of seagulls. We see him fully for the first time. As he settles down he begins speaking, but his words behind the mask are not clear; some fragments can be heard, such as "birds on the grass." As he speaks to what appears to be the seagulls, he points, as he often does, for emphasis. Only seconds after assuming this position, a seagull alights onto his hand (see Figure 9.12). It is a beautiful moment, particularly because it was not

Figure 9.12 William Scott, Film Capture, *Beautiful Peace on Earth*, Creative Growth Art Center

planned, and a startling visual symbol of the transformation of Vader, as Scott recasts him in goodness. The black shininess of the mask and the white dove-like appearance of the seagull consummate the message of the short film.

Scott/Vader is startled by the seagull, and utters an exclamation. The seagull flies away but returns a few moments later to his now outstretched hand, and then flies to the ground. The photographer captures the moment again in slow motion accompanied by an exhilarating and mystical instrumental sound track. Scott/Vader leaps to his feet, stretches out his cape and says, "It's a nice day outside, a nice day outside," this time with more emphasis and meaning. The photographer cuts to a new scene in which Scott/Vader is feeding the seagulls hot dog buns. He turns away in slow motion and the sound track returns with a deep and melodic voice singing, *Beautiful Peace on Earth*.

FINAL THOUGHTS

> *He's painted away his disability, he's painted away the neighborhood, he's painted away the trauma, and this is the life he wants to have. If he can go back and paint that moment, his reality will be different because he's erased history.*
>
> (di Maria, 2015)

The long hours and years that the artists have invested in their work together is what most art critics and observers cite as Creative Growth's disruption of the outsider category. Spruill, Scott, and Miller have developed as artists over the years in large part because of their proximity to each other. The five-day-a-week studio practice in a disability community is the stimulus that drives the artists to tell their stories. Sometimes their stories are explicit, such as in the captioned commentary that accompanies Scott's work. At other times the viewer must enter into a surrealistic-symbolic dialogue with the artist, such as with Miller's work, which gracefully balances texts and images. Spruill's work is the most accessible of the three artists because of his mobility within popular culture and access to social life. His comic strips tell the story of longing, ambition, reluctance, and the internal contradictions of this complex artist. The artist in the following chapter, whose identity is withheld, is also a narrator of lust, longing, escapism, and evasion, all of which are highly contradictory and yet remain assertive and inevitable.

Race is implicit in both Scott and Spruill's work, both being re-imaginings of the Bay area reclaimed by African-American inspired music, religion, and aesthetics. Scott is more deeply political, employing both government and religious institutions as assumptive partners in his re-envisioned, ecologically and socially just San Francisco. But knowing that he would need supernatural intervention to accomplish his goals, Scott also calls upon forces of the universe. Hence the "citizens" of this new city are buoyed by a powerful energy, uniting them in this super-human task. No one is excluded or marginalized by race or (dis)ability; everyone has a part to play in his utopian vision.

Scott and Spruill re-invent the way African-Americans are perceived and, at the same time, how they represent their place in their community, history, and the world. Therefore, a comparison might be made to a new generation of Black artists. Artist Glenn Ligon and the director and

Figure 9.13 William Scott, *In Another Life*, Creative Growth Art Center

curator of the Studio Museum of Harlem, Thelma Golden, are credited with coining the term *Post-Black*, cemented during the "Freestyle" exhibition in 2001. How might Scott and Spruill fit—or not—into the outsider and Post-Black labels? Their work is about being Black in a white-dominated world, and in Scott's case, the reclaiming of a predominantly white American city about to expire, but rejuvenated with the intervention of wholesome Blackness. How might the self-taught artists embody Black culture given the definition of Post-Blackness as the way artists understand their content as it relates to their identity as Black people? (Golden, as cited in Toure, 2011). Toure (2011) explains this ambiguous position as being rooted in but not restricted by Blackness. Scott is rooted in the Black community yet he is not restricted by the injustices he observes. His visionary plans of reconstruction and his many potential identities are his way of jettisoning the past into a just future. Given the climate of race in America, his friendly police series is particularly ironic, yet he remains peacefully confrontational.

Scott's works might be described as un-self-conscious versions of Kehinde Wiley, a self-defined Post-Black artist who is also a master of realistically rendered paintings. His costumed portraits recall historical white heroes recast as contemporary Black men, such as Alexander the Great with a sword and emblemed T-shirt, Ice-T as Napoleon on his throne, and "Colonel Plantoff on His Charger" with sweatpants and running shoes. But Wiley's works are ironic parodies, while Scott's re-enactments have a religious belief in possibility. And while both make art about power relationships, Scott's visionary works replace unequal power with a consensual, democratic take over. While Wiley borrows the trappings of wealth and power, Scott wears costumes that signify a renewed interest in civil service in a rejuvenated society. But both artists represent the dignity of Black men and women in real and imagined settings. Scott's seriousness about his position as an artist with a forceful social influence is equivalent to Wiley's and other contemporary African-American artists. His images behave as incantations—that with enough viewers and listeners, these messages will tilt the balance of injustices.

NOTES

1. Scott says that penthouses are undemocratic, and Higgs interprets his removal of penthouses as a powerful symbol of class warfare about privilege and wealth.
2. Higgs said in an interview in June 2014 that masks are often used by artists who have not been exposed to art history "as a recurring motif in their work about self and other" (personal communication, June, 12, 2014)
3. Later, on page 27 in a footnote, Watts offers a more florid definition of myth: "'In the beginning,' is *en arche* or in *principio*, the same as the 'once upon a time' which begins all folk/tales. Mythology is the representation of the supernatural, the unthinkable and unknowable, in terms of sensible images having spatial and temporal dimensions, apart from which the mind cannot think at all" (p. 27).

4. Jung was also an artist, his imagery arising from self-induced fantasy.
5. In keeping with the premise of this book, I quote a particularly elegant footnote from Watts (1968), "It is really the most astonishing *hybris* to suppose that the highest wisdom is constituted by the standpoint of conscious reason, for we hardly begin to understand the neural processes without which the very simplest act of reasoning is impossible. The entire possibility of logical and scientific thought rests upon a structure which was formed unconsciously, which we do not understand, and cannot manufacture. Should the finger accuse the hand of clumsiness?" (p. 18).
6. In Jungian terms, the shadow, or dark side, is an integral part of life. As part of human development, theorizes Jung, it is crucial to confront the Shadow, the first test of courage on the inner way. To become a whole person, human beings must recognize and confront their weaknesses rather than deny, externalize, or blame them on others, as Darth Vader ultimately did.

REFERENCES

California College of the Arts. (2007). *San Francisco world's fair.* Retrieved from: https://www.youtube.com/watch?v=5v5jamf_qdk

Campbell, J. (1991). *The power of myth.* New York, NY: Anchor Books.

Creative Growth. (2013). *Peace worlds.* Retrieved from: https://www.youtube.com/watch?v=GmROlJ7AbGw

Di Maria, T. (2015). Proceedings from *An Inclusive World: Bridging Communities.* Queens Museum, Queens, NY.

Elkins, J. (2004). *On the strange place of religion in contemporary art.* New York, NY and London, England: Routledge.

Hayward Goes Wayward. *Southbank Centre.* Retrieved from: http://www.southbankcentre.co.uk/sites/default/files/press_releases/alternative_guide_to_the_universe_press_release_final.pdf Higgs, M. (2011, May 16). *Conversations with Matthew Higgs.* In *The Museum of Everything: Exhibition #4.* Retrieved from: http://musevery.com/exhibition4/pdfs/MatthewHiggs.pdf

Hirschman, H. (2000). *Heroes, monsters & messiahs: Movies and television shows as the mythology of American culture.* Kansas City: Andrews McMeel Publishing.

Iaccino, J. F. (1998). *Jungian reflections within the cinema: A psychological analysis of sci-fi and fantasy archetypes.* Wesport, CT: Praeger.

Jung, C. G. (1981). *The archetypes and the collective unconscious: Collected Works of C. G. Jung* Vol. 9. Part 1. Princeton, NJ: Princeton University Press.

Outsider Art Fair 2016, William Scott. Retrieved from: http://outsiderartfair.com/artist/1084

The San Francisco world's fair of 2007. Retrieved from: http://curatorial- practice.blogs.cca.edu/?page_id=735.Watts, A. (1968). *Myth and ritual in Christianity.* Boston, MA: Beacon Press.

Yentob, A. (2013). (Director). *BBC: Imagine: Turning the art world inside out.* Retrieved from: http://www.bbc.co.uk/programmes/b03js57h

10 R.B., Gender, and Policy

Curators and critics have compared R.B.'s work to Henry Darger's. Like the obscured sexual identity of R. B's Victorian harlequins, Darger's naked Vivian Girls are similarly transgendered. Also, like R.B., Darger's androgynous figures are caught in a narrative loop, although Darger's story has a trajectory while R.B.'s is episodic. Both display a trait common to many "outsider artists," who use imagery "to anchor themselves in a world of their creation, and to minimally anchor themselves in the symbolic order through the help of a cadre of friends that can 'hold' them in this space, or enable the space to exist" (jagodzinski, 2012, p. 179.). The uncategorizable sexual figures of Darger and R.B. are also linked to outsider iconography of invented signifiers that have idiomatic meanings. In an interview with The Museum of Everything, Higgs (2011) says that the issue of language, or art as a common language, is the challenge of all forms of self-taught art in which the logic of language no longer holds reign: "In each case it seems as if the world produced in these workshops is *speaking* with a completely idiosyncratic dialect or accent, consequently its subtlety and nuance is specific" (p. 9). In my interview with Higgs, he underscored the difference between the shared language and art historical conventions, and the theories of MFA students, who usually share similar family and educational experiences. People with disabilities are usually excluded and therefore exist outside of these conversations. Creative Growth honors their independence from rules and conventions, allowing for over 162 disparate and nuanced voices to co-exist. "They resist the temptation to create anything homogenous, to mold these individual voices into something that's more legible" (personal communication, June, 12, 2014). This is particularly true for autistic artists such as R.B. who invent their own language. Many of her notebooks are filled with neologisms, a private language that she will speak fluently when she wants to communicate.

Without language, the familiar signs that neurotypicals use to frame, tame, and stabilize the world are absent from or transformed in R.B.'s paintings. jagodzinski (2012) theorizes that individuals such as R.B. exist in Lacan's realm of the Real, a molecular level of the body and unconscious activity that enables autists to make unusual connections with physical space and matter. These are the free-form associations that Lucy Blackman and Tito Mukhopadhyay capture, as discussed in Chapter Five (this volume). They are unstable, untamed, and fluid, formed from reflex memories and idiosyncratic associations, sometimes transposing non-material sensory perceptions into physical schemata:

> Like the chaos of the unconscious, the Outsider artist rummages through the *debris* of his immediate environment, and finds whatever he or she can lay hands on to use so that the narrative that emerges assembles these bits and pieces of found material into the creation of one's own *double*. They enter into a world where subject|object distinction vanishes, where dream|reality twists as in a möbius strip. (p. 180)

Outsider artists have been heightened to categories where they would not have gone a short time ago. Their work, once considered base and irrational, was not encouraged until met with Hans Prinzhorn's keen eye. Like the base materialism of Bataille and Stoekl (1985), their work was unmeritorious, having no relationship to the ideal of Art, and "foreign to ideal aspirations" (p. 51).

Unlike a popular notion about outsider artists, R. B. *knows* she is an artist. This might be true for all the exhibiting artists at Creative Growth, even those who have the least linguistic skills, such as Dan Miller. I observed these artists participating in the creation ritual, a ritual that is not perseverative or compulsive, as autists' artworks are often described, but rather a conscious awareness of inventions and mark- and shape-making that brings new forms into being. They look, as many journalists have commented, like any other art students, but without the stultifying consciousness of the market place that turns art into a kind of sameness (Higgs, 2011).

FEMINIST PERSPECTIVES OF DISABILITY

R. B.'s work might be more fully appreciated within feminist perspectives of disabled female "life-writers." They are changing the course of disability theory, following the lead of the 1970s and '80s feminist narrators who challenged the objective meta-narrative of the social sciences. Feminist ways of knowing exposed the privileged male perspective of devaluing and "othering" female life stories (Thomas, 1999). This epistemological shift achieved two important results, according to Carol Thomas (1999), by

> [F]irst, bringing the study of aspects of women's lives centre-stage (herstory) and in so doing unsettling notions that some areas of life are "private" or "pre-social;" and second, challenging the epistemological foundations of the social sciences, especially the belief that there is such a thing as scientific knowledge of the social which is unconnected to the

social conditions (structural, cultural, ideological) of its own production. (p. 69).

In a universalist worldview, emotion, experience, and autobiography are antithetical to academia (Stacey, 1997). Feminists disrupted the prevailing view from nowhere by locating the author, or the "writing self," in a situated space. The embodied view of the world from and of the body has changed how we think and talk about disability. Postmodern Feminist standpoint theory has increased the status of the experiencing subject and encouraged authors, such as Nancy Mairs (1997, 2002), Anne Finger (1990), Susan Nussbaum (1997), and others, to share the double bind of femaleness and disability. Without embodied stories, conceptualization of disability easily remains static (Swan, 2002). For example, the nature of space and time is called into question from the lived experience of the blind (Hull, 1992, Fittapaldi, 2004), or the definition of language itself from the perspective of the Deaf (Davis, 1997, 2002; Lane, 1992).[1] Disability affects one's daily sense of body in space, whether impairment is neurological, physical, or intellectual (Wexler, 2011).

Critics within the disability studies field, however, are concerned that personalization of disability, and particularly impairment,[2] erodes the hard earned focus on oppressive and exclusionary social and built structures. For feminists this argument perpetuates and enforces the dualistic position of the public versus the private; disability studies as *either* about the personal restrictions of impairment *or* systemic social barriers. Most importantly, the denial of the personal in disability studies disavows the social causes of oppression and its affect on self-identity and agency (Thomas, 1999). Thomas describes the ironic effect that the omission of social oppression has in aspects of self-esteem, relationships, family, and sexuality, as "'open season to psychologists and others who would not hesitate to apply the individualistic/personal tragedy model to these issues" (p. 74). Finally, Thomas argues that the erasure of the personal would inhibit the advancement of a theoretical construction that includes structure and agency, the social/cultural with the intimate.

According to the feminist view that initiated these discourses, the female disabled identity is often considered the double bind of patriarchal internalized determinants of the normative social female roles with the added devaluation of intellectual, neurological, and physical impairments.[3] In her life story, the author may re-write these representations within her own embodied experience. But these narratives are not, writes Susannah Mintz (2007), simply manifestos of resistance to medical, social, and economic oppression, although they are included in them, "they are also open-ended histories of embodiment, tales about anomalous physicality that emphasize a poetics as much as a politics of disability identity" (p. 4). In the subsequent sections, I return to R.B. and examine how the poetics of her visual narratives make her work intensely political within the history of disability and sexuality in the United States.

THE DISABLED BODY, SEXUALITY, AND FETISHISM

Sideshow Freakishness

Higgs calls R. B.'s Glam Rock watercolors her adolescent period, influenced by popular culture and other adolescent impressions and motivations. What he gleaned from her later mature period was the way she translated her adolescent interests in Glam Rock and horror film into the strange Victorian, dandyish world of California (M. Higgs, personal communication, June 12, 2014). The figures are slim and sinewy, often half-dressed with flowing hair and direct gazes, up-ending the postmodern gaze behind their masked faces. They sit or lounge in private watercolor spaces, under street lights or in bedrooms, their staging and theatrical postures reminiscent of the carnivalesque and spectacle.

In his review of R. B.'s work, Joseph Mosconi compares the clownish faces of the female figures of this later period to performers in carnival sideshows. To suggest a comparison of disability to the carnivalesque of the nineteenth century sideshow opens up a long and complex legacy of the disabled body and the extreme devalued position of the individual in this context. The representation and presentation of "freakishness" can be traced to stone age cave drawings of mysterious births, which became the monsters of early Greeks, the freaks of P. T. Barnum, and are today medically defined as the physically disabled (Garland Thomson, 1997). In the one hundred years of its existence, the freakshow defined what was antithetical to the emerging mobile, white, male, middle class, able-bodied American. Rosemarie Garland Thomson describes the first of P. T. Barnum's human curiosities, an ancient, physically disabled Black woman, as the embodiment of enfreakment, the body enveloping and obliterating "the freak's potential humanity. When the body becomes pure text, a freak has been produced from a physically disabled human being" (p. 59).

The transition from the sideshow to the operating theater is exemplified by Dr. Frederic Treves's (1923) autobiography and the theatrical staging of the *Elephant Man*. Leslie Fiedler (1979), well known for his book *Freaks: Myths and Images of the Secret Self*, analyzes the reason for the play's wild success as an old-fashioned celebration of horror and pity, and an audience of normals' simultaneous deliverance from guilt. Treves's patient Merrick is a Victorian "showfreak" who under the doctor's experimentation became a medical curiosity; but it is "perhaps the curiously tender male bonding between doctor and patient that is its true erotic center" (Fiedler, 1996, p. 39). Above all, their relationship remains the mythic trope of enlightened science and its triumph over the terror and loathing of the disabled other.

Fiedler also traces the fascination with freaks before and upon the death of the sideshow to their enshrinement in classic works of art, such as Goya's *Giant* and Velasquez's *Las Meninas*. Along with kings and courtesans,

Velasquez and Goya also depict dwarfs and other physically deformed fellow-humans kept for their amusement (Wexler, 2005). Fiedler recognizes the obvious: historically, the arts have failed to tell the truth about the Other, or how the Other perceives herself. R. B.'s depictions and representations of non-normative sexuality write new codes and definitions of human interaction, a Deleuzian becoming, imagining, and possibility of new forms of human relationships that Margrit Shildrick (2012) describes: "The so-easily silenced whisper of a kinship that would be denied—for it unsettles the foundation of western subjectivity—is growing into a roar that marks a new understanding of embodiment which owes much to Deleuze" (p. 142). A Deleuzian way of rethinking disability, according to Shildrick, is to acknowledge both normative and non-normative bodies in the process of construction and transformation, contingent on the social environment and, particularly, "the queerness of all sexuality" (p. 143).[4] R. B. touches us at our ambivalence about boundaries, social codes of morality, and normality that delimit our humanity. Her sexual ambiguity hints at the hypocritical, tragic, and comic condition of neurotypical codes of behavior.

ANDROGYNY AND SEXUALITY IN R. B.'S WORK

R. B.'s anomalous bodies, about which Shildrick (2012) writes, audaciously challenge normative heterosexuality. The transgressive nature of disability—the anomalous body as deviant—is contested in the playful relationships of R. B.'s hermaphrodites. They confidently stare back at the viewer, securely positioned in their world of free-form sexuality.[5] The viewer then appropriately takes the position of the voyeur, fetishizing the androgynous figures that R. B. makes accessible. Like Spruill, R. B. does not apologize for the inappropriate or transgressive performance of her sexualized figures. And because of the appealing and consuming vision that she paints, the viewer is seduced and norms are abandoned. Shildrick points out that the denial of abnormal sexuality arrests the growth and development of the disabled identity, sex being a rite of passage and integral to self-image, and in its "literal and metaphoric sense, that which brings the embodied subject into being" (p. 24). If some forms of embodiment are deemed to have more integrity and unity than others, R. B. wields a potent rebuttal in her seductive artworks as objects of desire that leave her audience breathless, and she in control of an unequal power relationship.

R. B.'s message echoes Shildrick's in which bodies and identities are in fluid and unstable relationships, never arriving, always becoming. R. B. invites us into the world of strip poker in one of the several paintings in which couples enjoy disrobing their formalwear. She usurps not only able-bodied and able-minded sexuality, but also invites the possibility of an uncertain sexuality, of non-heteronormativity, blurring the distinction between perverse and normal, as well as inviting the symbolic participation of the viewer.

R.B. is an expert in this sleight of hand that turns a century of sexual repression and surveillance over anomalous Others on its head. In a culture that is uncomfortable with the erotic, a sexualized disabled body has been especially absent in the western imagination. Heterosexual sex is reserved for the able-bodied and able-minded, all others being threats to disrupt the symbolic order (Shildrick, 2012). The uncertainty of abnormality intensifies the risk and vulnerability of sexuality, yet the horror that pursues the notion of abnormal sexuality also invites fascination. R.B.'s uncanny control over the pleasure of the normalized imagination beckons the neurotypical and able-bodied viewer to enter her world. The effects that the paintings have on the viewer lead me to speculate that she is aware of her products. She re-introduces the carnivalesque as a mutual transaction in which performer and viewer meet in an equal and powerful gaze that signifies agency and participatory subjecthood.

The Sexualized Other

Sex and disability, writes Robert McRuer and Anna Mollow (2012) in their Introduction to *Sex and Disability*, are terms that are not often seen together in text or heard in discourse. Of the many reasons for this omission, the most obvious is the emphasis of health and beauty in the imagination of western popular culture, and the designation to individuals outside the realm of desire to levels of freakishness. But "what if disabled people were understood to be both subjects and objects of a multiplicity of erotic desires and practices?" (p. 1).

Sexuality is typically dominated by the medical and psychological professions that fetishize the disabled as objects and, until recently, rarely encountered in the voice of the disabled subject (Shakespeare, Gillespie-Sells & Davies, 1996).[6] But whether infantilized or dismissed as asexual, the subject of sex and disability is most often surrounded by unease and therefore comfortably ignored. As demonstrated in second-wave feminism, the omission of personal experiences such as sexuality as private is, in itself, political (McRuer and Mollow, 2012).

Tobin Siebers (2012)[7] writes that the representation of disabled sexuality in discourse reveals the fragile separation of the private and public as well as exposing the long history of its paternalistic surveillance. He contests the public and private sphere binary, the role this separation plays in regulating sex, and the normative control exerted by traditional institutions such as marriage and family. He defends the expression of sexuality as not only a civil right but also as critical to personal identity, political agency, and happiness. He makes a distinction between "sexual culture" and "sex life," the latter being an ablest term that by definition implies that control and privacy are not available to the disabled.

The disabled do, however, participate in a sexual culture because they exist as sexual beings. A healthy dose of sexual iconography at Creative

Growth indicates a substantial sexual culture, be it political, humorous, or fanciful. The most blatant representations are made by Nick Pagan, such as his rug titled *Power to the Boner #1*, depicting an anthropomorphized penis in a college sweater with fist held high in solidarity. Sexual possibility is palpable in the Creative Growth studio, where artists flirt and find partners. The artists who live at home with their families, such as Spruill and Scott, are usually the most independent. They are, nevertheless, excluded from full access to normative sexual freedom and control implied in the definition of "sex-life." The potential for a sexual partnership is forever on the horizon and, as discussed earlier, both social stigmatization and individualistic limitations are barriers to fulfillment. Siebers's (2012) intervention of sexual culture provides "a deeper, more sustained idea of how sex and identity interconnect. . . . It means to liberate sex, allowing it to overflow the boundaries of secured places and to open up greater sexual access for people with disabilities" (p. 39).

Like Siebers, McRuer and Mollow (2012) resist the notion of heteronormative sex by broadening the definition to include pleasurable social interactions that might not typically be perceived as erotic. While Siebers used a wheelchair and his concern was with physical access, the invisible disabilities—as the intellectual and developmental disabilities are often called—have their own brand of obstructions. What underlies both kinds of disabilities, however, is the deterministic *ideology of ability*, which can be globalized to all abilities that provide social and physical access to sexuality, sexuality being the privileged domain of ability. Healthy offspring is also assumed out of reach for both the physically and intellectually/developmentally disabled. Reproduction is not only a marker of sexual status and privilege, but also signifies the potential to pass them on to one's children (Siebers, 2012). Disabled women, especially, are looked upon as less than female and dismissed as mothers, manifested in so-called "voluntary" sterilization[7] in the late nineteenth and early twentieth centuries, which achieved the dual purposes of institutional order and eugenic control (Trent, 1994).

Disabled individuals are considered to be part of a sexual minority often viewed as "perverted" and thus co-opted by queer theory, their conflation sometimes described as queering disability studies (McRuer & Mollow, 2012).[8] Yet, to be "queer" is to choose, while the label "intellectual disability" is given (Adams, 2015). Although their legal and social battles are similar to the experiences of homosexuals, the intellectually disabled exist in various states of dependency. Privacy and consent, like other basic rights, are the privilege of the abled. Consent is given in privacy and people with intellectual disabilities are permitted almost none, whether they live with a family or in group homes (Adams, 2015). In addition, consent implies competency, and so the label inherently prohibits its possibility. Although rare, young people with developmental disabilities have been granted more freedom, as recently represented in films such as the 2010 documentary *Monica and David*. However, even here questions about the limitations of an intimate life persist, the couple's life circumscribed by live-in parents who mean well in trying to protect them from social stigma. Supporters of intimacy and independence for people with intellectual or developmental disabilities, however, suggest that the right to risk social stigma is a freedom that should not be sacrificed (Desjardins, 2012).

Anne Finger (1992) is often quoted as saying that sexuality is the greatest source of oppression and pain for the disabled population, more difficult to talk about or attempt to change than all other forms of exclusion. Reflecting on this statement with McRuer and Mollow many years later, Finger suggested that more than civil rights, cultural change is needed. McRuer and Mollow theorize that the battlefield of identity politics has moved in the past twenty years from historical and social constructs toward the self, or the representation of self in film, autobiography, performance, and social media. While groundbreaking films such as *Monica and David* are ultimately conservative in imagining non-normative sexuality, they are nevertheless signs of cultural change that lay the foundation for future forms of representation in which people with intellectual disabilities enjoy alternative, erotic, or "queer" forms of intimacy (Adams, 2015). The more recent *Autism in Love* (2015), directed by Matt Fuller and produced by Carolina Groppa, might be the first of new documentaries and films that propose the possibility of sexual independence. Other than the parent interviews and off-camera questions and prompts by the director, who does not identify himself, the autistic protagonists are doing the talking. The film is free of the neurotypical narrator, voiceover, or informational segments by experts who interpret or speak for the protagonists. The changing dynamics of the characters and the relationships with their partners are given full representation. As the documentary progresses, Fuller's relationships with the autists grow, closing the divide between filmmaker and subject. His lack of knowledge about autism, and therefore lack of preconceptions, allows for the unobstructed revelation of the autists' personalities, although they never appear to be coaxed or prompted. Groppa's interest began as an assistant to Ira Heilveil, professor of psychiatry at UCLA medical school. Her engagement in the research of romance in the autism community ignited her desire to tell their stories in film. The result is not only a re-examination of love in the autism community, but the re-examination of love as defined by neurotypicals.

THE DISABLING CATEGORIES

That R. B.'s figures are set in the nineteenth century is additionally ironic, since it is this era that Foucault targets as the genesis of the obsessive categorizations of normative sexuality and desiring bodies. "The recurring problem of the nineteenth century is that of discovering the core of monstrosity hidden behind little abnormalities, deviances, and irregularities" (Foucault, as cited in Shildrick, 2012, p. 113). Shildrick suggests that the legacy of toned-downed ambiguities of the nineteenth century is recast in the designated "abnormal" bodies and minds in the twenty-first century, and manifests in judicial and social policies, biomedicine, and psychiatry. Over the last century these sites have achieved a sense of civilized inclusiveness and assimilation while erasing disability in the effort to normalize and control transgressive Others.

Foucault is known for his exposé of government control and the disciplinary processes of institutions. With techniques of normalization, institutions construct and contain the disabled body. Changes in the law, even when beneficial to disabled populations, according to Shildrick, have also been significant in policing the boundaries of the disability category, such as the consequences "that normalization, which demands homogeneity—named in the juridicial domain as equality before the law—inherently risks effacing difference, at the very moment of appearing to recognize it" (p. 115). The law behaves within a normative context, and in addressing discrimination does not give disability rights freely and, therefore, constructs and designates the disability identity within this context (Brown & Halley, 2002, Shildrick, 2012). Ambiguity is the result of these constructed signifiers of abnormality, which for Shildrick is the most damaging to the disabled identity.

Thus, the problem of marginalization and isolation within the institution in the mid-twentieth century existed as a new and subtle problem: the ambiguity and erasure of identity as a result of the social and governmental policies of rehabilitation and integration. To legislate, says Stiker (1997), is to codify into law a universalist norm. To the able-bodied, who are observer-invariant, conformity to the norm might seem natural and good; however, "the specific extension of rights accruing to disability cannot be counted an unproblematic good, but as an intensification of the disciplinary grasp of biopower" (Shildrick, 2012, p. 115). And with each implementation of the law in the relief of the disabled person, says Shildrick, she is re-designated as a devalued person. Rather than the responsibility of society to conform or adjust, it is the other who must normalize in order to attain civil rights and benefits:

> To call on the law *as* disabled is scarcely a challenge to the normative standards of ablebodiedness that tacitly underlie the liberal humanist notion of a legal subject—that is, one who exercises independent agency—but serves rather to unavoidably consolidate the power of the system that constitutes and sustains such binaries in the first place. (p. 116)

FINAL THOUGHTS ON DISABILITY STUDIES AND SPECIAL EDUCATION

I turn now toward the policies of special education in the public school system, which readily uses the terminology of difference in its social codes, institutional language, and other euphemisms to demarcate the "different" and "diverse" individual from the "norm." Among such thinly veiled terms are "at risk," and "English language learners," which hide the dominant white standard while suggesting the presence of a normative student (Baglieri et al., 2011). Disability studies in education examines the enforcement of the norm under social, political, and cultural influences that have been made invisible by its appearance of inevitability. The highly stratified public school system reflects a classed society, from the privileged at the highest rank to the working-class at the lowest (Baglieri et al., 2011). To be ablebodied, normal, and white is a powerful identity that begins in childhood.

The responsibility of the individual to adjust to the physical and social obstacles and barriers rather than the other way around is certainly true in education in which children with disabilities are relegated to special classrooms or schools. The term "special" is ironic, for it is unabashedly a euphemism. Simi Linton (1998) writes that the dictionary definition of "special" belies the reality that neither the children nor the curriculum, which the term designates, surpasses what is common. Instead, the term "special" thinly disguises the deep ambivalence, antipathy, guilt, or disdain hidden within. Linton points out that it is not that special education classroom instruction is necessarily inferior, but that it is not voluntary, which sets up the isolating and stigmatizing conditions for disabled children. Segregated classrooms are not worse because they contain disabled children, but rather because they are restricted environments. The benefits of their small populations and individualized instruction "are often overshadowed by the limited types of interactions children can have with one another" (p. 63).

Linton suggests that the status quo of special education correlates with the absence of research in higher education by disabled researchers. Typically, the disabled individual is the subject of research and rarely the investigator. The structure of research, therefore, sets up a dichotomy. This disparity, well studied in the social sciences in terms of the power structures and social relations of race and gender in research production, has led to the isolation of disability in the applied fields of social work, health rehabilitation, and special education. Although the landscape is changing, the absence of disability studies as a field of study in most universities insures that the practices of special education will remain entrenched in its current form. "And if we do not imagine 'disability' as a broad, general subject that shapes the humanities, it is all the less likely that we will manage to imagine disability as a broad, general subject that shapes public life and public policy" (Berube, as cited in Linton, 1998, p. viii). The structure of the academic fields within the university often inhibits the crossing between applied fields and liberal arts. These fields are typically taught by practitioners who cast people with disabilities as patients, students, or clients. The bifurcation of special education and regular education into separate systems further establishes the disabled learner as separate. This has been true in my experience, and with the current mandates of the Common Core Curriculum inching its way into teacher education, the modest gains that have been made in disability studies might be lost in this field.

Disability studies is positioned to critique under-analyzed rehabilitative practices sustained in and driven by a network of political and economic policy in reaction to social needs rather than ideology. Initiated by the disabled population, it began in contradistinction to the medicalized perspectives of disability and traditional curricula with the purpose of displacing the authoritative voice with the self-determination of disabled people. Rather than the practical approach of the applied fields, it is an inquiry-based study that questions the reliability of the definitions and categories of disability, particularly the narrowed view that the individual is the source of the problem and in need of a cure. Because of this lack in the applied fields, disability studies emphasizes the totalizing and oppressive effects of essentialist beliefs in the inevitability of biological destiny:

> Practices exist that limit freedom, infantilize people with disabilities, force dependency, create and perpetuate stereotypes through the use of tools such as testing and diagnosis, constrict pleasure, and limit communication and political activism among disabled people. (Linton, 1998, p. 82)

The deficit model is dominant in the applied fields, borrowed from the medical fields that describe individuals' limitations and impairments rather than contextualizing disability in the broad category of the social environment. Linton often points out that disability is conceived as an individual phenomenon, deviating from a supposed universal and neutral position. Disability studies re-contextualizes these assigned pathologized roles of disabled people as constructs and products of social and political networks. It re-positions disability from a health or medical issue to a politically and socially oppressed cultural group, valorizes the individual in the context of identity and community, and enters the field as a discipline of conceptual study.

Reclaiming Inclusiveness

In the *Teachers College Record's* "[Re]claiming 'Inclusive Education' Toward Cohesion in Educational Reform: Disability Studies Unravels the Myth of the Normal Child," Susan Baglieri et al. (2011) review how in the United States the notion of inclusive education is limited within the discourse of special education. The authors use the lens of disability studies in education to broaden the term to include a democratic conceptualization of special education that services all students who are potentially marginalized by poverty, ethnicity, social class, religion, and gender. They find the source of the problem in the institutionalization of normalcy and, as a result, the emergence of a service delivery model of special education that primarily labels and places students with disabilities. They call the "normative center" a self-sustaining practice that artificially de-centers students who fail to work within the rigid standards of the circumscribed "norm."

Roland Barthes's (1972) theory of the mythic meaning of images and words, in which a hidden set of rules and conventions specific to a group appear to be natural and universal, might be useful in unpacking the term *inclusion*. The use of institutional language establishes an appearance of inevitability in and the rightness of "special" labels and placements. The reoccurring familiar terminology of special education obscures and, at the same time, legitimates inherent asymmetrical power relations. Under these conditions, the benign term *inclusion* in public schools has taken on the connotation of not belonging, such as in the frequently used "inclusion kids." The authors of the *Teachers College Record* suggest that the mythology of the normal student needs to be examined if current practices are to be replaced with more democratic methods of serving students. Inclusion in public education is typically understood as the placement of students who have been labeled with a disability. They reconceptualize the term within an international discourse of critical disability studies in which policy operates in the hidden form of a white ideology of institutionalized racism and ableism. Re-conceptualizing inclusion therefore means aspiring to a democratic education wherein all students participate in a non-discriminatory setting that is welcoming of diversity.

Through the lens of disability studies, the acontextuality of the student in special education discourse is given particular notice. Baglieri promotes the Elementary Inclusive Education Preservice Program at Teachers College, Columbia University, as a model of re-contextualizing inclusive education within a democratic community. The program is in alliance with disability studies education from its position that inclusive education is based on inquiry, ideology, and moral decision-making rather than the sole practice of placing and labeling students. On their website the program states:

> Rather than understanding inclusive education to be focused solely on the integration of students with disabilities in classrooms alongside nondisabled peers, our understanding of inclusive education involves active and deliberate participation on the part of teachers in the process of transforming schooling as a whole. We thereby embrace and value human differences as constituting a richness in our societies to be reflected and celebrated in our classrooms. This also means affirming the right of every young person to equal opportunities for active participation in an education that addresses her or his capacities and needs in a community wherein respect for all is cultivated with intention and care. Thus, we are committed to resisting the many ways in which students experience marginalization and exclusion in schools. (Teachers College, para. 2)

Public education practices must be re-examined for the connotative meaning that *inclusion* has unwittingly developed. Rather that belonging, as Baglieri et al. suggest, it has come to mean not belonging. As long as the mythic normative child has the central position from which other students are measured, barriers to learning will obstruct the fair education of all children. For example, the implicitly exclusionary method of accommodation for "non-typical" students is equivalent metaphorically, says Jay Dolmage (2008), to a side door. "Instead, all students and teachers, coming to the conversation with varying abilities, must redefine what they are able to do together . . . emphasizing the right of every student to be the re-creator of the world," which means envisioning an egalitarian public school that engages all learners rather than privileging dominant learners (p. 23). For inclusion to work, it must be altered by changing our fundamental assumptions about how we construct the spaces in which children learn.

NOTES

1. Deaf with a capital "D" signifies deaf individuals who identify with their culture and use primarily sign language. This standpoint is in opposition to the audist position of the deaf who chooses to be in mainstream culture and primarily lip read to communicate (see Lennard Davis, 1997).
2. The "impairment versus disability" debate within disability studies has evolved in the past years with renewed discussion of the place of impairment. The fear of feeding the "tragedy" model of suffering has caused resistance in disability scholars to engage in a discourse with impairment. Thomas (1999) also describes the problem of critics who conflate impairment with the personal.
3. Mintz (2007) lists beauty, sex appeal, and marriage as a few of these determinants of female success and "according to which disabled women are necessarily construed as failures, less than whole, and even vaguely inhuman" (p. 93).
4. "Queer" is defined in opposition to normality rather than to homosexuality in this context.
5. The staring back in R. B.'s work is more like the erotic gaze that Rosemarie Garland-Thomson (1997) distinguishes in *Extraordinary Bodies: Figuring Physical Disability in American Culture and Literature* as sexual rather than the stare directed at the disabled.
6. The omission of sexuality is felt even in disability studies, McRuer and Mollow point out. Shildrick's pioneering book in 2009, *Dangerous Discourses of Disability, Subjectivity and Sexuality* might be the first to deeply explore this subject.
7. Tobin Siebers passed away on January 29th 2015. He was a long-standing Chair of the Initiative on Disability Studies, V. L. Parrington Collegiate Professor, and Professor of English Language and Literature and Art & Design at the University of Michigan.
8. McRuer and Mollow (2012) write that disability scholars who write about the violence of exclusion "are in their resistance to this violence and exclusion, engaged in imagining disability in ways that exceed or violate norms of propriety and respectability. In ways, that is, that are queer" (p. 32)

REFERENCES

Adams, R. (2015). Privacy, dependency, discegenation: Toward a sexual culture for people with intellectual disabilities. *Disability Studies Quarterly, 35*(1). Retrieved from: http://dsq-sds.org/article/view/4185/3825

Baglieri, S., Bejoian, L.M., Broderick, A.A., Connor, D.J., & Valle, J. (2011). [Re]claiming "inclusive education" toward cohesion in educational reform: Disability studies unravels the myth of the normal child. *Teachers College Record, 113*(10), 499–516. Retrieved from: https://www.tcrecord.org/library/abstract.asp?contentid=16428

Barthes, R. (1972). *Mythologies* (A. Lavers, Trans.). New York, NY: Hill and Wang.

Bataille, G. and Stoekl A. (Eds.). (1985). *Visions of excess: Selected writings, 1987–1962* (A. Stoekl, Trans.). Minneapolis: University of Minnesota Press.

Brown, W., & Halley, J. (Eds.). (2002). *Left legalism/left critique*. Durham, NC: Duke University Press.

Codina, A. (Director). (2010). *Monica and David* [Motion picture]. HBO Documentaries. United States.

Davis, L.J. (1997). Constructing normalcy. In L. J. Davis (Ed.), *The disability studies reader* (pp. 9–28). New York, NY: Routledge.

Davis, L.J. (2002). Bodies of difference: Politics, disability, and representation. In S. L. Snyder, B. Brueggemann & R. Garland-Thomson (Eds.), *Disability studies: Enabling the humanities* (pp. 100–108). New York, NY: The Modern Language Association of America.

Desjardins, M. (2012). The sexualized body of the child: Parents and the politics of "voluntary" sterilization of people labeled intellectually disabled. In R. McRuer & A. Mollow (Eds.), *Sex and disability* [Kindle DX version]. Retrieved from Amazon.com

Dolmage, J. (2008). Mapping composition: Inviting disability in the front door. In C. Lewiecki-Wilson & B. J. Bruegemann (Eds.), *Disability and the teaching of writing: A critical sourcebook* (pp. 14–27). Boston, MA: Beford/St. Martins.

Fiedler, L. (1979). *Freaks: Myths and images of the secret self*. New York, NY: Touchstone.

Fiedler, L. (1996). *The tyranny of the normal: Essays on bioethics, theology, & myth*. Lincoln MA: David R. Godine.

Finger, A. (1990). *Past due: A story of disability, pregnancy and birth*. Seattle, WA: Seal Press.

Finger, A. (1992). Forbidden fruit. *New Internatiionalist, 233*, 8–10.

Garland Thomson, R. (1997). *Extraordinary bodies: Figuring physical disability in American culture and literature*. New York, NY: Columbia University Press.

Groppa, C. (Producer) & Fuller, M. (Director). (2015). *Autism in love* [Motion Picture]. ACG Entertainment Production. United States.

Higgs, M. (2011). *Conversations with Matthew Higgs*. Retrieved from: http://www.museumofeverything.com/exhibition4/pdfs/MatthewHiggs.pdf

Hull, J. (1992). *Touching the rock: An experience of blindness*. New York, NY: Vintage Books.

jagodzinski, j. (2012). Outside the outside: In the realms of the real. In A. Wexler (Ed.), *Art education beyond the classroom: Pondering the outsider and other sites of learning* (pp. 159–185). New York, NY: Palgrave Macmillan.

Lane, H. (1992). *The mask of benevolence: Disabling the deaf community*. New York, NY: Alfred. A. Knopf.

Linton, S. (1998). *Claiming disability, knowledge and identity*. New York: New York University Press.

Mairs, N. (1997). *Waist-high in the world: Life among the nondisabled*. Boston, MA: Beacon Press.

Mairs, N. (2002). *Sex and death and the crippled body: A meditation*. In S. L. Snyder, B. Brueggemann & R. Garland-Thomson (Eds.), *Disability studies: Enabling the humanities* (pp. 100–108). New York, NY: The Modern Language Association of America.

McRuer, R., & Mollow, A. (Eds.). (2012). *Sex and disability*. [Kindle DX version]. Retrieved from Amazon.com

Mintz, S. B. (2007). *Unruly bodies: Life writing by women with disabilities*. Chapel Hill, NC: The University of North Carolina Press.

Mosconi, J. (2007). Appealing biography. *Fillip Publication*. Retrieved from: http://fillip.ca/content/appealing-biography

Nussbaum, S. (1997). Mishuganismo. In K. Fries (Ed.), *Staring back: The disability experience from the inside out* (pp. 367–401). New York, NY: Plume.

Shakespeare, T., Gillespie-Sells, K., & Davies, D. (1996). (Eds.). *The sexual politics of disability: Untold desires*. London, England: Continuum International Publishing Group.

Shildrick, M. (2012). *Dangerous discourses of disability, subjectivity and sexuality*. London, England: Palgrave Macmillan.

Siebers, T. (2012). A sexual culture for disabled people. In R. McRuer & A. Morrow (Eds.), *Sex and disability* (pp. 37–53). Durham, NC: Duke University Press.

Stacey, J. (1997). Feminist theory: Capital F, capital T. In V. Robinson & D. Richardson (Eds.), *Introducing women's studies* (pp. 54–76). London, England: Macmillan.

Stiker, H. J. (1997). *A history of disability*. Ann Arbor, MI: The University of Michigan Press.

Swan, J. (2002). Disabilities, bodies, voices. In S. L. Snyder, B. Brueggemann & R. Garland-Thomson (Eds.), *Disability studies: Enabling the humanities*, (pp. 283–295). New York, NY: The Modern Language Association of America.

Teachers College, Columbia University: Elementary Inclusive Education in the Department of Curriculum & Teaching. Retrieved from: http://www.tc.columbia.edu/curriculum-and-teaching/elementary-inclusive-education/about-us/

Thomas, C. (1999). *Female forms: Experiencing and understanding disability*. Philadelphia, PA: Open University Press.

Treves, F. (1923). *The elephant man and other reminiscences*. London, England: Casssell.

Trent, J. W. (1994). *Inventing the feeble mind: A history of mental retardation in the United States*. Berkley, CA: University of California Press.

Wexler, A. (2005). Identity politics of disability: The other and the secret self. *The Journal of Social Theory in Art Education, 25*, 210–224.

Wexler, A. (2011). The siege of the cultural city is underway. Adolescents with developmental disabilities make "art." *Studies in Art Education, 53*(1), 53–69.

Index